WEBMASTER

DEVELOPING

REAL-WORLD
INTRANETS

Dan and Judith Wesley

CORIOLIS GROUP BOOKS

Publisher	Keith Weiskamp
Project Editor	Toni Zuccarini
Copy Editor	Beth Demain
Cover Artist/Design	Gary Smith
Interior Design	Michelle Stroup
Layout Production	ProImage
Proofreader	Charlotte Zuccarini
Indexer	Mary Millhollon

The Coriolis Group, Inc.
7339 E. Acoma Drive, Suite 7
Scottsdale, AZ 85260
Phone: (602) 483-0192
Fax: (602) 483-0193
Web address: http://www.coriolis.com

1-57610-001-4: $39.99

Printed in the United States of America

10 9 8 7 6 5 4 3 2 1

Contents

Chapter 6   Information Content: The Data Sources   119

Chapter 7   Developing Web Pages   139

Chapter 12   The Data: Interfaces, Delivery, and Indexing Tools   265

Chapter 13   Bundled Solutions for Intranet Development   305

Part 4   An Intranet Blueprint   319

Chapter 17   Themes, Trends, and Technologies   389

Appendix A   Acronym Extensions   397

Appendix B   Intranet Resources   405

Appendix C   All Things Hypertext   419

Appendix D   What's on the CD-ROM   467

Index   469

Acknowledgments

Many people have helped make this book a reality and deserve our sincere appreciation:

Frank Hanlan, who got us together with Keith Weiskamp at Coriolis, and started something we had to finish; Morgan Wesley, who spent innumerable hours surfing to find the information to build the product tables, and did research for the Appendices; Dave Huet, who provided moral support, and occasionally some good advice; Shawn Golmon, who kept Dan's frequent sweeping generalizations about technology in check; Glen Cleveland, who gave us a new understanding of the term "technical obsolescence"; and Greg Skafte, our Unix/Network/Internet/Web guru, who not only understands Unix, but likes it.

Our thanks also goes out to the many people who contributed to the book's contents by providing their time, ideas, and/or material: Skip Kerr (Grower Direct Fresh Cut Flowers), Gary Fendler (Aetna Health Plan), Steve Whan (BC Hydro), Mike Tierney (Hewlett Packard), Serge Lezhnin (Ural State University), Susana Fernandez Vega (CERN), and Jean-Yves Le Meur (CERN).

Thanks, too, to our family and friends, who provided support and encouragement during the tough chapters, and ran all the errands that we couldn't find time for. We'd like to include Denny and Marilyn and their staff at Muddy Waters Cappuccino bar, where we had our office away from home, complete with good blues music, food, excellent coffee, and on more than one occasion, an extension cord for the notebook.

And last, but certainly not least, our editor at Coriolis, Toni Zuccarini, who patiently let us work our way through the writing process.

Introduction

What's Covered in the Book

Like the Internet itself, the intranet phenomenon has engulfed the computer industry and the business community. It has been proclaimed by some to be the *silver bullet* (a myth), the *answer-to-all-problems* (an even larger myth), and as nothing more than a *fad*, or *hype*, by others (the greatest myth of all).

Through the course of this book we hope to dispel these myths by providing an understanding of what intranets are, why they came to be, and the benefits they can provide. You'll gain an understanding of why thousands of companies around the world have embraced this technology, and why, in computer industry parlance, intranets are "hot."

Having done that, we'll examine what's involved in building an intranet, looking at areas such as hypertext design considerations, database integration, and security. We will also discuss the various tools that can be used in intranet development, and present some representative products from each of the different categories of software.

After providing some guidelines that can be used for planning, developing, and implementing an intranet in your organization, we'll cover the various aspects of intranet maintenance. The last section looks at what's involved with connecting your intranet to that larger network of networks—the Internet—and at some significant themes, trends, and technologies for the future.

Our Audience

We've attempted to reach as broad an audience as possible without diluting the technical aspects to the point where it would be useless to a computer professional. The book, then, is geared toward readers with a moderate to high level of technical skills, such as managers who want to find out what an intranet is, and what is involved in building one, as well as computer professionals who need to acquire an understanding of the topic from a technical perspective.

The Computer Platform

Rather than attempt to write a book that covers the topic of intranets from the perspective of every computer platform, we've focused on the Windows NT environment. (I don't hate Unix; I'm simply more familiar with NT.) However, many of the concepts and approaches presented are platform-independent, in keeping with the Internet's open systems philosophy.

What You'll Gain

This book is intended to provide the information that you need to make an informed decision about proceeding with an intranet project, and to help you select products that can be used for developing an intranet application or publication. Unfortunately, some of the product information will be out-of-date by the time you read this. All we can do is apologize beforehand, fall back on the excuse that this is an unavoidable shortcoming of computer books in general, and hope that you find the rest interesting and useful.

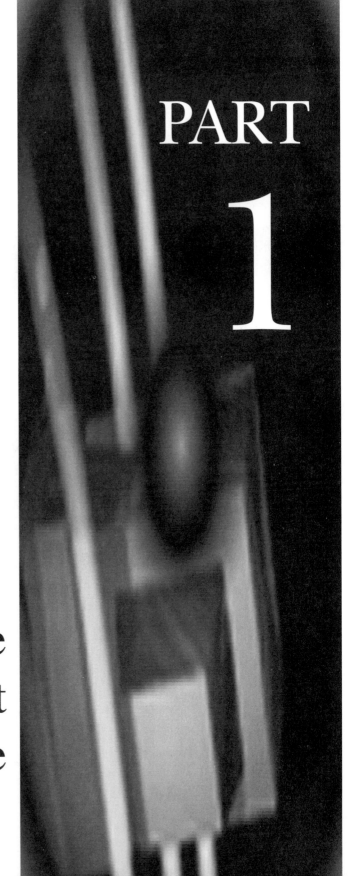

PART

1

The Intranet Advantage

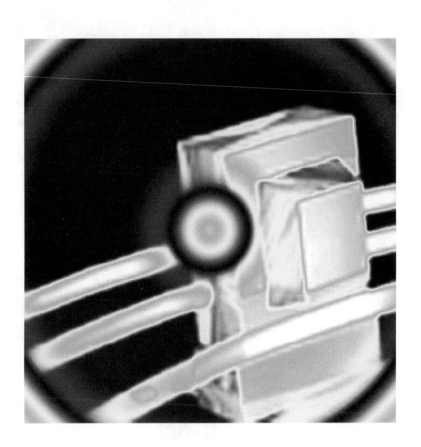

1

The Information Dilemma

1

The Information Dilemma

O ne of the difficulties with computer terminology is that any definition of a new concept tends to be shaped by the experience of its author, or influenced by marketing. Clarity becomes even more difficult when labels are created and become part of the common idiom. Intranet, a word coined to describe the use of internetworking standards and technology within an organization, is no exception.

An intranet is an electronic information and communications system running on an internal computer network. The system uses Internet protocols, standards, and tools as a means to create, distribute, find, and retrieve textual and non-textual information.

To lay the basis for an examination of this new Internet application, we review the current state of information sharing in the organization, along with its inherent problems and what is required to solve them. A brief overview of the Internet's standards, technologies, and functions, which provide the technical foundation of an intranet, is presented.

The Information Boom

The modern office is in the midst of an information production boom, made possible by the availability of high-performance, low-cost computers. This, in turn, has supported the development of more powerful and sophisticated software programs which, when combined with the PC, make it possible to host mission-critical business applications on platforms other than the mainframe or minicomputer. Without a doubt, the PC has become a ubiquitous and essential tool in today's office.

Keeping pace with the proliferation of PCs have been networking technologies that make it possible to connect computers in an array of Local and Wide Area Networks (LANs and WANs). These networks support distributed data storage and processing across hardware platforms and international boundaries. It would seem to be an ideal situation: We now have the ability to create and distribute all the data and information we need to run a business—or do we? While the degree of interconnectivity at the physical and data transport levels has made significant advances, the same cannot be said of the application and presentation levels—how data is created, stored, and communicated.

On the PC platform, the vast store of data we have to deal with is created by business applications that use different data storage formats, or by an assortment of personal productivity programs that are used to produce reports, graphs, presentations, and so on. Regardless of how the data is created, it's usually stored in a proprietary format particular to the software used to create it. On my PC, for example, there are files that have been created by Word, Excel, Powerpoint, CorelDraw!, Visio, Paintshop Pro, and an assortment of HTML (Hypertext Markup Language) editors. Generally speaking, moving data between them is far from seamless or transparent to the user.

The "not invented here" attitude that has come to characterize competing standards is, perhaps, strongest in the area of software products. While there is a degree of coexistence, or at least reasonable conversion capability between most packages, PC software in general continues to be highly proprietary. When was the last time you were able to load a WordPerfect document into MS Word and get 100 percent error-free conversion? The issue of data format compatibility is even greater if you're trying to move data between different types of software applications, such as from a word processing document to a spreadsheet, each of which has come from different vendors.

Moving from the application to the presentation level, or user interface, the situation only gets worse. The Windows environment has certainly contributed to ease of use by providing some consistency and a degree of integration, but you've probably discovered that not all Windows programs are created equal! If a business needs a common interface that uses data from several different sources, it must be custom-developed, usually an expensive and time-consuming exercise that is very difficult to cost-justify.

The Pace of Change

The standards issue is further exacerbated by continuous and rapid technology change in both the software and hardware sectors of the computer industry. Have you also felt that you're in continuous upgrade or replacement mode?

In the software industry, there's a yearly deluge of new products and software upgrades. At one time, you might have expected to receive a couple of minor upgrades during a year, followed by a major upgrade every 12 to 16 months. It's now pretty well accepted that software will be released with bugs in it, to be followed by an ongoing series of patches until the next major upgrade. In a speech at Carnegie-Mellon University, Rich Rashid of the Microsoft Corporation indicated that on average, Microsoft releases 50 new products every year, and upgrades existing products every 18 to 24 months to maintain their revenue stream. Given this quick turnover of software products, it is very difficult for companies to keep pace, and the associated costs, particularly for maintenance, support, and training, continue to rise.

Hardware production differs somewhat in that component flaws aren't as common as software bugs; but, in the race to keep ahead of the software developers and competitors, new hardware products are appearing as quickly as software. In hardware, too, it's becoming increasingly difficult to maintain technical currency, and even harder to justify these new costs. During a recent outsourcing project for the provision of desktop computing and its support, the issue of technical currency was so contentious that it was a major factor in the decision to reduce the outsourcing's scope to only providing support services. Jim Forbes raised this issue in an interview with Agnes Emregh for the January 29, 1996 issue of *Electronic Buyer's News*: "'Staying abreast and anticipating new technology is much more important than it's ever been,' declared Agnes Emregh, vice president of Computer Products at NEC Technologies, Inc., Boxborough, Mass. The current pace of technology has reduced the design life of some PC products to as few as six months, she noted, a major change in a market where until 1993, products had lives of up to 13 months or more.'"

This short life span means that any standards on which you've based your technological architecture are also likely to change frequently or, even worse, disappear completely, creating new legacy systems virtually overnight. So, despite all the technological gains, companies are ending up with "islands of information." Figure 1.1 displays this "information dilemma." These valuable resources can't be exploited fully for the benefit of the organization, and have reduced investment return while increasing maintenance costs, requiring further investment.

What's Required

In order to resolve the information dilemma, you need to find a technological solution that satisfies each of the following criteria as much as possible:

- **Technical Stability**—The stability required in the office is best provided by technology that is mature and not subject to continuous and dramatic upgrades. Any changes that are introduced should be of an evolutionary nature, and, as such, allow for a more systematic modification of the computing environment.

- **Flexibility**—The desired solution should have the flexibility to accommodate business or technical changes. This is best provided by technology based on widely supported and mature standards, such as international standards, and designed from an open systems point of view. It should not be proprietary or platform dependent.

- **Integration**—Ideally, your system should be able to provide users with the highest possible level of integration between the various business

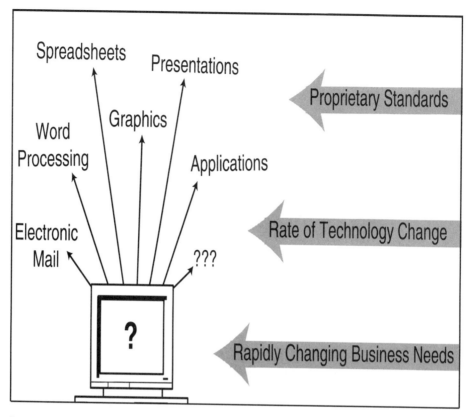

Figure 1.1   The information dilemma.

applications and the productivity tools that are already in place. This means a common presentation layer, or interface, is necessary. The system should be able to display data and information in different formats, including word processing, spreadsheet, or presentation graphics. At another level, this technology should be able to access data and information distributed throughout the organization on different platforms and in different geographical locations.

- **Investment Leverage**—Over time, your company has invested a significant amount of money directly into the acquisition of technology and, indirectly, through investing in employee training or hiring computer professionals to create and maintain your data. The technology we're looking for, then, should leverage this investment by building on the existing technical infrastructure, employee skills, and existing data.

- **Obsolescence**—While some obsolescence is inevitable, a mature, flexible technology that is evolutionary in nature provides a measure of currency, and protects against the need for continuous investment in upgrades and employee retraining.

- **Cost**—The solution that you're looking for should be cost effective in terms of acquisition and implementation (including training). The cost factor also applies to ongoing licensing, maintenance, and support costs. Companies often seem to miss these latter items when trying to cost-justify a technology project.

- **Scalability**—It's a fact that systems and applications grow, but it is very difficult to project the rate and magnitude of growth in any given computing environment. Therefore, it's essential to select a solution that has reasonable growth capability, and is not limited by proprietary components or standards.

Not surprisingly, no one product is robust enough to satisfy this list of requirements; the answer to the information dilemma can't be found in a shrink-wrapped package displayed on the trade show circuit. Nevertheless, it is possible to meet the communications- and information-sharing needs of the workplace, and it has been for some time. The solution simply requires looking in a different direction and reevaluating the possibilities of an established technology—the Internet.

The Internet in a Nutshell

When the Internet's builders began working on the internetworking project that was to become the Internet, they were presented with a series of challenges. Some were imposed by the technology of the day, others by the agency funding the project. Since an intranet is the application of Internet standards and technology within an organization, it will be useful to review these challenges and the solutions to them. Although the magnitude differs, the basic nature of the problems faced in today's office computing environment hasn't changed. The focus has shifted from the level of hardware connectivity to applications and data issues, but there still remains the need to connect diverse systems and move information between them as effectively and efficiently as possible.

Early Challenges and Their Solutions

The model for the Internet came from a 1964 paper prepared by the RAND Corporation in response to military concerns about the possibility of the Cold War getting hot. It proposed a command-and-control network based on two principles: there would be no central point on the network that enemies could target, and it would be designed on the premise that the network itself had the possibility of being essentially unreliable at any time. They were to accomplish these goals by building a network in which all nodes were equal in status, and blocks of information would be divided into smaller pieces called packets. The individual packets could be sent by different routes to avoid nodes that were no longer operational.

In 1969, the Advanced Research Projects Agency was commissioned to build a network based on this model, using packet switching theory. The first issue the agency had to deal with was a vast array of computer hardware distributed over scattered geographic locations. These would require a set of protocols that could be mounted on the different architectures, allowing them to talk to each other. The Network Control Protocol (NCP) was developed, and by 1971, the network (ARPANET) consisted of 23 host computers. In 1972, the first public demonstration of ARPANET, consisting of 40 connected machines, was presented at the International Conference on Computer Communications.

Work then proceeded on developing a mobile network that could use data lines, radio, and satellites to handle transmissions between nodes. The problem of getting transparent host communications across multiple packet networks led to the development of the Transmission Control Protocol (TCP), which was implemented concurrently at Stanford; Bolt Beranek and Newman, Inc. (BBN); and University College, London. The new protocol was first demonstrated in 1977, when a triple network Internet consisting of ARPANET, the Packet Radio Net, and the Atlantic Packet Satellite Network (SATNET) was created. They sent test data from a mobile radio node across a continental network, across an intercontinental satellite network, and then back into a wireline network.

Although TCP was a robust protocol and had a very reliable delivery rate, packets did occasionally get lost. Retransmission resulted in significant system degradation, particularly when voice data packets were sent. It was reasoned that if the existing packet was divided into much smaller packets, transmission time would be significantly reduced; consequently, the level of system degradation resulting from retransmission would also be reduced. TCP was redesigned and split into two protocols. The TCP component was used for passing packet information, such as the number of packets being sent and their sequencing, between the hosts. The second component, the Internet Protocol (IP), related to the individual packet and carried the data and the addressing information necessary to get it to the destination. These two protocols came to be referred to as one—TCP/IP. In 1982, the Department of Defense endorsed TCP/IP as their networking standard and, as a result, the Internet was first defined as a connected set of internets (networks using TCP/IP). In 1983, all the ARPANET hosts were switched from NCP to TCP/IP.

Protocols and Standards

Internet protocols, unlike those in the commercial computing world, have been function-driven, rather than market-driven. They are also characterized by an approach to design based on the lowest common denominator, and as such, are the least proprietary in the computer industry. Most of them have resulted from Request For Comment (RFC) documents or Internet Drafts prepared for the Internet Engineering Task Force (IETF). These were circulated throughout the international technical community, giving them a distinctly global flavor. The net effect is a collection of protocols and standards that epitomizes an open-systems approach to computing and has the highest degree of cross-platform compatibility and portability.

The Origin of the Internet RFC

In 1969, the first Request For Comment (RFC), called "Host Software," was published by Steve Crocker, at that time a graduate student working at the UCLA Network Measurement Center. (Crocker later went on to found CyberCash, Inc., where he now serves as the Senior Vice President of Development.) Since then, the RFC has become the standard vehicle for reviewing and publishing protocols. Another of the Internet pioneers, Vinton Cerf, founder of the Internet Society (ISOC) and regarded by many as the "Father of the Internet," relates the story behind the first RFC in his article "How the Internet Came to Be:"

In April 1969, Steve issued the very first Request For Comment. He observed that we were just graduate students at the time and so had no authority. So we had to find a way to document what we were doing without acting like we were imposing anything on anyone. He came up with the RFC methodology to say, 'Please comment on this, and tell us what you think.'

Table 1.1   Internet Protocols

Protocol	Description
File Transfer Protocol (FTP)	Covers the transfer of files from one host to another
Hypertext Transport Protocol (HTTP)	An application level, object-oriented protocol for the distribution of data in various formats
Internet Gopher Protocol	Covers distributed document search and retrieval
Internet Group Multicast Protocol (IGMP)	Extensions defined to IP for the support of internetwork multicasting
Internet Message Access Protocol 4 (IMAP4)	A client/server protocol for manipulating remote mail stores
Internet Protocol (IP)	Covers transmission of blocks of data between the source and destination, as well as fragmentation and reassembly if required
Multipurpose Internet Mail Extensions (MIME)	Redefines the format of message bodies to enable exchange of multipart messages and textual or nontextual body content
NetBIOS	A standard for the transmission of IP datagrams over NetBIOS networks
Network News Transfer Protocol (NNTP)	Allows information in USENET format to be exchanged over the Internet
Point to Point Protocol (PPP)	Defines a standard method for transmitting multiprotocol datagrams over point-to-point communications links

(Continued)

Table 1.1   Internet Protocols (Continued)

Protocol	Description
Post Office Protocol 3 (POP3)	Permits a workstation to dynamically access a mail drop on a server host and retrieve messages
Secure Sockets Layer Protocol (SSL)	An Internet Draft describing a security protocol for private communications over the Internet
Secure Hypertext Transport Protocol (S-HTTP)	An Internet Draft describing a protocol for sending secure messages using the HTTP method
Serial Line Internet Protocol (SLIP)	Enables the transmission of IP datagrams over a serial line
Simple Mail Transfer Protocol (SMTP)	Covers the transfer of electronic mail between host machines
Telnet Protocol	Specifies remote terminal access to host machines
Transmission Control Protocol (TCP)	A host-to-host communications protocol for use in a packet-switched communications network

The most common of these protocols are summarized in Table 1.1, and relevant RFCs are provided on the accompanying CD-ROM.

Internet Tools and Their Functions

The software technology developed by the Internet user community has evolved continuously as its needs grew and changed. A good example of this dynamic is the development of the Telnet protocol and software, which enables terminal connection to a remote host. Since the computing resources of the day were fairly scarce, especially in the supercomputer category, the ARPA project team decided that giving researchers this remote computational capability would prove invaluable to the research community. Over the next couple of years, it became apparent from the volume of data traffic that the network was being used primarily for electronic communications between researchers, not for shared processing. From the beginning, the Internet was viewed as much as a communications vehicle as a tool for resource sharing and information distribution by its users.

Communications

Computer communication is generally divided into two subcategories: batch and real time. The batch mode applies to any situation where the exchange of information between the sender and the recipient takes place at different points in time, for instance, if I compose a message this morning, send it, and you read it this afternoon. Real time communication, like a telephone conversation between two people, is immediate. While there are other communications tools available, the following are the most likely to find their way into the office environment.

ELECTRONIC MAIL (BATCH)

Electronic mail, or email, appeared in the early 1970s, but the actual specification for mail was put forward in RFC 733, published in 1977. Email continued to grow in functionality through the 1980s, adding features such as electronic address books and folder systems. Mail content continued to be limited to text, which contained no special characters or format controls, until the Mutipurpose Internet Mail Extensions (MIME) specification was set by RFC 1521 in 1992. This protocol provided support for multi-part messages and tabs in the message body, and generally revolutionized email on the Internet by providing the capability of using mail messages as a transport agent for non-textual information. Now, any information that can be stored as a computer file can be transported over the Internet as a mail attachment. Email has emerged as the communications workhorse of the '90s and is without equal in terms of providing low-cost, interpersonal communications.

LIST SERVICES (BATCH)

More commonly referred to as mailing lists, list services are simply a means of providing automated distribution of email messages to a large number of users over the Internet. In addition to facilitating distribution, list server software also automates the addition and removal of subscribers (mailing list recipients). List services take two forms: one broadcasts information to which no response is required, and the other presents moderated discussion where participants can reply to messages they've received. In the second case, replies are returned to the list server computer and redistributed to other list members. Either way, a list service provides a very economical and effective way to broadcast information over a network.

USENET (Batch)

Although it is text-based, like email and mailing lists, the USENET has its own protocol (NNTP) for transferring information over the Internet, and requires specialized software to handle activities such as creating, reading, and replying to news articles. Often referred to as the bulletin board of the Internet, USENET organizes the information sent (posted) into categories called newsgroups. Each topic area has its own newsgroup name, and participants can select the topics they wish to read, or the particular electronic discussions in which they want to participate. It should be noted that USENET facilitates online discussions, and is not to be confused with online conferencing, which requires specialized software that supports real-time interaction between discussion participants.

Audio, Voice, and Video (Real-Time)

Since the first audio and video multicast broadcasts took place over the Internet Multicasting Backbone (MBONE) in 1992, transmission performance and quality has advanced rapidly. Given the low cost of long-distance communications over the Internet, it's not surprising that these additions to interpersonal communications have attracted attention from the business community. The market potential in this area is evidenced by the rapid appearance of commercial software since 1995, supporting audio, voice, videophone, and video conferencing.

Resource Sharing and Information Distribution

The dissemination of information on the Internet has progressed from the sharing of computational resources to the distribution of information in many different formats, including documents, computer program files, data files, and graphics. With the exception of the World Wide Web, the items in this category are software programs as well as protocols.

Telnet

The Telnet specification for remote-terminal access to a network host was published as RFC 318 in 1972. As mentioned earlier, this was a response to the need to share computational resources among researchers on the network. At that time, a limited number of supercomputers were available to meet the emerging processing demands. It made sense to have the necessary programs or data installed on one of these machines, and then have users log on from another node on the network to carry out their processing activities.

FILE TRANSFER PROTOCOL (FTP)

RFC 454 appeared in 1973 and established specifications for file transfers between hosts on the network. FTP was a logical extension to Telnet—if users could connect to remote hosts, it would be helpful to have the capability of transferring files between the connected hosts. These file transfers would eliminate the need to physically transport tapes across the country, thereby reducing costs and shortening the time frame required to load programs or data and complete computations.

GOPHER

The main issue driving the development and release of the Gopher specification covering search and retrieval of distributed documents was ease of use. The Internet had been identified as an ideal vehicle for providing a campus-wide information system at the University of Minnesota, with one exception—it was too complicated for most of the intended information providers and consumers. The project's backers put forward a very simple user specification: The proposed solution must be flexible and easy to use.

The computer systems group responded admirably, meeting not only the user requirements, but also ushering in the client/server computing concept to the Internet. The Gopher protocol and software were released in 1991, at which point the scope of information distribution on the Internet underwent a significant change.

For the information providers, there was now a tool they could use to construct a menu-based system, with links from specific menu items to local or distributed documents. There was also a menu displayed on the screen from which users could select items by typing a number.

For the systems staff running the computers, Gopher provided a more effective means of utilizing the available computer resources. Prior to this time, any connection to a host using Telnet or FTP meant that a port, or connection point on the machine, was tied up until that particular session was finished; the Gopher client/server approach (much, much more on this topic later) maintained the connection only until the information requested by the user (the client) was sent by the host computer (the server).

You can appreciate how the client/server approach greatly increased the capacity of host systems to distribute information to users on the network. It also meant that a document linked to a menu item on a given Gopher server could reside on a host computer in a distant location.

THE WORLD WIDE WEB

At the same time work was underway on Gopher, the staff at the CERN (*Conseil Europeen pour la Recherche Nucleaire*) European Laboratory for Particle Physics in Switzerland was working on an alternative approach to information search and retrieval. While ease of use was a consideration for that project, the staff also paid attention to the way people processed visual information, and to the nature of the data that made up document content sent over the network, such as data that extended beyond the scope of textual documents distributed using a Gopher server.

Using menus to present information to users was regarded as too linear, and was not consistent with the way we process visual input. The World Wide Web's architects argued that if you observe a person reading, you'll notice that his eyes are drawn to key words or phrases, and that they are likely to skip randomly over the page or through the document. A system for presenting information, then, should try to match this reality as closely as possible. The result was a model based on the idea of a document page as a way of delivering information. Rather than menu items, the user was presented with highlighted key words or phrases that, when activated, would retrieve other pages linked to them. This hypertext concept, which had been around in theory since the 1970s, was implemented by using a subset of a text formatting language called Standard Generalized Markup Language (SGML). This subset is Hypertext Markup Language (HTML), and uses a tool called a browser to display text and hypertext documents on the screen.

Like the Gopher developers, the World Wide Web project team supported the client/server approach. However, they decided to set out a specification that was not limited to documents, but could also reference and retrieve *objects* over the network. The result was the Hypertext Transport Protocol (HTTP), a specification for the movement of objects between host computers.

The World Wide Web became firmly entrenched on the Internet and set the direction for future distributed information systems when a browser called Mosaic was released in 1993. Mosaic provided the capability of displaying non-textual file types such as graphics and audio, thereby extending the boundaries of the document page. Since that time, HTML and the browsers for viewing HTML pages have been enhanced to the point where a full range of multimedia information can be distributed and displayed over the network, and hypertext is now generally referred to as hypermedia.

Looking Inward: The Internet Becomes an Intranet

In 1995 (or perhaps before—who knows the moment when a wave becomes a wave), systems staff who had set up corporate Web sites on the Internet engaged in some lateral thinking, and realized that these sites could be used to distribute information within the workplace. In fact, Web sites could be built inside an organization and not be connected to the Internet at all. From this brainstorm, intranets were born (the person who coined the word is unknown, although several have offered to take the credit). Intranets are networked office environments made possible through the use of Internet protocols and tools, as shown in Figure 1.2. Although World Wide Web technology is the most visible and publicized aspect of corporate intranets, it is only one of the Internet's many resources that can be useful. The entire collection of protocols and tools, which together reflect the ongoing mission of the Internet's formal standards bodies (W3 and IETF) to provide wide-scale, heterogeneous connectivity and communications, furnishes the building blocks for solutions to the corporate information dilemma.

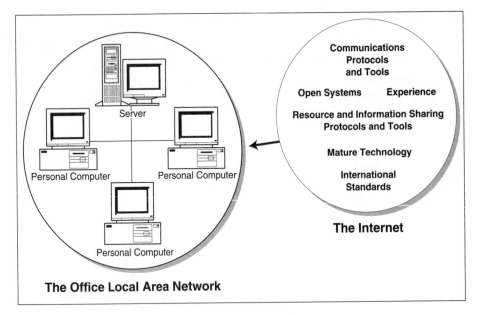

Figure 1.2   Moving the Internet inward.

What Parts of the Internet Can You Use?

Web servers are grabbing all the attention as far as intranets are concerned, but you don't have to, nor should you, exclude the rest of the Internet's protocol and tool collection. Each one, in a given situation, can add to your organization's communications and information infrastructure, making it more effective, flexible, and robust.

List services (mailing lists), for example, provide an inexpensive way of getting email-based messages to the lists' subscribers. This text-based email format also skirts the frustration of time-consuming slow links or modems. A good illustration of a list service is Gleason Sackman's Net-Happenings, a mailing list with more than eight thousand subscribers interested in keeping up with happenings on the Internet. On a daily basis, they get a collection of messages about Web sites, software, books, and so on. They can go through these messages and choose the ones they want to follow up on for more information. In addition to the mailing list, Gleason has provided a Web site with an archive of all the messages sent since the list was started. If a user has missed some messages, has accidentally deleted them, or simply wants to find additional information, he can go to the site and do a keyword search. This effective use of two of the Internet's tools allows users the choice of either having information broadcast to them or obtaining it on command.

As you can see, each of the Internet tools has its use, and as part of the intranet planning activity (Part 4, An Intranet Blueprint), each should be assessed in the light of business processes, business requirements, and above all, your users.

What Are the Basic Requirements for an Intranet?

The minimum basic requirement for an intranet is a local area network whose operating systems (Network and PC) can support TCP/IP—in other words, most networks will work. Any additional requirements will be based on the capacity of the existing system, relative to the scope and complexity of the intranet you envision. Likewise, the necessary employee skill sets will be determined by the nature of this intranet. After you've finished this book you will probably find that, for the most part, your project team already has the basic skills needed, and very little specialized training will be required.

2

Client/Server Computing
for the Networked Office

Client/Server Computing for the Networked Office

The Internet provides the protocols and tools that companies can use to build a technical infrastructure for internal communications, including creating and distributing information throughout the organization. Since the Internet is not constrained by data type or the hierarchy of a menu-based design, the World Wide Web provides a flexible platform for delivering and presenting a full range of multimedia information content. This multimedia, distributed information system is based on the client/server computing model, which we will examine in detail.

Distributed Computing

Before we delve into the client/server model, we need to lay the foundation for an understanding of client/server technology with a brief overview of distributed systems. This concept, originally referred to as *distributed processing*, resulted from the realization that CPU usage did not have to be confined to one computer or one location—by using high-speed data communications lines, processing could be distributed over many geographically dispersed computers. Distributed computing spread rapidly, driven by rapidly changing business requirements and supported

25

by improved computer and telecommunications technologies. The scope of the concept also expanded to include shared and distributed processors, devices (such as printers), and files. Later, applications also were included in distributed computing. Since the scope of the model had grown, the catch-phrase distributed processing was replaced by the term *distributed systems.*

These systems are characterized by:

- **Resource Sharing**—The various computer resources that have been identified are shared over Local, Municipal, and Wide Area Networks.

- **Open Systems Architecture**—The standards and protocols in use are not proprietary; access to the system is open to different computing platforms and manufacturers' equipment types.

- **Scalability**—The system is capable of expansion without degrading either the system's overall performance or the performance of any of its components.

- **Concurrency**—Applications and databases can be run at the same time on different parts of the system with no loss of data integrity.

- **Fault Tolerance**—The system will continue to function even if individual computers or parts of the network fail.

- **Transparency**—The system appears as a single entity, leaving the user unaware of the existence of the network, the location of the applications, or the location of the data.

Client/server technology was developed to facilitate the *resource sharing* requirements of distributed systems.

Client/Server Computing

Client/server provides a conceptual model and technical framework, such as hardware and software, for supporting the distributed processing and data storage requirements of today's office. Its origins and precise definition, as well as its creators' initial intent, are somewhat elusive, since they're clouded by consumer perceptions, the trade press, and the vendor marketing juggernaut. Despite this confusion, it is possible to provide a basic definition and lay out the client/server technical and functional model with some accuracy. But first, it's important to know some background information on conventional client/server computing.

Conventional Client/Server

As early as 1986, Sybase, a database software developer, used the term *client/server* to describe its own software product, which could provide a link between host databases and applications. The PC was only slightly more intelligent than the dumb terminal, and it wasn't until the 1990s that client/server computing really gained momentum. In the early '90s, many things happened in the computer industry to provide the motivation and impetus to push client/server computing to the forefront of computer topics, where it remains one of the industry's hot items.

As business computing moved into the 1990s, there was a tremendous change in application variety, with computers being used in a myriad of ways to support various business processes. Since corporate computing was still predominantly mainframe-based, the many applications in a business were combined (in the name of integration), resulting in complex, monolithic systems. And, while computing horsepower was a non-issue, these huge systems could not be readily modified. Time, resources, and cost were major issues. This inflexibility, along with the fact that the demand for these applications far outstripped the capacity of the central Management Information Services (MIS) groups, led to general user frustration with the pace of systems development, and a feeling of isolation from the systems group.

During this same period, businesses themselves were undergoing significant and rapid changes: restructuring, downsizing, and re-engineering. This meant that a computing infrastructure had to be flexible and responsive to business changes, while at the same time containing or reducing computing costs. Obviously, the mainframe-based head office data center could not meet these demands.

While all these changes were going on, significant events took place in the PC world, notably performance increases and cost decreases. The resulting flood of PCs into the office environment, plus advances in local and wide-area networking technologies, resulted in a large installed base of networked microcomputers capable of much more than simply serving as replacements for typewriters, adding machines, and dumb terminals. Increased PC processing capability, coupled with powerful and relatively inexpensive new software tools, made it possible to develop applications very quickly (compared to the mainframe world). The resulting proliferation of PC applications created a new challenge: accessing data and applications spread across two or three platforms, while using a single workstation with a common interface. Given the new computing landscape and the legitimization of the PC platform, the client/server model was the logical answer. The forces that contributed to the move to client/server are illustrated in Figure 2.1.

Client/Server in a Nutshell

The client/server model and its supporting technologies have become incredibly complex, making it very difficult to put forward a broadly accepted definition. However, as a basic definition you can say that:

> *A client/server environment is one in which data sources and applications are distributed, but can be accessed by a* client program *that sends a request for service to one or more* servers, *which provide the requested services.*

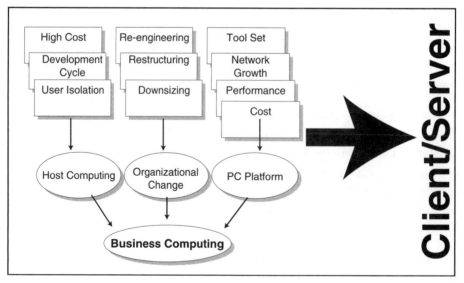

Figure 2.1   The dynamics of client/server computing.

At its simplest level, client/server can be shown by the following example: On a Local Area Network (LAN) where there's a file server and several PCs, the file server has a word processing program shared by all users on the network. If one of the users wants to use the word processor, she can click on the icon (assuming there's a graphical interface), and the request will be sent to the server. The server, in turn, responds to this request for service, and sends the program to the PC that made the request (the client). The client program then loads and starts the word-processing program.

In this illustration, the service provided by the file server is the delivery of requested files to the client. Even in this very simple situation, there is interaction between the client, with its own operating system, interface, and/or client program, and the server, which has its operating system and the LAN's Network Operating System (NOS).

We'll build on this model further by examining the three main components of a client/server environment, the server, the middleware, and the client, in more detail.

The Server

In general, servers run continuously, waiting for client requests, which are sent over a communications session. These sessions can either be dedicated to clients, or dynamically allocated from a pool of sessions. A server must also concurrently service multiple clients and provide different levels of service priority. It also needs to trigger and run any background tasks (such as file downloads in off-peak hours) that are unrelated to the primary purpose of the server.

In addition to the file server in our example, there are several other specialized types of servers:

DATABASE SERVER

The database server provides services that allow the client to interact with a database. The client must send the request in the format required by the Database Management System (DBMS) it uses. (A database using the Structured Query Language (SQL), for example, would have to receive valid SQL commands in order to process the request.) Each request is treated individually, processed against the database, and the results are passed back to the client. An example of this would be a request for a specific record, or a record update.

TRANSACTION SERVER

A transaction server stores procedures and executes them at the request of the client. Using the previous SQL example, the transaction server would have a procedure containing a series of SQL statements that would be executed as a single transaction against the database when the server received the client request. While more efficient than a simple database server, the entire procedure can fail if just one of the statements fails.

GROUPWARE SERVER

This class of specialized servers is used to provide services related to messaging and document exchange, such as work flow or workgroup computing. Lotus Notes is a good example of a groupware server.

OBJECT SERVER

This type of server supports object-oriented applications, where the client requests specific objects. The Object Request Broker (ORB) supports network interaction between the application and an object.

Figure 2.2 illustrates each of the server types, as well as the client calls that would be sent to request a service from individual servers. It also shows all the server programs hosted on a single computer—while this may occur occasionally, it's unusual. The number of servers in use will, in fact, depend on the nature of the individual applications and the capacity of the computer being used as a server. Another determining factor is, of course, performance.

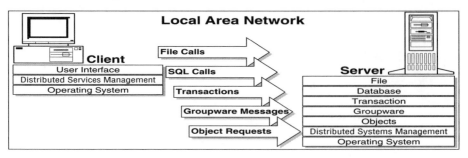

Figure 2.2   Client/server LAN with different server types.

In the client/server LAN illustrated in Figure 2.2, you can see that the client might send service requests to multiple server programs, each one of which expects to receive messages in a specified, and usually proprietary, format. You will also notice that on the client side, there is a user interface (Windows, for example), the PC operating system, and an application called Distributed Systems Management (DSM). DSM runs on every node on the network, and manages the flow of information between the clients and the servers. On the server side, there are various server programs, the DSM, and the operating system.

The Middleware Muddle

This definition of middleware was supplied by writer John R. Rymer in an April 1996 *Byte* magazine article, "The Muddle in the Middle":

"Middleware *n* 1: stuff that links clients and servers (helpful, but vague) 2: the slash in client/server (not helpful, but clever) 3: software to manage communications with databases (clearer, but do all client/server applications involve database transactions?)."

Middleware

Sitting between the client and the server is a collection of protocols and programs that makes communication between the two possible. It's generally referred to as *middleware,* and has been used to describe anything that isn't specific to the client or the server. Middleware basically provides:

- **Client/Server Connectivity**—The programs and protocols that constitute middleware provide a mechanism for applications to communicate across the network.

- **Platform Transparency**—Middleware handles platform-specific encodings so that the client and server do not need intimate knowledge of each other.

- **Network Transparency**—Application programmers can let the middleware handle any low-level networking choices without developing network-specific routines for the application.

- **Application and Tool Support**—Middleware provides Application Program Interfaces (APIs) that provide hooks for applications and servers.

- **Language Support**—Database middleware provides transparency across different database dialects, such as SQL, and generic middleware supports the use of different programming languages to create various pieces of the application.

- **Database Support**—Transparency across different storage formats is achieved by hiding DBMS differences, or by providing support from both proprietary and standard APIs.

The middleware component of the client/server architecture is divided into three layers: transport, Network Operating System, and applications or services. Figure 2.3 shows these layers, as well as the DSM component that manages information flow. (The DSM sits on the client and server, and in the middleware.)

THE TRANSPORT LAYER

The transport layer consists of transport protocols (protocol stacks) that provide end-to-end communications across LANs and WANs. By using interconnect technology such as routers, bridges, and gateways, it is possible to transport multiprotocol traffic seamlessly across networks. These protocol stacks, such as TCP/IP and Novell's Internet Packet Exchange/

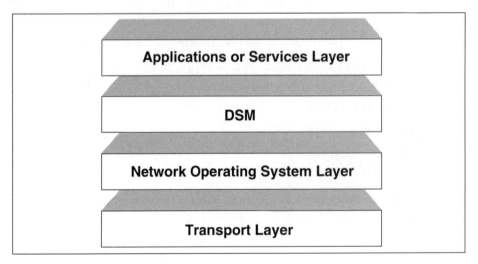

Figure 2.3 Middleware layers.

Sequenced Packet Exchange (IPX/SPX), provide a link between the PC network card, that card's logical network driver, and a transport-independent API that links to a specific application. The role of each of these elements is as follows:

- **Network Card**—This card, also called a Network Interface Card, or NIC, provides the physical link between the PC and network cabling.

- **Logical Network Driver**—This program provides a single interface between the network card and the protocol stack that manages the adapter card to send and receive data. The two most widely accepted standards for network drivers are Open Data-link Interface (ODI) from Novell, and the Network Device Interface Specification (NDIS) from Microsoft/ 3Com, both of which are designed to let different protocols use a single network card.

- **Application Program Interface**—The API layer is a transport-independent interface that allows developers to connect their programs to a single interface that supports multiple protocols.

THE NETWORK OPERATING SYSTEM LAYER

This software connects all resources (such as printers and file directories), and facilitates their sharing over the network. The NOS layer also coordinates communications activities between applications on the network.

THE APPLICATIONS OR SERVICES LAYER

As we've already noted, this layer handles service requests to the specialized servers that are needed to provide different functions for applications on the network, and returns the appropriate responses.

There are, of course, differing views of the middleware component and what it should include. Rymer, for example, in his *Byte* article, regards the protocols I've described as part of the transport layer as nothing more than low-level transport protocols and, as such, shouldn't be regarded as middleware. You can see that even one piece of the client/server model can be difficult to define, and easy to debate. It is possible, however, to find agreement with the fact that middleware's scope, function, and complexity is constantly changing.

The Client

The client portion of client/server is a program, which, through its interface, sends requests to the server for specific services. In turn, the request's results are displayed on the client's screen. (In the client/server configuration illustrated in Figure 2.2, the client has a Graphical User Interface (GUI), but it should be noted that interfaces can come in two additional flavors: non-GUI and Object Oriented User Interface [OOUI].) From the user's point of view, the technology is straightforward and easy to use. Development, on the other hand, is much more complicated, since no single interface will service all the applications required on a system. Here, too, cost, complexity, and proprietary standards raise their ugly heads.

FAT CLIENT

Traditional client/server applications, such as file and database servers, moved the bulk of the processing activities to the client side of the model. The increased power of the PC made this possible, and it reflected the prevailing belief that the mainframe was dead, and that everything should be done on the PC. In fairness to the early client/server developers, the middleware idea hadn't really crystallized, and certainly no software existed to support it. A benefit of having fat clients is that they provide a great deal of flexibility, and give users the opportunity to create their own applications. Figure 2.4 shows the benefits of both fat and thin clients.

FAT SERVER

The converse to fat clients is usually found in applications that use groupware and object servers. Fat server applications have the advantage of easier deployment and management, as well as their ability to reduce overall network traffic. More recently, though, developers have discovered that fat clients aren't necessarily a good thing, given the cost of continuous client upgrades (from 486s to Pentiums, from Pentiums to multiprocessors, and so onwards and upwards) to keep things running smoothly. At the same time, the "mainframes are dead" hysteria has subsided somewhat, and MIS groups are getting back to some basics: the *functional requirements* and *nature of the application* should be the major factors in deciding how and where to distribute processing. This, coupled with the sophistication of new middleware, means there are now more, and better, options for distributing the load between the client and server.

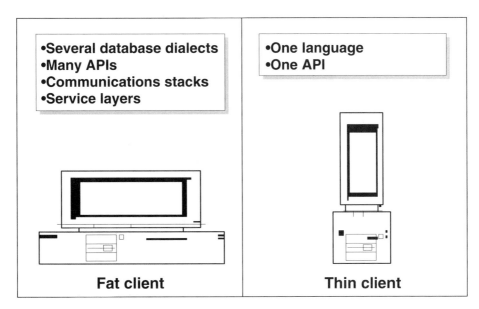

Figure 2.4 Fat vs. thin clients.

Benefits, Weaknesses, and Issues

It's easy to appreciate the complexity of the client/server world, even using the simple model shown in Figure 2.2. Try to picture a scenario where there are multiple LANs and specialized servers distributed throughout an organization, and across two or three hardware tiers. Complete the picture by adding several databases, online transaction processing, and a management information system (to name only a few of the possible applications) to this technical infrastructure. Given this staggering complexity, it is easy to appreciate the problems involved in developing and maintaining client/server applications.

As in any computer technology, client/server has its strengths and weaknesses. Some advantages include reduced hardware and software costs and more technological options to choose from, resulting in a higher level of flexibility. And, since the PC platform is the focal point of the software industry, most of the progress in software development is happening in the PC realm. Also, client/server applications are scalable, allowing reallocation of computer resources as needed.

But on the negative side, this technology is not without its limitations and risks. With broadly distributed, complex client/server applications, the support costs are significantly greater than in a mainframe host environment. This complexity adds to the management and security issues, and highlights the area of system reliability. A related issue is system performance and tuning—the more parts the system has, the greater the possibility that something might go wrong, and the more places where a bottleneck problem might arise. One analyst has described client/server as a bottleneck in motion. From a cost perspective, the Gartner Group, an internationally-recognized computer consulting and trend analysis firm, prepared cost-of-ownership studies which indicated that client/server systems are 40 percent more expensive to produce and maintain than traditional systems.

Another important issue is the proprietary nature of client/server components, especially the middleware. Products in this category, like others, have a market-driven life expectancy. Good market share adds to their shelf life; poor market share erodes it. This creates legacy client/server applications that may be only a couple of years old. The last issue concerns the client side of the equation at the presentation level (user interface). The Windows desktop provides a reasonable, iconic view of the world, but different client programs must still be used to access various applications and databases. A common, ubiquitous interface or applications view has not been available to tie everything together for the user—until now. The World Wide Web's client/server model and hypertext page view of information provide what commercial software developers have been trying to achieve since the beginning of this decade: openness, scalability, extensibility, data integrity, and transparency.

The World Wide Web and Client/Server

When Tim Berners-Lee was working at CERN in the late 1980s, he encountered a situation that frustrated computer users then and now—having to use different workstations, procedures, and commands to access information on different systems. He reasoned that it must be possible to use a single interface that would let users access all these different kinds of information. His finished proposal for dealing with this issue, "World Wide

Web: Proposal for a HyperText Project," laid the foundation for the creation of the World Wide Web and its supporting protocols. The following goals and objectives from that document illustrate his approach to the problem, and provide a good model for the type of client/server computing required by the workplace:

It will aim:

- To provide a common (simple) protocol for requesting human read able information stored at a remote system, using networks.

- To provide a protocol within which information can automatically be exchanged in a format common to the supplier and the consumer.

- To provide some method of reading at least text (if not graphics) using a large proportion of the computer screens in use at CERN.

- To provide and maintain at least one collection of documents, into which users may (but are not bound to) put their documents. This collection will include much existing data. (This is partly to give us first hand experience of use of the system, and partly because mem bers of the project will already have documentation for which they are responsible).

- To provide a keyword search option, in addition to navigation by following references, using any new or existing indexes (such as the CERNVM FIND indexes). The result of a keyword search is simply a hypertext document consisting of a list of references to nodes which match the keywords.

- To allow private individually managed collections of documents to be linked to those in other collections.

- To use public domain software wherever possible, or interface to proprietary systems which already exist.

- To provide the software for the above free of charge to anyone.

The project will not aim:

- To provide conversions where they do not exist between the many document storage formats at CERN, although providing a frame work into which such conversion utilities can fit.

- To force users to use any particular word processor, or mark-up format.

- To do research into fancy multimedia facilities such as sound and video.

- To use sophisticated network authorization systems. Data will be either readable by the world (literally), or will be readable only on one file system, in which case the file system's protection system will be used for privacy. All network traffic will be public.

The client/server model that Berners-Lee envisioned was elegant in its simplicity. On the client side, there was to be a common interface to display the information—an interface that was not platform-dependent or proprietary—so that the existing server side would remain, for the most part, in its present form. The key, then, was in the middle. This required an addressing scheme, a common protocol, and format negotiation. Format negotiation meant that the client and server did not change the format of the information, but simply used a method to transport it. The information, whether text or graphics, was treated as an object. Figure 2.5 is based on a model used in a presentation Berners-Lee gave in 1991 and 1992, and shows the client/server he envisioned for an *intranet* at CERN, which he called the World Wide Web.

Web Specifications

The essence of the World Wide Web is encapsulated in three basic specifications, which we'll examine briefly. The details can be found in the RFCs included on the accompanying CD.

HyperText Transport Protocol (HTTP)

Designed to run as a layer on top of TCP/IP (but not exclusively), it is the core communications protocol between the client and the server. HTTP allows the client to send a list of the types of data it understands and the data transfer protocol to be used. Through this format negotiation, the server can reply in a suitable way, using the correct transfer protocol, such as Gopher or FTP.

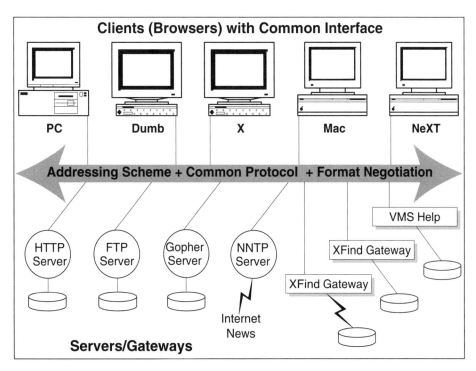

Figure 2.5   The World Wide Web client/server model.

UNIFORM RESOURCE LOCATOR (URL)

This is used to specify object locations on the network. It specifies the access method, such as HTTP or Gopher, the server location (domain name or IP address), the directory name on the server machine, and the object identifier. For example, the URL for the Berners-Lee seminar I referred to earlier would be:

http://www.w3.org/pub/WWW/Talks/General.html

Reading this from left to right you have:

http://—the access method, Hypertext Transport Protocol;

www.w3.org/—the server location, as a domain name;

pub/WWW/Talks/—the directory path;

General.html—the name of the object, in this case an HTML document.

Hypertext Markup Language (HTML)

This is used to construct hypertext documents (essentially, text files with embedded links to other documents), thereby allowing the user to see and access various types of information at other locations. HTML is a derivative of SGML, which is used to provide document structure and formatting codes for text documents, making these documents readable across a variety of hardware platforms and software programs. There are codes (called tags) placed in the source file, which are used to provide structure, control document and text appearance, insert objects such as images, and specify anchor points with links to other documents or objects. We'll be examining HTML in more detail later in the book.

The Client or Browser

The browser's role is twofold: it functions as a file viewer, and it serves as a client program for sending requests to a server on the network. As a viewer, it interprets the HTML tags in a file and displays the formatted document on the screen. Highlighted links (a word, phrase, or picture) can be activated by positioning the cursor on the link and clicking the mouse button. This triggers the browser's client role, and a request is sent to the URL specified in the hypertext link statement, thus initiating a Web client/server transaction that has four distinct steps: connection, request, response, and close.

- **Connection**—The client sends a signal to establish a connection with a specified server.

- **Request**—Once a connection is established, a request is sent to the server. This request contains the following information: the protocol the client is using, the name of the object to retrieve, the location of the object on the server, how the server should respond (for example, reply using HTTP), and what command the client will use to retrieve the object (such as GET).

- **Response**—If the server can fulfill the request according to the client's parameters, it sends the object to the client.

- **Close**—After the object has been received, the connection is closed.

By providing an addressing scheme, a common protocol, and a format negotiation, a user on any workstation can access different kinds of servers on the Internet. Take Gopher (a client/server system itself), for example, where everything the user can see or access is a menu or a document. Normally, when using Gopher client software you would see a list of items on the screen, with a number in front of each and some descriptive text. The user selects items by typing the item's number, and then pressing the Enter key. In the hypertext world, each item's descriptive text is displayed as a hypertext link (underlined text), as shown in Figure 2.6.

The browser, then, provides a user interface that acts as a universal client program for servers on the Internet, and as a viewer for displaying the different types of information located on these servers.

The Server

Berners-Lee saw the role of the server in the client/server model as very straightforward, having only to respond to client requests. The proposal

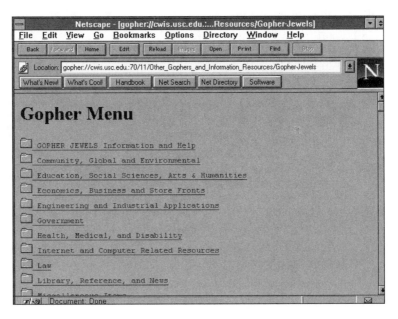

Figure 2.6   Gopher menu at the University of Southern California.

for a HyperText Project describes the operations between the client and server. According to Berners-Lee:

"A link is specified as an ASCII string from which the browser can deduce a suitable method of contacting an appropriate server. When a link is followed, the browser addresses the request for the node [a text object] to the server. The server therefore has nothing to know about other servers or other webs and can be kept simple."

The Middleware

Although we've talked about the middle between client and server on the World Wide Web, there is no middleware, as we understand it, in the commercial client/server world. If anything can be called middleware, it is the World Wide Web itself, and some analysts have gone so far as to suggest that middleware, as a specialized type of software, will disappear completely.

The World Wide Web delivers on the promises of client/server by providing a scalable, low-cost, flexible, and open system for business computing. Above all, it's amazingly simple.

Electronic Publishing

3

Electronic Publishing

Since its inception, the growth of the World Wide Web has been nothing short of explosive. According to figures released in *On The Internet* (a publication of the Internet Society), there were 30,000 Web sites in November 1995, and this number doubles every two months. This explosive growth is due in part to the Internet's ease of use, and also to the rich medium it provides for handling all kinds of electronic information. For the Internet community, the World Wide Web is the vehicle of choice for publishing, distributing, and managing information. The combination of proven standards and a rapidly growing selection of tools make it ideal for electronic publishing in today's organization; therefore we consider the publishing model to be more suitable for the modern organization than the traditional MIS information system.

The World Wide Web and Electronic Publishing

To understand the framework of Web publishing, it will be worthwhile to examine the conceptual basis of the World Wide Web and its implementation in more detail. In searching for the solution to CERN's information retrieval and display requirements, Tim Berners-Lee went to the available research on how we naturally read. It showed that our visual processing experience is based on the printed page. When someone reads a book, report, or magazine, his or her eyes scan across the page in both directions, as well as up and down. The material's content, format, and key words or phrases influence the person's eye movement. As a result, people do not, for the most part, read in a linear fashion, but skip forward and backward to pursue the information threads they want to follow. Working from these facts, Berners-Lee concluded that Gopher (client/server, but menu-based) was clearly not the answer to CERN's needs—the presentation of electronic information should be modeled on the page rather than a menu-based format.

The next piece of information he added was the observation that books, magazines, and so on have links that allow a reader to navigate through the material. These links can be found in the tables of contents, indexes, glossaries, footnotes, and references to other sources. Working from these points, or to these points from key words in the text itself, readers can move around in a document according to their needs. Now what Berners-Lee needed was a way to emulate the paper page, but in electronic form. The answer was *hypertext,* whose roots can be traced back to an article that President Roosevelt's key scientific advisor, Vannevar Bush, wrote for a 1945 issue of *Atlantic Monthly.* In it, he called for linked information retrieval machines that would help deal with that era's information explosion. The word hypertext was coined in the 1960s by Ted Nelson, creator of a global hypertext model called Xanadu. In his book *Literary Machines,* Nelson defined hypertext as follows: "I mean *non-sequential writing*—text that branches and allows choices to the reader, best read at an interactive screen. As popularly conceived, this is a series of text chunks connected by links which offer the reader different pathways."

Working with these concepts, Berners-Lee finalized the format of CERN's distributed information system—pages with active links that would allow the reader to pursue paths of information in any linear or nonlinear fashion he might choose, within the boundaries of the author's design. All that remained to be done was to develop a way to construct and view the pages. Extracting the commands he required from the existing SGML, Berners-Lee created a subset, to which he added the abilities for linking to and retrieving other documents (objects) on the network.

Figure 3.1 shows a hypertext page as it is displayed by a text-based browser. The active links are the highlighted text (on screen this is achieved by having the links more brightly displayed than normal text). The cursor (shown in Figure 3.1 as a dark bar over the word HOME) is moved from link to link by using either the Up/Down arrow keys or the Tab key. When the link phrase "Cut Flower Defects and Diseases" is highlighted by the cursor, then activated by pressing the Enter or Right Arrow key, the object referenced by the link is retrieved and displayed on the screen. The result of this particular link activation is shown in Figure 3.2.

MIME and Hypertext

The next major evolutionary step toward broad electronic publishing capability was taken when the MIME specification was published in 1992. MIME, which defined data types and how they should be treated, provided the ability to insert and display nontextual information content.

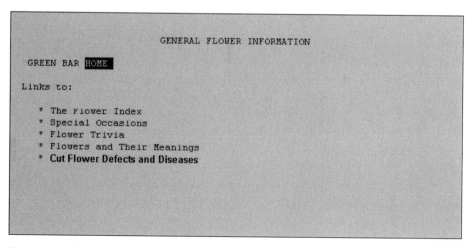

Figure 3.1   A hypertext page displayed with a text-based browser.

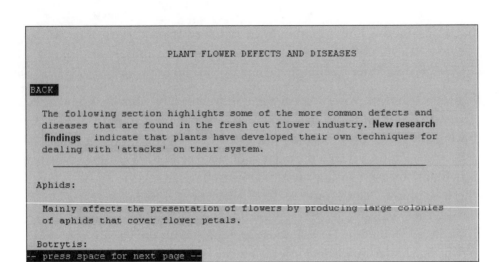

Figure 3.2   The result of link activation from Figure 3.1.

Synergy on the Internet

When the World Wide Web first appeared on the Internet in 1991, the browser could only display a limited number of data types: hypertext and text. The following year, two researchers working independently from the World Wide Web project submitted RFC 1341, titled *MIME (Multipurpose Internet Mail Extensions): Mechanisms for Specifying and Describing the Format of Internet Message Bodies.* The MIME RFC simply proposed extensions to the Simple Mail Transport Protocol (SMTP). However, when combined with the Web protocols, it made true universal readership possible.

The MIME specification allows the attachment of nontextual files by encoding the file in a special format. Information about the content type and length is put in the message header, which is parsed by the recipient software. If the recipient is MIME-compliant, it starts the appropriate program to handle specific types of data in the attachment. The MIME standard sets out 7 basic data types:

- application
- audio

- video

- image

- message

- multipart

- text

Within each of these types, there are subtypes based on the specific way data is represented and stored by a given software program. For example, the image data type contains subtypes for different graphics representations, such as the Graphics Interchange Format (GIF).

It was the MIME specification that moved the World Wide Web from simple hypertext to a multimedia vehicle called *hypermedia*. Within months of the introduction of this specification, staff at the National Center for Supercomputing Applications (NCSA), lead by Marc Andreessen, one of the summer programmers employed at the Center (who later went on to found Netscape Communications), developed Mosaic, the first graphical browser for the World Wide Web. Mosaic increased browser functionality for the page creators and the readers using the World Wide Web. Page authors could now include static graphics images with the text, thus gaining more options for expressing and conveying information. From the readers' perspective content was enriched, and since the browser's interface was graphical rather than command-line driven, the browser was much easier to use. Our previous text-based browser page samples (Figures 3.1 and 3.2) are shown in Figures 3.3 and 3.4 as they would appear when displayed by a graphical browser. On these pages the active links are indicated by underlined text (usually seen as blue on the screen). The mouse is used to move the cursor to the "Cut Flower Defects and Diseases" link, and by clicking the left mouse button the link is activated. Figure 3.4 shows the result of activating the link.

In Figure 3.3, the image displayed on the right-hand side of the screen contains a logo and has the phrase "home page" written on it. The graphic itself is defined as a hypertext link to the Grower Direct home page, which means that the user can click on the picture to retrieve and display the home page.

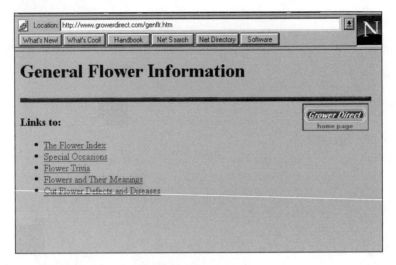

Figure 3.3 A page display using a graphical browser.

Web Publishing

We've seen how the Web's specifications and tools enable an author to create documents which equal, and in some cases surpass, the capabilities of the paper-based world. There are several features of publishing on the World Wide Web that make the resulting documents stand out from other electronic publishing systems. One such feature is the creation process itself. By having the tools to reference and link to other sources of data, an author can create new information. The results of this synthesis are dynamic rather than static, allowing the publisher to respond quickly to the readership's changing needs. This is illustrated in Figure 3.5, where:

- The user (1) links to **www.w3.org**, and that home page is displayed on the user's screen.

- The publisher (2) at CERN provides a series of links from the CERN home page to related pages (3) to (5).

- One of the CERN pages (4) contains Internet statistics obtained by a link to page (6) at another publisher's site (7) (**www.netree.com**).

- Whenever information is changed at (6), the information is dynamically updated at (4).

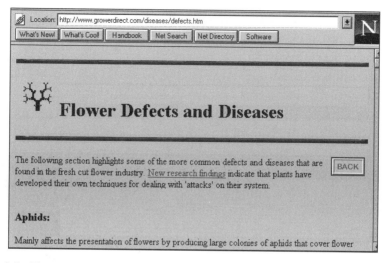

Figure 3.4 The result of link activation from Figure 3.3.

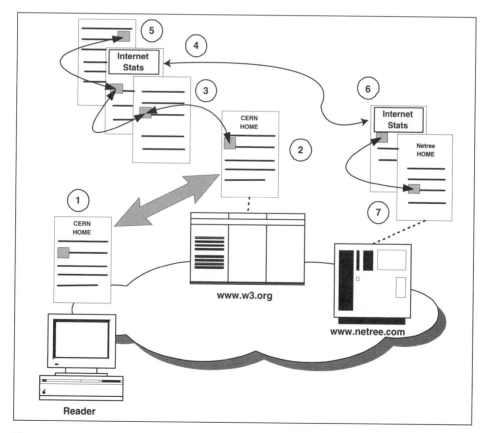

Figure 3.5 Accessing and distributing a Web document

Another positive feature of Web publishing is distribution—the publisher doesn't have to send a document out to readers. Instead, assuming they have access to the World Wide Web and know how to reference a given document, readers "come to the material" (even though the material is actually sent to them). They can do this when they want, for as long as they want, and as often as they want. The World Wide Web, then, provides information on demand to its users. It goes without saying that the final publishing and distribution costs are insignificant, and in terms of distribution, the World Wide Web is unequaled, having the potential to reach readers in most countries around the world in a matter of minutes.

Finally, Web publishing is flexible, scalable, extensible (has the ability to add other features, functions, data types, objects, and platforms), and nonproprietary, thereby giving the publisher a wider range of options for providing information to readers. The publisher doesn't require sophisticated and costly tools to create a document, nor are highly specialized in-house skills needed (beyond basic HTML coding and the ability to write). The same can be said of readers; with Internet access, a browser, and minimal training, they can link to, and retrieve, the information they need.

Information in the Workplace

When computers were initially used in the workplace, any data, and the information that could be created from it, took the form of reports. These reports were typically narrow in focus and very limited in scope—sales reports for the marketing group, financial reports for the accounting group, and so on. Furthermore, it was rare to find data from different areas combined to create a single report. This paradigm was a reflection of the corporate culture of the time, and of the technical limitations that made using data from a variety of sources difficult and expensive. The period was also characterized by the direction of the information flow itself, which was, for the most part, vertical through the corporate layers. Recently, the situation has changed dramatically as a result of such things as the massive deployment of the PC and the wholesale resizing and restructuring of the corporate world. In Figure 3.6 we've illustrated the typical activities involved in the production of a paper document intended for company-wide distribution, such as a policy and procedures manual.

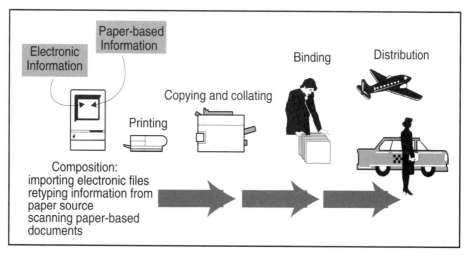

Figure 3.6   The production and distribution of a policy and procedures manual.

On Corporate Change

As computerization at the desktop level swept the office, employees became less and less dependent on the Information Technology (IT) group (formerly called the MIS group—IT is a popular new label for the same function). The PC ushered in user empowerment, first at the information creation level (word-processing reports and spreadsheets) and then, later, at the applications level. This trend continues unabated, as the tools needed to create fairly sophisticated and complex PC applications become easier to use. With the rise of the knowledge worker and local expert, dependency on the IT group lessens even more, with the systems professional becoming the last resort, only to be called on when there's a severe technical problem to fix. Another aspect of this dynamic is a general shortening of development time for office applications. This trend is not surprising when you have robust user tools and a diminished IT role in the development cycle—there are fewer meetings and fewer people involved. The net result of these corporate changes is a greater volume and diversity of data being produced by employees in all parts of the organization.

At the same time, as the workforce has become more independent, the organization itself has undergone significant changes which not only support the desktop revolution, but have likely accelerated it. The downsizing, rightsizing, restructuring, and re-engineering dynamic means that the boundaries separating the various parts of the organization have had to at least blur, if not disappear. There are fewer bodies to do the same amount of work—if not more—and the notion of the team approach, or workgroup computing, is now firmly entrenched in the office. The workgroup model also provides the degree of flexibility the modern company requires to remain competitive and stay in business.

The Changing Nature of Information

The fundamental nature of information creation and distribution is changing. The data and information needed to support the organization today, and in the future, is characterized by the following:

- *Scope and Sources*—The content is broader, focusing on the needs of the organization as a whole, and is drawn from a variety of sources.

- *Data Types*—Data is no longer limited to text, but also includes images, audio clips, and video clips.

- *Availability*—Information is available on demand, as needed by consumers.

- *Presentation*—The interface, or presentation layer, is easy to use and capable of supporting full multimedia delivery of information.

- *Stability*—The information is not static, but changes dynamically.

- *Movement*—Information moves around the organizational structure, rather than only moving vertically up the organizational ladder.

A New Model for Workplace Information Processing

Prior to the technology and information boom we've described, it wasn't necessary to have a sophisticated structure for producing, distributing, and managing information—life was simpler then. With information now becoming the lifeblood of an organization, a structure is needed to cope with, and effectively use, this resource. The challenge is to find a model that can accommodate the characteristics described above, and at the same time be flexible enough to change in response to its environment. We suggest looking to the publishing industry for this model, because regardless of the nature of a business, every organization creates and consumes information.

The function of the publishing company is to create and distribute information, just as the function of the communications system within a business is the creation and distribution of information. In much the same way, in both cases, data is collected from a variety of sources, arranged in a certain format for the readership, and distributed by a specified time. In addition, the World Wide Web, the tool of choice for constructing intranets, is built on the document-publishing paradigm.

The Nature of Publishing

Let's take a look at the staff and functions needed to produce a publication such as this book. At the same time, we'll correlate them to the activities of a business information system.

The various publishing houses have their own approaches to projects, and different types of publications (daily newspapers, periodicals, and so on) have their own special requirements. Nevertheless, in general, the essential activities are: writing, research, various editorial work, production, and printing. A publishing project team consists of people responsible for each of these tasks, and, like any other business, there may be some job overlap, or individuals doing double duty. It's worth noting that teams must be flexible, and that their makeup and individual roles will change from project to project.

For example, an editor working directly with a writer on one project could well be working as a copyeditor on another project. We'll examine these activities and roles in more detail, and then see how they can correlate to information activities in an organization. Figure 3.7 illustrates the typical processes and people involved in the production of a publication such as a book.

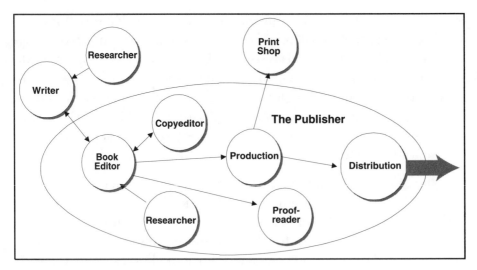

Figure 3.7   The publishing model for book production.

In Figure 3.7, the publishing industry staff are shown in the circles and their lines of communication are shown by the arrows. Figure 3.8 shows the corporate organization as a publisher. We'll work through this model, examining each of the publishing components, as well as seeing how these functions and activities might map to information production in other lines of business. (We assume at least a moderate degree of computerization.) For ease of comparison, the following functions and activities are separated into two categories: *Publishing* and *Business.*

THE PUBLISHER

Publishing—The publisher is responsible for ensuring that the final product meets the needs of the information consumer, and has the final say on what information is produced and distributed.

Business—In the business world, the publisher is the CEO, the policy-maker who sets out the objectives of the company as a whole and provides the corporate view that the communication systems and their content are based on. Depending on the size of the organization, and how decentralized decision-making powers are, some aspects of this responsibility may be delegated to the managers, or management teams, who oversee specific areas of the business, developing systems with the overall objectives of the organization in mind.

THE EDITOR

Publishing—The editorial staff's overriding objective is to make sure the writer stays on track, schedule and subject-wise. Among its other duties are ensuring that the project has adequate and appropriate resources (staff, equipment, and budget), that the product meets established quality levels, and that the content is consistent with the publisher's philosophy or mission. There's usually an editor who works directly with the writer, providing advice, assistance, and direction when required, and who does some, or all, of the manuscript editing. The editor will also track the manuscript, managing its routing between the writer, the editor herself, the copyeditor (if one has been assigned to help with editing), and the production department.

Business—The focus of the editorial function is somewhat different in the corporate setting, since the end result of document publishing is providing information rather than selling a product. In the publishing industry, style is equally as important as content, whereas content is of paramount importance in business. Consequently, the role of editor falls to management, whose job is primarily to provide project resources, scheduling, and project coordination. Copyediting tends not to be defined as a distinct task; both manager and writer deal with questions of writing style as they arise. Evaluation by content specialists may, however, be a requirement in the publication process.

THE WRITER

Publishing—It all starts with the writer, whose job is to produce the copy for a book, magazine, or other publication. The writer organizes the information and writes about it in a style that meets the book's objectives; for example, to educate, inform, entertain, and so on. Objectives are met if, and only if, the audience understands the content as the author presents it, and realizes its anticipated benefits. The writer is usually responsible for providing any artwork required. While, in the case of line art, the Production area typically redraws anything submitted, it is not responsible for creating original drawings.

Business—Whether in the publishing industry or any other type of business, the role of the writer remains the same—to impart specialized knowledge to an audience. While some larger companies have communications groups with writers on staff, by and large, corporate documents are produced by staff members with the specialized knowledge required. As is the case with the editorial function in a business environment, the writer's focus is different than that of an author writing for a publishing house. Content is the first concern, sometimes even to the extent of sacrificing the finer points of writing style. The employee/writer may also act as her own copyeditor and proofreader. Typically, any artwork is outside the scope of this role; it is sent to an outside contractor, since most businesses do not have staff artists.

THE RESEARCHER

Publishing—Researchers may be used to supply the writer with any special information or background needed, either by conducting project-specific research or by virtue of the fact that they are experts in a given area.

Business—The function of researchers in both publishing and business is to supply specialized information to the writer. However, where a researcher may need to collect and organize the information required, the content specialist within an organization already has it at hand. In addition to providing information or data, the specialist's job may also be to ensure that publications are presented in the appropriate format for the audience.

PRODUCTION

Publishing—This group lays out the book, creates and places line art, and selects the font types and sizes to use.

Business—The corporate equivalent to the production department is found in the IT group. This role is the responsibility of the computer graphics or multimedia specialists and the programmers who are required to build any necessary interfaces from a document to other data sources, such as databases.

THE PROOFREADERS

Publishing—These members of the team check for typos and other errors after the work has passed through the editor, copy editor, and production.

Business—The proofreading role may fall to anyone within the organization, but it is probably best given to someone from the area for which the publication has been produced.

THE PRINT SHOP

Publishing—The printers produce the book after they receive the finalized manuscript.

Business—The organization's printing function is carried out by the technical staff who install the completed document on the server so that it can be accessed by readers.

DISTRIBUTION

Publishing—Distribution of completed publications or books to the consumer is the work of the shipping department. Given the massive volume of products that are shipped, this function is one of the most resource-intensive, cost-consuming aspects of the publishing industry.

Business—Once a document has been installed on the server, all that remains for it to be distributed is for the IT staff to set server, directory, and file permissions to permit access to authorized users.

The publishing model in Figure 3.8 provides a sound framework for managing the production and distribution of information within any organization, and for facilitating a team-based approach to creating publications. Given this new model for information systems, plus the technical benefits

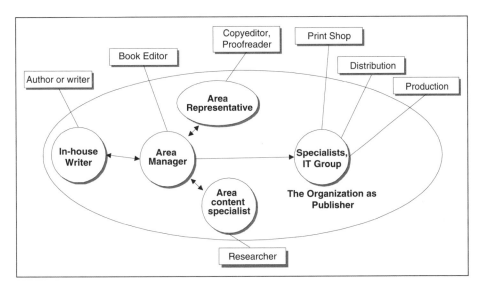

Figure 3.8   The publishing model applied to the corporate information system.

gained from the Internet, you can begin to understand why major corporations have chosen this route to meet their information and communications needs. In the next chapter, we'll look at the business reasons for
adopting this technology, and profile some of the companies that have
already implemented intranets.

Intranets at Work in a
Business Environment

Intranets at Work in a Business Environment

If intranets are just another example of media and marketing hype, why are companies like AT&T, Federal Express, and VISA installing them, and why does Netscape estimate that over 50 percent of its Web software is sold for use on intranets—not for connecting to the World Wide Web? How are intranets being used to solve the long-standing problem of effective internal corporate communication, and how might this Web technology fit into your organization? In this chapter, we'll examine these questions, show you how a variety of companies, large and small, are employing intranets, and look at the limitations of this technology.

Here Today, Here Tomorrow

It's clear from the activities of the vendor community, the software industry in particular, and data gathered from the business community at large, that the intranet phenomenon is not a passing fad; it is, instead, the beginning of a revolution in corporate information sharing. This revolution is already having an impact on the way people share information and collaborate in the office, the way business is being conducted, and the role of IT in the organization.

Some Statistics and Forecasts

- Of the total Web server license sales in 1995 (worldwide), 55 percent were for intranet use, and 45 percent were for Internet use. (International Data Corporation)

- A survey of 50 major corporations indicated that 66 percent already have an intranet in place, have plans to build one, or are considering the possibility of doing so. Thirty-four per cent have no intranet activity planned. (Forrester Research)

- The intranet server software market is expected to grow from its 1995 size of $476 million to $4 billion in 1997. (Zona Re-search)

- Within 5 years, there will be 199 million Internet users, and 3.5 million intranet Web servers installed. (International Data Corporation)

Before looking at why companies throughout North America are embracing the intranet idea so vigorously, let's stop for a moment and consider the reasons an organization invests in any technology: to solve a problem, to improve operations, and/or to reduce costs—all of which contribute to gaining a competitive advantage.

Problem Solving

Usually, the first reason new technology is considered by a company is to solve a problem. Somewhere in the organization, something isn't happening the way it should, or as well as it should. This is exactly the situation that Aetna Health Plans (AHP), a division of Aetna Inc., found itself in about a year ago.

The AHP Intranet Project

Gary Fendler, the Assistant Vice President of Strategic Communications for AHP, and currently a team leader for Aetna Health Plan's intranet projects, provided us with the following background on the AHP environment, and explained how the company used Web technology to solve its communication problem.

AHP provides managed health care services across the United States. It has offices in every state, and of the approximately 24,000 employees involved in managed care, between 17,000 and 18,000 have desktop computers. Before the installation of an internal Web site, the staff with PCs had access to an email system that employed Microsoft's MS Mail program to distribute information within the company. However, each time information requiring corporate-wide distribution was sent out, overloaded systems crashed throughout the organization. As a result, delivery was either delayed or incomplete; employees received information late, or not at all. The company worked around the problem by sending email out in waves. That reduced the number of system crashes, but the delays remained (company-wide distribution took half a day, on average), and some employees still weren't receiving information. Obviously, the email system was simply not adequate to handle the email volume.

In addition to sending email in waves, the company tried getting around their problem by sending information to middle management, with instructions for them to handle further distribution to its staff. Unfortunately, this often resulted in information gridlock—a not-uncommon situation in a corporate environment—and employees were still not consistently receiving the information they needed.

A project team, sponsored by a senior executive in AHP Strategic Communications, identified the use of an internal Web site as the solution, and went to work constructing the organization's first intranet. It was an unqualified success, and since the company newspaper went online (which, coincidentally, yields cost savings in printing and distribution), similar work has been done in Human Resources (an online policy manual), and in Marketing (a newsgroups application to gather and distribute information, providing competitive intelligence for AHP staff).

> The intranet solution has already provided many benefits for AHP, such as reduced costs for the production and distribution of information, and full employee access to unfiltered information. Employee morale has also improved because the new communication system has helped to remove the sense of isolation common in large organizations.

AHP's intranet experience is similar to that of many other organizations. What started out as a solution to one problem has grown to encompass other activities within the company, thereby providing more benefits than originally anticipated.

Improved Operations

Another reason for deploying new technology is to improve or enhance existing operations. Information flow and its management is at the core of today's business processes; improve information-related activities, and you can enhance, revitalize, and perhaps even reinvent your operations. The intranet profiled in the next case was aimed at providing better internal support, and as a consequence, improved customer service.

Improving Customer Service at Hewlett-Packard

Mike Tierney and his team at Hewlett-Packard (HP) provide support for internal "customers." They supply the expertise and up-to-date information needed by the first-line support engineers who deal with HP's database product customers on a daily basis. Before their local intranet existed, it was a constant scramble to make sure the engineers had the most current information about various DBMS products, such as the current software versions, and the next product release. This material was distributed as a blanket electronic newsletter via email, and the support engineer then had to search through his electronic collection of newsletters to find specific product information in response to customer requests. Other staff, who had no use for the information, received it as well. Now, by making newsletters available at a Web site, the cost of distribution has been reduced, and a complete archive of product documentation is available for the HP staff who need it.

At the same time, Mike's team has been converting the classroom-course material they provide about DBMS internals to online tutorials—making it possible for engineers to get training without taking a five-day classroom course. This has been a good news/bad news experience for the internal support team; the unit used to generate internal revenue based on the attendee head count of each course, but that revenue stream no longer exists. On the other hand, the benefits of an internal Web site outweigh the lost revenue. In Mike's own words: "If we knew that it would be a net financial loss to our group, I think we'd go ahead and do it anyway."

In this example, a relatively minor enhancement to a communications procedure achieved three things: it enabled the second-line engineers to provide information more effectively, made it possible for the first-line engineers to do their job more efficiently, and improved customer relations. Plus, the Web technology made new applications, such as the online training program, possible.

Cost Reduction

The use of technology to reduce costs is an area where it's often difficult to show proof of success—particularly in the case of sophisticated and expensive technology, with its hidden training and support costs. Web technology is not one of these cases; the cost reductions are visible, tangible, and can be realized over a short period of time. Our next example illustrates this point, and shows how Internet technology can be used to deal with technical obsolescence, as well. This example comes from the British Columbia Hydro and Power Authority Limited (known as BC Hydro to its customers), a public utility responsible for the creation and supply of electrical power throughout the Canadian province of British Columbia (about the same land area as Texas and Oklahoma combined).

The BC Hydro Intranet

Steve Whan, a computer professional in BC Hydro's Network Computing Services (NCS) division, had been investigating the Internet for about a year. He was trying to determine if any of the technology could be of use in a multiplatform environment (IBM mainframe host, Macintosh computers, and Intel PCs) that was broadly distributed over some 330,000 square miles. In addition to the broad geographical area involved, bandwidth for individual sites on the network varied greatly, according to location. Steve focused on the World Wide Web, and realized that it would provide an ideal method for undertaking several projects NCS had in mind.

As a proof-of-concept project, Steve's team converted the Information Management Manual to an online hypertext document. The manual, which had to be distributed to 140 locations throughout the province and consisted of 508 printed pages, provided a testing ground for resolving the problems inherent in the production, distribution, and revision of a large paper document.

The entire project took only three weeks, and a review of the business case showed that the cost savings on this one manual recouped BC Hydro's investment in a server, the software, and the manpower required for the conversion. Future savings would also be realized, because the information could be kept current without the cost of reproducing the entire manual on a regular basis.

This project set the stage for the next project—the replacement of BC Hydro's VM/PROFS mainframe, an expensive-to-run electronic office mail system that was moving rapidly towards obsolescence. Steve and his team developed a prototype for a hypertext-based, common user interface that provided access to a variety of PC-based operating systems and applications (Windows 3.x, Windows 95, MS Mail, MS Word), and that would furnish a suitable replacement for PROFS. Since running the prototype with 300 users in April of 1996, BC Hydro is well on its way to having more than 5000 employees across the province online, using this common desktop interface. Figures 4.1 and 4.2 show the home page for the BC Hydro intranet.

The company's current intranet activities are directed toward mission-critical information. As part of its mandate, BC Hydro is responsible for the operation of 30 hydroelectric dams in the province, and the maintenance procedures for critical equipment at these dams must be kept up-to-date. Because of the critical nature of these procedures, all revisions must be validated and distributed in a timely manner, neither of which can easily be done using a paper-based or email system. Consequently, a project is being initiated to develop a Web site-based repository that will make these procedures available on the BC Hydro intranet. Phase One of the project will be the conversion of 1,800 of the most critical procedures to documents in Adobe's pdf format, with the balance (approximately 1,200) to be converted at a later date.

Figure 4.1 The first screen of the BC Hydro intranet home page.

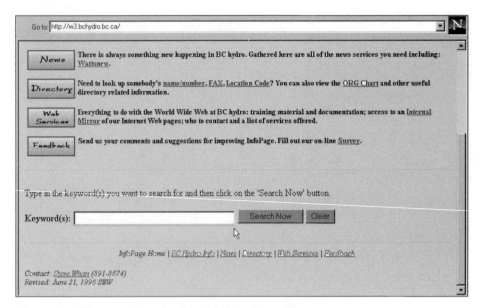

Figure 4.2 The second screen of the BC Hydro intranet home page.

There are thousands of similar examples of companies all over North America who have automated the production and distribution of company manuals, and have realized immediate cost benefits without incurring a massive investment in new technology. Most, like BC Hydro, started with simple hypertext documents and nothing fancy—no extensive gateway programming or multimedia applications—just basic documents that could be produced easily and quickly, to produce a fast return on their investment.

The Intranet Technical Advantage

The technical advantages provided by an intranet are, as we've seen, made possible by the various Internet protocols and software programs that have evolved over the last couple of decades. These aren't the latest hot item— sometimes called "killer apps"—to come out of Silicon Valley (although some of the products designed for use on the Internet are definitely in that category). Rather, they are mature, proven approaches to distributed computing and information handling, all based on a global internetwork that exists on a scale that's never been seen before.

We've alluded to the features, advantages, and benefits of Internet technology in previous chapters, but a more in-depth coverage will help you fully appreciate its features.

Nonproprietary

The standards and protocols used on the Internet comply with or support those developed by international standards bodies, such as the IEEE and the ISO. Furthermore, the very nature of the Internet (not-for-profit and global in outlook) means that all technical research and development is based on a open systems philosophy. The original goal was, and continues to be, the advancement of platform-independent computer and telecommunications technology. By default, this means that an Internet-based environment is flexible and able to accommodate different hardware architectures.

Reliable

As we've indicated, the Internet is not an overnight phenomenon, but rather is the result of the ongoing evolution of a collection of technologies. The tools, techniques, and protocols are the result of work done by some of the leading figures in various fields, and are subject to the rigors of international scrutiny. And remember, this network of networks was originally designed to withstand a nuclear attack!

Scalable

From the outset, continued growth was presumed to be a central feature of this internetworking project. Every aspect of the Internet, including connectivity, Gopher client/server, and the World Wide Web, can be upscaled; the only practical limitation is the ability of your technical infrastructure (computer hosts and network) to handle the increased processing and transmission requirements.

Extensible

Another assumption made by the Internet community is that things change. Protocols, then, must be able to change as well, extending their current capabilities to provide more functionality. HTTP, a protocol designed to handle objects that at the time were restricted to text files, is a good example of extensibility. When non-text files such as graphics, audio, and video clips arrived on the scene, the HTTP was able to deal with these new objects.

The net result of all these features is an enabling technology that organizations of any size and type can use to quickly build and deploy applications—applications that cost less than traditional information systems and provide tangible returns on investment in a short time frame.

An Enabling Technology

Applied within a company as part of an intranet, Internet technology can be used to accomplish tasks that, until recently, have seemed outside the realm of possibility for many organizations. These organizations, shackled by legacy systems, proprietary technology, and increasing technical complexity, and under pressure to be responsive to rapidly changing business needs—without affecting the bottom line—have embraced intranets. In the following sections, we've highlighted some areas where intranets fill an enabling role, as well as some of the benefits to be gained from their use.

Common Desktop Interface

Hypertext/hypermedia are used to provide a ubiquitous, common interface to an organization's applications and information—an interface based on a familiar view of information, the printed page. This interface is easy to use, requires minimal user training, and reduces overall training and maintenance costs. In addition, productivity is increased by simplifying the users' computer environment.

Data and Applications Integration

The combination of the HTML, HTTP, and CGI protocols makes it possible to pull data and information from diverse information repositories and applications, regardless of the hardware platform they reside on. No commercially available product can do this as completely, readily, or as inexpensively as an intranet can. The proprietary solutions available usually entail significant programming or conversion activity, and very often, result in a company having to completely switch over to a given vendor's product line.

Integrating Communications and Information

In the past, it was only possible to merge communication and information at the PC desktop level, where a few products provided some integration between email, scheduling applications (calendars), and a limited number of productivity tools, such as word processors and spreadsheets. Internet technology goes beyond linking a small collection of software programs, to developing applications that integrate electronic communications—such as email—with data that is dynamically gathered from a variety of sources (such as document repositories, databases, spreadsheets, and audio-visual collections).

Client/Server

As we've already pointed out, the traditional approaches and tools for developing client/server applications are complex, proprietary, and expensive. Organizations that have made a significant investment in client/server now question whether or not promises made by this technology's proponents have been delivered, and wonder if there will be an appreciable return on their investment. Because of the controversy, many other companies have avoided client/server altogether. They thereby fail to realize any of the benefits this model can, in fact, provide in a distributed, cross-platform computing environment. Now, however, client/server applications, as implemented on the Internet with Web protocols, are portable, flexible, scaleable, and have low total development costs.

Business Process Re-engineering

Business process re-engineering can be a very complex, cost-intensive undertaking. On the other hand, as we saw earlier in this chapter in the Hewlett-Packard example, it can be as simple as changing the way information is distributed. Most business processes are based on information flow, in the form of messages, memos, or reports. Any technology that can alter or enhance the information flow within an organization can be used to re-engineer business processes. An intranet provides the framework to deliver information, and the various tools available to work with that information can be used to alter its flow, content, characteristics, and quantity.

Data Utilization

Each of the numerous and varied data stores within a company requires specific tools for managing its contents; traditional methods for accessing and integrating these valuable resources are proprietary, expensive, and, for the most part, provide an incomplete solution. Fully utilizing corporate data provides a major opportunity for leveraging the organization's investment in technology, and is vital for today's businesses. Internet protocols provide a cost-effective and efficient means to access data repositories, as well as a presentation method (hypertext pages) and a means to distribute the information effectively throughout the organization (Web servers). Applications based on Internet technology provide a low-cost, flexible, and nonproprietary means to extract and manipulate corporate data; this allows the information provider to synthesize new content for company use in a variety of ways, through utilizing the corporate data resource to its fullest advantage.

Workgroup Computing

Prior to the intranet phenomenon, the tools required for workgroup computing, especially the category of software called groupware, were typified as limited in selection, and very expensive. The best known of these products, Lotus Notes, is without doubt the pacesetter for groupware products. Unfortunately, as robust as it is, this particular software is effectively out of reach for many companies because of the cost (a current estimate is $200 per workstation). Now, a similar level of functionality can be achieved using an intranet (combining different elements such as email, Web pages, and workflow software), for approximately $40 per user workstation. A good illustration of this cost savings is provided by Eli Lilly, a major pharmaceutical company. Having decided that Notes would provide more complexity than it needed for sharing and reviewing data, Eli Lilly linked 3,000 employees on an intranet, at a cost of only $80,000.

User Empowerment

The migration of technical tasks from the domain of the computer professional to various user areas is a result of two things: users' increasing technical sophistication, and computer software itself. During the past several years, PC users have become increasingly knowledgeable and proficient in resolving their computer problems, as well as in developing the applications they need. They have, as a result, acquired a variety of self-taught skills, ranging from basic hardware support to programming. The software available for the PC platform has supported this trend as well; for instance, Web server software, like O'Reilly's WebSite, can be installed and configured easily by any of these "power" users.

Like the PC, intranets play an empowering role by moving technology into the hands of the users, and away from the central IT group. For example, the simplicity of the Hypertext Markup Language makes it possible for staff outside the systems group to develop their own information systems and online manuals; as a result, users are no longer completely reliant on computer professionals to build applications. It is true that some aspects of Web site development, such as CGI scripting or setting up a Web server, require a high level of technical experience. However, even these tasks are handled more and more often by the nontechnical staff in an organization.

Investment Leverage

Internet technology enables an organization to increase its return on investments by building on the hardware, software, applications, and human resources already in place. In most cases, the implementation of an intranet doesn't require a large investment in new hardware and software, or in significant technology upgrades. Once installed, the intranet infrastructure can be used to tap into existing stores of data to gather, generate, and distribute information throughout the organization. It is particularly effective for providing an interface to legacy systems, without the need for extensive programming, and can protect this investment by circumventing the need for wholesale replacement of these systems.

Specific Applications

There are many different areas within an organization where intranet applications can be deployed, and Table 4.1 is by no means definitive; it seems that the only real bounds on uses for this technology are budget and imagination.

Table 4.1   Potential Intranet Applications in an Organization

Area	Description
Corporate Culture	Newsletters, announcements, awards, employee suggestions, and promotions
General Administration	Holiday scheduling, time reporting, and expense claims
General Communications	Centrally available information as an adjunct to email
Help Desk, User Support	Use of workflow software to route and track reports, and provide Frequently Asked Question (FAQ) repositories on a variety of subjects; for example, virus detection software
Human Resources	Telephone lists, training/conference information and registration, online training, benefit information, placement or competition information, employee performance reviews, and employee personal data updates
Information Management	Searchable document repositories
Inventory Management	Stock status, and office equipment and furniture available for re-distribution
Publishing	Multipoint authoring and document distribution (directories, manuals, policies, procedures)
Research and Development	Collaborative work (white boards and draft circulation), information repositories (internal and external), and status reports
Sales and Marketing	Price lists, product catalogues, competitive intelligence, contact lists, client information retrieval, and product announcements and reviews
Technical Support and Development	Information repositories regarding company applications, code libraries, development status reports, and software distribution

Real-World Intranets

Literally thousands of companies, large and small, have installed intranets over the past two years to meet their internal communication needs. The following are samples of the ways Web technology can be used within an organization.

CAP Gemini Sogeti

CAP Gemini Sogeti, the French computer consulting and service giant, installed its intranet (known as the Knowledge Galaxy) in September 1995. The system not only provides a communications link between the company headquarters in Paris and its many subsidiaries, but it also acts as a repository for software tools, includes a database of projects in progress that allows collaborative work among employees, and provides a large collection of Web pages containing the most up-to-date information available on computer technology. And, as an addendum to the intranet's business uses, the company has provided its Paris employees with an Internet café that allows them to surf the Internet for recreation.

Home Box Office

At Home Box Office (HBO), a premium service provider for cable television companies, a 500-user intranet connects staff to the company's corporate movie database. The database contains a vast store of information—every movie ever made, its cast, its director, what its revenues were, new movies in progress, and much more—used to make programming decisions. Web technology has also made it possible to combine this information with a Nielsen Ratings database needed to develop HBO's marketing campaigns. In addition, all the company's regional sales offices are linked to the intranet, giving them immediate access to the marketing material for each campaign as it's finalized. HBO is now working toward establishing a company-wide intranet that will allow all staff entry to virtually all corporate information.

Eli Lilly & Company

It would be difficult to find an organization that gets more value from intranet technology than Eli Lilly & Company, the giant pharmaceutical manufacturer with offices and laboratories around the world. The 3,000-

workstation intranet they set up in 1995, which links workers in 24 countries, has already made a significant contribution to streamlining the company's work in dealing with the intricacies of scheduling worldwide clinical trials of new drugs, and the multitude of regulations surrounding the testing and marketing of pharmaceuticals. The Web site, which is also used, among other things, to provide information repositories for researchers, distribute current information to marketing and sales staff, and develop new projects, has been so successful, the company plans to have 13,000 employees linked worldwide by the end of 1996.

Genetech

Genetech, noted for its pioneering work in biotechnology, has also adopted the intranet concept in a big way. Originally, the company looked at Web technology as a means to improve user access to information, which was distributed across three computer platforms (Macintosh, Windows, and Unix)—each with its own syntax and quirks that made access difficult and time-consuming. The Web's protocols and tools suited its needs, and since this technology was brought into Genetech, virtually every department in the organization has put up Web pages to facilitate information-sharing with other staff. Internal newsgroups and bulletin boards are heavily used as well. The company's latest project involves the use of Web technology to assist in the manufacturing process. They're working on a prototype-graphing application that pulls data from laboratory instruments and sends it to hypertext pages, where the data is represented as graphs.

McDonnell Douglas

From an environmental perspective, perhaps the biggest corporate tree-saver is McDonnell Douglas, the aircraft manufacturer. Each day, it produces four or five service bulletins, each averaging twenty-five pages in length, for distribution to the company's customers around the world. The yearly page count for these service specifications is in the neighborhood of 4 million pages—that's lot of trees! By making this information available electronically, the company has reduced paper usage, reduced costs (production, distribution, and storage), and perhaps even saved lives. The paper-based system was heavily reliant on the many postal systems throughout the world, meaning that often, crucial information in a service document took two or three weeks to reach a customer—time when a mishap could occur.

National Semiconductor

In another manufacturing sector, an intranet-based information system allows National Semiconductor, whose chips are used in many types of electronic devices, to bring products to market more quickly by publishing information faster. Its internal information system enables employees working on projects to quickly get at the most current information they need to do their job, thus reducing cycle times during development. The system also provides the company with the ability to integrate activities among its various manufacturing operations throughout the world, which increases its ability to identify and deal with production problems before they get out of hand—or worse, go unnoticed.

VISA International

The well-known financial-services company, VISA International, began its foray into the intranet world with an online directory of its contacts in member banks. Before putting this directory online, some 1,200 VISA employees relied on a two-volume paper directory (reported to be nearly four inches thick) to obtain contact information. With more than 19,000 banks in the directory, it was impossible to keep the data current—revised directories distributed to staff were out of date by the time the print run was finished. The online directory, on the other hand, gives employees immediate access to current information as it's updated. Based on its success with the electronic directory, VISA is now investigating the idea of building a separate intranet, to give member banks online access to the fraud-alert bulletins currently sent on diskettes.

Federal Express

Our final example highlights the potential cost savings provided by an intranet, and looks at the Federal Express intranet experience. The overwhelming success of the FedEx World Wide Web site on the Internet (shown in Figure 4.3), which enables customers to track their own packages, inspired management to look for opportunities to use Web technology in-

Figure 4.3   Federal Express' Internet site.

side the organization. As a result, it's working on a project to make the company's procedure manuals available to employees on an internal network. According to Susan Goeldner, manager of Internet Technologies at FedEx, the company could potentially save as much as $120,000 each year by putting just one manual (printed twice yearly) online. With these kinds of savings, and at least eight other manuals that could generate similar cost reductions sitting on bookshelves, it's little wonder that intranets are a popular idea at FedEx.

These are just a few of the possible examples of how organizations are using intranet technology, but even this small sampling will give you some idea of the scope of the applications possible, and of how intranets can reduce the effects of distance, facilitate collaborative work, speed up development cycles, and produce cost savings. In the following chapters, we'll show you what's involved in constructing your own intranet—its key components, the tools required, and some guidelines for its development.

PART 2

Building Blocks— The Critical Elements

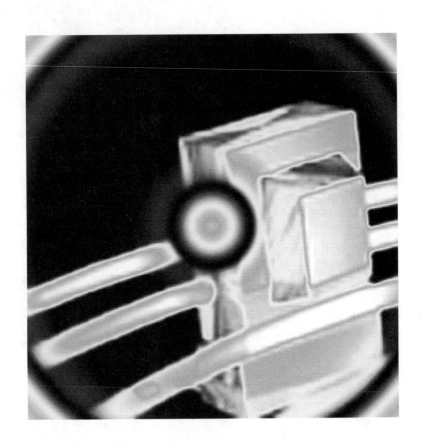

CHAPTER

5

The Technical Environment

5

The Technical Environment

The technical environment required to host your intranet application is an existing Local Area Network. LANs are complex entities consisting of a collection of hardware and software components that need to interact with each other, but, for ease of reference, we've split the coverage of this basic LAN configuration into three main parts: the workstation, the server, and the network. Later in the chapter, the option of connecting your intranet application to an existing database is examined, along with the associated alternatives and issues. We will close by taking a look at some of the intranet design options that are available.

Basic Intranet Configuration

The basic configuration we're going to look at assumes you'll be using an existing LAN running Windows NT Server as the Network Operating System. Figure 5.1 illustrates a simple intranet architecture consisting of a client, a database, and a LAN server.

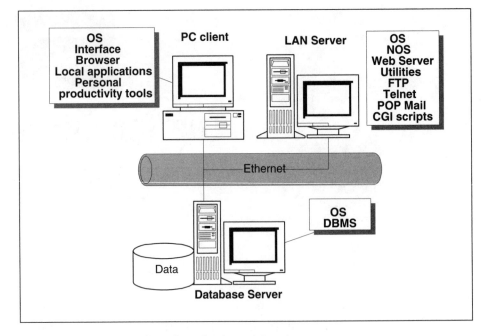

Figure 5.1 Basic network configuration for an intranet.

The Architecture of the Individual Computers

Architecture is used to describe the components of a computer and how these parts interact with each other. The intended use of a computer is a determining factor in deciding which architecture will deliver the performance that is needed; a server, for example, will have far different requirements than a desktop PC. When dealing with computer architectures, there are three parts of the system that must be considered: the Central Processing Unit (CPU), the bus architecture, and the disk controller.

CPU

A given processor doesn't necessarily support all operating systems and applications. For example, most Motorola processors (680x0, PowerPC) don't support Windows NT, whereas the Pentium, Pentium Pro, and Alpha processors do. The actual processor architecture will determine the instruction set used by the processor, the clock speed, and the number of instructions per second available to both the OS and the application. Good examples of architectural differences are the DEC Alpha and the Intel Pentium chip; if both are 100MHz CPUs, the DEC Alpha has more processing power. Architecture also affects power consumption (the Alpha requires more), and this may be an issue, depending on the intended location of the server. Finally, the architecture determines the cost of the machine—for example, when all considerations are taken into account, the Pentium is less expensive than the Alpha.

THE BUS ARCHITECTURE

Bus architecture describes the numerous ways of moving data between the various system components, such as the CPU, memory, video cards, and hard drive. There are many bus areas in a computer, but bottlenecks in data transmission are most likely to occur in the Input/Output (I/O) system, which provides the main data path between the video adapter, the hard drive, memory, and the CPU. The mostly widely used bus architecture is the Industry Standard Architecture (ISA) based on the IBM PC AT computer. The ISA bus provides an 8-bit and 16-bit data path (at a normal speed of 8 MHz), which is adequate for slower devices in the computer, such as the serial port or the printer port, but far too slow for display adapters and fast hard drives. Since 1987 there have been several alternate bus architectures developed with a view to increasing the speed of data throughput to the CPU.

Microchannel Architecture (MCA)—Microchannel was introduced by IBM in 1987 and promised higher data throughput rates. It was slightly faster, at 10 MHz, than the AT bus, and provided a 32-bit data path. This architecture also featured a technique called bus mastering, which enabled the controller on an expansion card to take control of the bus for I/O operations, thereby freeing up the CPU for other processing. MCA looked promising, but a combination of factors, notably the cost of microchannel machines, high MCA adapter card prices, incompatibility with existing ISA adapter cards, and IBM licensing policy, limited its widespread acceptance. (IBM treated MCA as proprietary technology and expected vendors to pay license fees for using it.)

Extended Industry Standard Architecture (EISA)—In reaction to MCA and the need to come up with a non-proprietary and less expensive architecture, other manufacturers developed EISA, an extension of ISA which expanded the data path to 32 bits, provided bus mastering, and maintained compatibility with ISA cards. The downside of ISA compatibility was speed, which remained stuck at 8 MHz (a serious limitation for supporting advanced video operations). Speed, system cost, and adapter card cost were once again limiting factors in the widespread acceptance of this new bus architecture. Bus design did not make any significant advances until large numbers of 486 CPUs were shipped, and the incongruity of having 33 MHz CPUs being stifled by 8 to 10 MHz data transfer rates was highlighted.

VESA Local Bus (VLB)—VLB was the first new design to appear in the wake of the 486s, and was developed by the Video Electronics Standards Association (VESA) to resolve the issue of video data transfer rates. VESA uses local bus technology, which means that the expansion bus is attached directly to the microprocessor. Higher data transfer rates were achieved by eliminating a number of intervening components and reducing the number of connections that were needed. VLB can provide 32-bit data transfer with speeds up to 132 MB per second. However, the continued success of VLB was hampered by several factors, including its design focus, the width of the data path, the number of expansion slots, and the nature of local bus design in general.

Being nonproprietary, other vendors designed non-video cards to use local bus, but since the VESA implementation was specific to video operations, these other cards simply didn't perform very well. The potential to grow a system by adding other cards was also an issue since VLB machines only had two expansion slots. Finally, local bus design is closely tied to processor design; therefore, any bus changes that are dictated by processor changes are difficult to implement—the Pentium proved to be the deciding factor in the fate of this bus architecture. Pentiums require a 64-bit data path, and by the time VLB had been modified (VESA II) in response to the P5 chip, Intel's implementation of local bus was well-established and had achieved market dominance.

Peripheral Component Interconnect (PCI)—Designed by Intel, PCI offers a high performance I/O bus that provides a 64-bit data path and speeds of 33 and 66 MHz. For expandability, there are three PCI slots and five ISA slots. This architecture's overall design means that PCI adapter cards require fewer chips so their prices are comparable to ISA cards, and a capability called Plug-and-Play is available. Plug-and-Play lets the operating system detect installed hardware and set various configuration parameters, such as interrupts and addresses, thereby eliminating the need for manual configuration when new cards are added to the system.

The characteristics of the different bus architectures are summarized in Table 5.1.

Disk Controller

The disk controller determines the number of drives that can be mounted in the server, the types of drives that can be used, and the overall data transfer rate between the hard drive and the bus. The three controller types are the Integrated Drive Electronics (IDE), Enhanced IDE (EIDE), and Small Computer Systems Interface (SCSI). IDE is an older controller technology, limited by its data access and transfer speed (it's a 16-bit system), and the maximum size of the drive itself. It is further limited by the number of drives the controller can accommodate. EIDE is a 32-bit system that provides higher access and transfer rates, and currently supports drive sizes up to 3 GB. SCSI controllers range from 16 to 32 bit, and of the three controller types provide the highest access and transfer rates. In addition, they can support more drives (devices) on one controller. The basic SCSI specification allows for six attached devices, while Wide-SCSI (a subset of the SCSI2 specification) can support up to fifteen devices per controller.

Table 5.1   Bus Architecture Characteristics

	ISA	EISA	MCA	VLB	PCI
Data bus (bits)	8/16	16/32	8/16/32	32	32/64
Data rates (MB/second)	10	32	10-160	132	132/264
Available connectors	8	12	8	2	3
DMA channels	7	7	15	N/A	System dependent
Auto-configuration	No	Yes	Yes	No	Yes

The Workstation (Client)

The workstation provides access to the information on the server through the browser program installed on it. If your intention is to use an existing PC as an intranet client, you will have to consider its:

- Compatibility

- Capability

- Capacity or sizing

Compatibility

Compatibility is a software issue that refers to the ability of the operating system (such as Windows NT or Windows 95) or the interface (Windows 3.1) to work with the application. Therefore, the system has to provide support for TCP/IP and be able to run the browser you've selected for your environment. At the browser level, this isn't really a major issue anymore, since all of the major browsers, such as Netscape and the multiple incarnations of Mosaic, have been developed to run on several platforms, such as Unix, DOS/Windows, and Macintosh. However, the various helper applications that may be required to run with the browser are not necessarily available for all platforms.

Capability

Another software issue, capability, relates to the ability of the workstation to run the client software you've selected. For example, if you're running Windows 3.1 on a PC, and haven't installed the 32-bit upgrade patch, the 32-bit version of Netscape simply won't work.

Capacity

The final item has to do with capacity, or sizing, and is a hardware issue. For the client PC, the two main components that concern us are the amount of memory and the size of the hard drive. Since the PC is already in use as a station on the LAN, it has to be able to handle not only the current operational requirements, with their processing and storage demands, but also the additional load the new application places on the machine. There are three basic types of intranet application: minimal graphics, database, and graphics intensive (or multimedia). The nature of these applications determine any additional PC hardware requirements.

Minimal Graphics—This type of application refers to Web pages with some graphics, but no animation, video clips, or sound clips. If the existing PC is Windows-capable, and you can live with its current performance, then it's capable of running most intranet applications. Hard drive space shouldn't be an issue, since browsers typically consume only 3 to 5 MB of disk space.

Database—Database applications tend to be less video-intensive and, as a result, are more forgiving in terms of your machine's processing and storage requirements. Exceptions do occur, particularly if the nature of the data pulled from the database is largely nontextual, such as graphics images or video clips. In situations where this happens frequently, the client must be a higher-performance machine.

Graphics Intensive or Multimedia—Graphics-intensive applications are strongly affected by the video card and the screen refresh rate and, consequently, require higher-performance computers. On some older PCs, a video card upgrade to 2 MB of video memory may be necessary. Multimedia, on the other hand, needs a sound card and speakers in addition to a fast video card; for these types of applications, we recommend a video card with at least 2 MB of memory. Also, given the volume of data being transferred, your PC should be a Pentium with at least 16 MB of RAM.

Most intranet applications run well on clients that are 33 MHz, 486 PCs with 8 MB of RAM. The hard disk space requirements aren't too onerous. Your browser will consume about 3 to 5 MB, and unless you're saving documents (which is counterproductive, since the whole point is to reduce, if not eliminate, the volume of paper generated in the office), the only additional space considerations may be for operating system (OS) paging or browser disk-caching. Large swap files for the OS should not be used unless the client station is low on RAM, such as a PC running NT Workstation with 8 MB of RAM. Disk-caching, like paging, consumes space on the drive, and is a technique used by Netscape and Microsoft Internet Explorer as a work-around for slow modem connections. Caching means that when a page is first retrieved, it's stored on the local hard drive. Then, if the page is requested again in the same browsing session, it's loaded into the browser from the hard drive, rather than pulling it off the server.

If hard drive space is not an issue, use caching to reduce the traffic load on your network. For files accessed on a frequent basis, consider the option of caching them on the local machine, rather than going to the server to get them each time. On larger networks, another option is setting up a Web server proxy to serve frequently-accessed material.

Up to this point, we've been talking about using existing workstations for your intranet. However, if it is necessary to purchase equipment, consider the fast Pentiums (133 MHz): prices continue to drop, and most are shipped as multimedia-ready machines. A fully equipped and configured PC reduces initial installation costs such as setup, configuration, and testing. The only thing to watch for is the amount of RAM on these units—although memory is relatively inexpensive, manufacturers still ship many machines that hold only 8 MB, and this isn't really adequate for today's operating systems and applications. Figure 5.2 presents some issues to consider when selecting a PC to use for your intranet.

The Server

The capacity and performance of the machine being used for a Web server will be affected by the number and types of applications being run, the number of users, and the NOS. The degree to which it can meet your

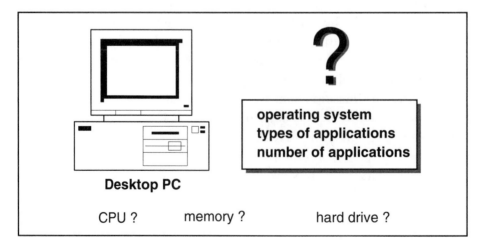

Figure 5.2 Determining factors in sizing a PC.

requirements will be determined by its architecture (processor, data bus, and controller), its scalability, and the degree of fault tolerance and redundancy it provides.

Scalability

At some point, it will become necessary to confront the issue of scalability and to increase the capacity of the server by adding more memory, another processor, or more hard drive storage. Since there are limits to the amount of memory you can add to systems, and since not all systems support multiple processors, the determining factor for processor-related growth is the motherboard itself. If the multiprocessor option is not possible, then the alternative is to replace the entire unit or distribute the workload across multiple servers. The latter option isn't necessarily the least expensive, since it's constrained by the current applications on the system—some software programs can't support load balancing across multiple machines, and others are difficult and costly to split. With a large Oracle database, for example, not only will significant programming effort be required, but multiple licensing arrangements must be made, both of which add to the total cost of this approach.

Fault Tolerance

Fault tolerance relates to the equipment's ability to continue operating, either after sustaining damage or having a component fail. This ability, or lack thereof, is centered on the CPU, the memory, and the hard drive. Different models of DEC and Hewlett-Packard machines, which are NT compatible, provide full fault tolerance—they have redundant power supplies, processors, and special error-correcting memory that isolates defective areas. It should be noted that the cost associated with fault tolerance is two to three times that of a nontolerant system.

Redundancy

Redundancy refers to standby capability and is provided either by machines or devices that can be quickly replaced, or by the ability to port applications and data to another computer environment (or in the case of critical systems, the ability to move the entire system to a backup computer). Redundancy is most commonly implemented with hard drives, and is achieved by the use of drive arrays (multiple hard drives) to store data. Using drive arrays not only provides protection from data loss, but coincidentally can improve server performance as well. The most common type of drive array implementation is called Redundant Array of Inexpensive Drives, or RAID.

A typical RAID implementation of the drive array concept is hardware-based, using RAID controllers and special drive arrays to implement disk mirroring and disk striping. Disk mirroring uses other drives to make identical copies of the file that is being written. The disk write and read in a two-drive array is illustrated in Figure 5.3. Recovery from a drive failure or media failure is shown in Figure 5.4.

With disk striping, the file is broken down into pieces that are distributed over several drives. The minimum array configuration consists of three drives, with data distributed on two of them while the third is used for error checking. Figure 5.5 illustrates the disk striping technique.

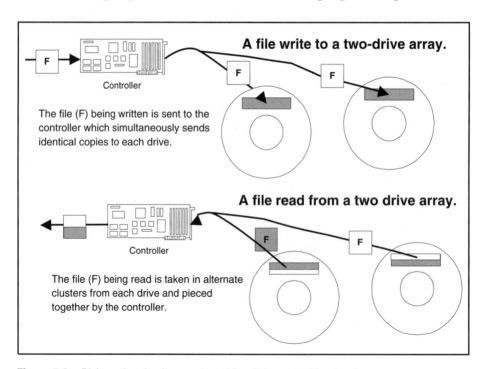

Figure 5.3 Disk read and write on a two-drive disk array with mirroring.

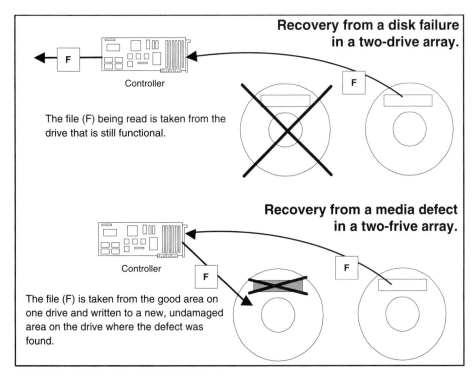

Figure 5.4 Recovery from drive or media failure on a two-drive disk array with mirroring.

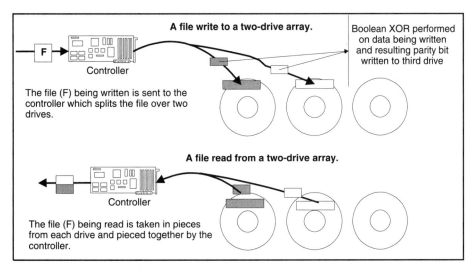

Figure 5.5 Disk read and write in a three-drive array with striping.

In the case of a drive failure or damaged media, the striping technique uses the reverse of the Boolean operation performed during a write operation to repair the damaged data.

RAID LEVELS

The methods of redundancy provided by RAID are described in terms of RAID *levels*. These levels range from 0 to 5 and reflect the reliability, performance, and cost of each method. Table 5.2 sets out these RAID levels, and also indicates which of the levels are supported by Windows NT Server.

RAID IMPLEMENTATION ON WINDOWS NT SERVER

The NT Server implementation of RAID is software-based, which means that conventional controllers and hard drives can be used, rather than incurring the expense of the hardware drive array solution. In addition to disk mirroring and striping, NT provides a third method of redundancy called *sector sparing*, so all write operations to a drive are verified in two parts:

1. Bad sectors on the drive are mapped out when they are detected during the verification process that takes place during file formatting. These mapped-out sectors are replaced by spare sectors on the disk.

Table 5.2   Windows NT Server RAID Level Support

RAID Level	Description	Windows NT Server Support
0	Disk striping	Yes
1	Disk mirroring	Yes
2	Bit-level striping with Error Correcting Code (ECC)	No
3	Byte-level striping with ECC stored as parity	No
4	Block striping with blocks stored on a single drive	No
5	Block striping with parity blocks stored over multiple drives	Yes

2. All write operations are checked to see if they are successful. If the operation is not successful, the bad sector being written is mapped out and the file is written to a spare sector.

Minimum System Requirements

Several factors affect your minimum system requirements. The OS itself requires a specified amount of RAM; for example, Windows NT Server requires a minimum of 64 MB to run reasonably well. There will also be demands from the Web server software, plus any other applications that may be running concurrently (perhaps a database or mail server). Some types of applications, such as multimedia, also increase demand on the server's processor and memory, as does the level of hard drive activity, or reads versus writes (as in the situation where users may be adding to a database). For a minimum server configuration we recommend a microcomputer with the following:

- 133 MHz CPU

- 64 MB of RAM

- PCI local bus

- SCSI controller and hard drive

 Use a dedicated server machine for your intranet Web site; you'll find that you need all of its capacity.

Impact of Adding Applications

The number and type of applications run, plus the user count, determine the impact of adding your intranet application to the server, as Figure 5.6 illustrates. Typically, the existing system load has peak periods—you need to know the time and the length of these peak intervals to determine present capacity. It may be that an existing server simply cannot accommodate the addition of another application.

A particularly important aspect of system load to keep in mind is the number of users; adding more will have a definite impact on the server. If you

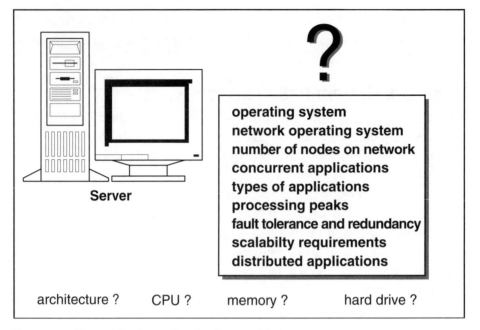

operating system
network operating system
number of nodes on network
concurrent applications
types of applications
processing peaks
fault tolerance and redundancy
scalabilty requirements
distributed applications

Server

architecture ?   CPU ?   memory ?   hard drive ?

Figure 5.6 Determining factors in selecting and sizing a server.

run a small pilot with 10 or 15 users, you won't add a significant burden to the machine (unless it's a full-blown multimedia application). However, the technical support staff will notice an additional 50 or 100 users—as will the current users, who will notice performance degradation.

Turnkey Server Solutions

For organizations that want to set up an internal Web server, yet don't want the burden of hardware and software evaluation, purchasing decisions, equipment installation, and configuring that is needed to get a server operational, help is available in the form of turnkey server solutions. A turnkey system is one that comes with all of the required software preinstalled and preconfigured on the computer; ideally, all that's required is to plug the computer in and turn it on. During the past year, numerous turnkey solutions have been assembled to provide either a general purpose Web server, or a communications server for remote access to the site.

The characteristics of the Windows NT-specific turnkey solutions are summarized in Tables 5.3 (a general purpose server) and 5.4 (remote access servers).

Table 5.3 A General Purpose Turnkey Web Server for Windows NT 3.51 InterServer Web-300

Configuration			
Processor	Pentium Pro		
Internet Services			
Web server	Microsoft Internet Information Server		
Email (SMTP/POP-2/3)	Yes		
FTP server	Yes		
Gopher server	Yes		
Network protocols	TCP/IP, NetBIOS, NetBEUI, IPX/SPX		
Web browser	Microsoft Internet Explorer		
Administration			
GUI tools	Yes		
Host and IP administration tools	Yes		
DNS administration tools	Yes		
User administration tools	Yes		
Remote administration tools	MS Server Manager, MS Internet Services Manager		
Security	OS and application level		
Backup utilities	NT Backup		
Web Publishing			
HTML editor	MS Word Internet Assistant		
Access Management			
Time limit on connection time	Yes	Yes	No
Inactivity timeout	Yes	Yes	Yes
Display user and port status	Yes	Yes	Yes

Table 5.4   Remote Access Turnkey Communications Servers for Windows NT 3.51

	Attachmate Corp. RLN 4.1	Citrix Systems Winframe/ Enterprise v1.6	Microsoft Corp. Microsoft Windows NT Server 3.51
IP address assignment	Port, Server pool, Client, BOOTP, DHCP	Port, Server pool, Client, DHCP	Port, Client, DHCP
Security			
Authentication	PAP, CHAP	PAP, CHAP	PAP, SPAP, PAP MD 80
Authorization Services	Security Dynamics, TACACS, Digital pathways, Enigma Logic, Banyan StreetTalk	Security Dynamics, NDS, NT Domain	Security Dynamics, ACM/400, NT Domain
Server			
Processor	Intel 486/66	Intel Pentium	Intel 486
LAN topology	Ethernet, Token-Ring LAN independent		LAN independent
WAN topology	ISDN, X.25, Async	ISDN, Frame Async Async	ISDN, X.25, Relay, T1,
Async/ISDN BRI per server	32/32	15/15	256/256
Serial protocols	PPP, RLNCP	PPP, SLIP	PPP, Proprietary NT RAS
PPP control protocols	IPCP, IPXCP	IPCP, IPXCP	IPCP, IPXCP, NBFCP, CBCP, CCP
LAN-to-LAN routing	No	Dial-up	Dial-up
Auto-detect incoming transport at port	PPP, ARA, RLN	Proprietary PPP, SLIP	Yes
Automatic port pooling	Dial-out	Dial-in, LAN-to-LAN routing	Dial-in

(Continued)

Table 5.4   Remote Access Turnkey Communications Servers for Windows NT 3.51 (Continued)

	Attachmate Corp. RLN 4.1	Citrix Systems Winframe/ Enterprise v1.6	Microsoft Corp. Microsoft Windows NT Server 3.51
Client			
Client OS supported	DOS, Win 3.x, Win95, OS/2	DOS, Win 3.x, Win95, WinNT, OS/2	DOS, WinNT, WinNT5, Win3.x, OS/2
Licensing	Unlimited	Unlimited	Per server, per seat
Remote control client	RLN WinFrame, RLN Applink	Citrix	None
PPP client	None	Funk	WinNT
IPX stacks	Netx, VLM, NDIS 2.x, PDS	Netx, VLM, NDIS 2.x, NDIS 3.x	NWLink
IP stacks	None	Microsoft TCP/IP	Microsoft TCP/IP
Dial-back	Yes	Yes	Yes
Roving Dial-back	No	Yes	Yes
Log-on/Install scripting	Yes/Yes	Yes/No	Yes/Yes
Dial-on-demand	Yes	Yes	Yes
Client auto reconnect	Yes	Yes	Yes

The Network

Through protocols and installed software, the network provides the physical connection between its users and the server. In other words, it provides the vehicle by which users can interact with the server, or with other nodes via the server. (Each computer on the network is a node, and the connecting cable is the link.) The current state of the network has an impact on the performance and capabilities of your planned system—what can be shared and accessed, its overall capacity, and its growth potential. We're going to look at:

- Networking standards

- Networking in general

- Network design considerations

- The Windows NT Network Operating System

While it's beyond the scope of this book to cover the major design issues and solutions in great detail, the networking basics we've provided will help you understand why impediments to your planned intranet may arise and how to deal with them.

 Find out what your PC's existing architecture is, and get a feel for its limitations and constraints. Ask the network people to do some performance monitoring to determine load, peak, and capacity.

Networking Standards

The two major standards for communications and local area networking are the Open System Interconnection (OSI) reference model and the Institute of Electrical and Electronic Engineers (IEEE) LAN standards (IEEE 802).

THE OSI REFERENCE MODEL

This model was developed by the International Standards Organization (ISO) to describe the flow of data from the physical connection to the network and, ultimately, to the user application. It sets out seven layers to describe a networking environment.

Figure 5.7 shows the OSI layers increasing in complexity from the bottom to the top of the chart, with the most basic functions, such as data bits on the network cable, at the lowest level. In this model, each layer provides services to the level above it, but is shielded from the details of the lower level, which implements the services. When the server and the LAN PC communicate with each other, it appears that communication takes place at the same layer; in actuality, the communication is between adjacent layers on the same computer.

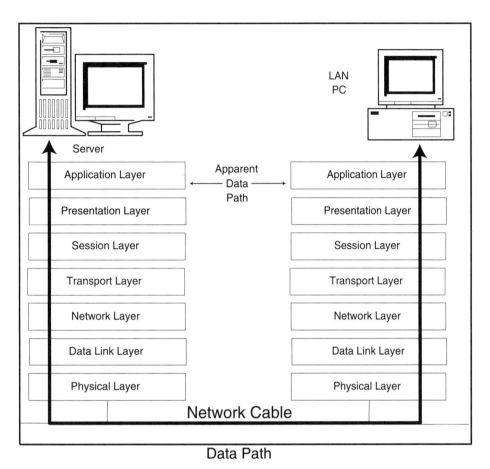

Figure 5.7 The OSI model illustrating communications between two computers.

Let's examine these layers and see what services each provides:

- The *physical layer* is responsible for the transmission of raw data bits over the physical medium (the network cable), and deals with the connection of mechanical, electrical, optical, and functional interfaces to the cable. It also determines how cards are connected to the cable, describes the topology used to connect computers, and defines the transmission techniques used to send the data over the network.

- The *data link layer* packages the bits into data frames (logical structured packets) that contain address information, and whose format is determined by the topology of the network. This layer is responsible for the error-free transfer of frames between computers.

- The *network layer* deals with message addressing by translating logical addresses and names into physical addresses on the network. It manages message routing based on priority of services and network conditions. It also deals with switching and data packet congestion on the network.

- The *transport layer* is responsible for packaging and repackaging messages by dividing long messages into smaller packets, or assembling small packets into larger ones. It acknowledges the receipt of messages and handles error recognition and recovery.

- The *session layer* allows an application on two separate computers to establish, use, and end a communications session. It provides name recognition, task synchronization, and security functions, and regulates transmissions between the computers.

- The *presentation layer* acts as a translator for data exchanged between two applications. It takes the data received from one application and translates it to a format that the receiving application can understand. This layer also provides services such as data transfer, encryption, and compression.

- The *application layer* provides a link between application processes and network services. It supports applications such as software for file transfer and electronic mail.

IEEE PROJECT 802

In February 1980, the IEEE started a project to identify and set LAN standards for networks with a data transfer rate not exceeding 20 Mbps. The activities of Project 802 (the 80 comes from 1980 and the 2 stands for the second month) resulted in the IEEE 802 LAN standards, which are summarized in Table 5.5.

IEEE 802 LAN STANDARDS

The IEEE 802 model defines two sublayers for the Data Link Layer: the Media Access Control (MAC) and the Logical Link Control (LLC). MAC, the lower layer, provides the computer's network adapter (interface) card with access to the physical layer. The LLC sublayer provides logical interface points other computers can reference, so data can be moved from the

Table 5.5   IEEE 802 LAN Standards

Standard	Covers
IEEE 802.1	LAN bridging
IEEE 802.2	Logical Link Control (LLC)
IEEE 802.3	Ethernet standardization
IEEE 802.4	Token bus standard
IEEE 802.5	Token ring standard
IEEE 802.6	Metropolitan Area Network (MAN)
IEEE 802.7	Broadband technical advisory
IEEE 802.8	Fiber-optic technical advisory
IEEE 802.9	Integrated Voice/Data (IVD)
IEEE 802.10	LAN security
IEEE 802.11	Wireless LANs

LLC to the upper OSI layers. Project 802 also resulted in three key standards for the network topologies:

- 802.3—defines standards for bus networks

- 802.4—defines standards for token-passing bus networks

- 802.5—defines standards for token ring networks

The IEEE also provides a definition of a LAN, setting out the characteristics that distinguish local area networks from other networking technologies, such as WANs. These characteristics are:

- A LAN supports peer communications between its nodes, unlike centrally controlled hierarchical systems like IBM's Systems Network Architecture (SNA).

- An emphasis is placed on geographic area; typically, it does not exceed a distance of five to seven miles, and it is usually found in a single building or in buildings located in close proximity.

- The physical communications channel has moderate data rates, unlike Wide Area Networks, which often use public-switched communications channels.

Networks in a Nutshell

Networks can be described in several ways, depending on one's point of view, the IEEE standard used, network topology, the cabling media, or the protocols used by the NOS. We're going to look at networks from the topology perspective, and relate the other descriptive elements to the network's topology. However, before proceeding with topologies, it is necessary to be aware of cabling types and media.

CABLING

The most common type of media for Local Area Networks is copper, which is used for two basic cable types: twisted-pair wiring and coaxial cable. The second medium is glass fiber which is used in fiber-optic cable.

Twisted-pair wiring is similar to telephone cable, and consists of a pair of copper wires twisted around each other; one strand transmits signals and the other receives them. Twisted-pair can be unshielded or shielded. Shielded twisted-pair (STP) has a protective sheath around the cable to reduce electrical interference and was preferred to unshielded twisted-pair (UTP) until the Ethernet standard was tightened up. Since then, UTP has become popular due to the cost differential between the two wiring types.

The second type of copper media is coaxial cable, which consists of a central conducting core, an insulating sheath, another conductor (braided wire mesh or solid sleeve), and an outer protective covering. Signals are transmitted down the central core and received through the second conductive layer. Coaxial cable is the medium used to provide cable television to homes, and although more expensive than twisted pair, has the advantage of being better protected from interference, as well as having much higher transmission speeds.

Fiber-optic cabling is used primarily in high-speed network backbones and consists of a central glass fiber covered by insulation and cladding. Fiber-optic is by far the most expensive medium. However, because it uses light pulses rather than electrical signals, it has the advantages of high speed, virtually no interference, and of being very difficult to tap into.

Topology

Topology refers to the cabling layout used for connecting all the nodes in a network. The three basic configurations are bus, star, and ring.

Bus Topology

As shown in Figure 5.8, a bus network is very simple, making it attractive as a networking architecture. Each node on the network is attached in series to the bus (the backbone), which is closed at each end by a terminator, creating what is called a segment. Segments can be joined together to extend the length of the bus.

Each node has an address assigned to it, and as messages pass along the bus, individual nodes examine the addresses of each message. The node retains any message addressed to it, and passes the others down the network to the next node. Signal transmission uses a technique called *carrier-sense*. Before a node transmits, it listens for activity on the channel; if it hears nothing, a signal is sent down the line. If the node detects a busy signal, it waits, and then checks for activity again. Since multiple stations on the channel are using the carrier-sense mechanism, it is called Carrier Sense with Multiple Access (CSMA). Because of transmission lags on the network, electrical interference, and messages queued at other stations, nodes do sometimes send messages with traffic on the line, causing a collision. Ethernet stations try to detect collisions as they occur, and when one is detected a signal is sent out over the network to alert all the stations of a Collision Detect (CD).

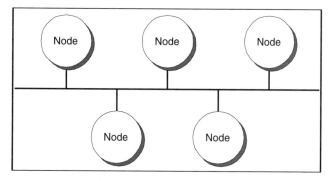

Figure 5.8 Bus topology for a network.

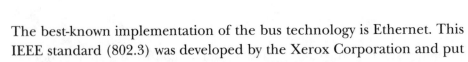

The best-known implementation of the bus technology is Ethernet. This IEEE standard (802.3) was developed by the Xerox Corporation and put forward as a proposal with the support of DEC and Intel.

The most common cabling specifications for Ethernet are: 10BaseT, 10Base5, and 10Base2 (also referred to as thin Ethernet). The transmission speed for all three is 10 Mbps.

10BaseT uses twisted-pair cabling in a star configuration, with a maximum segment length of 100 meters. Since most commercial-grade phone wiring installations have at least 2 pairs of extra wires, it's possible to use this existing wiring to cable a network.

10Base5 uses a bus topology and shielded twisted-pair cabling from the node to the bus (referred to as the Attached Unit Interface (AUI) cable). The backbone, or bus, uses thick Ethernet cable. The maximum length for the AUI connection is 50 meters, while the top length of a segment is 500 meters. No more than 5 segments can be connected together, each with a maximum of 100 attached computers.

The last major specification, 10Base2, uses a linear bus topology, which means that no cables run from the computer to the bus as they do in a 10Base5 network. The bus is coaxial cable (commonly referred to as thin Ethernet), and allows a maximum segment length of 185 meters. There can be 5 segments connected, each with up to 30 computers.

Despite the reality of collisions on a bus network, it is still the most economical (in terms of cabling and network equipment) and the easiest type of network to install. Its major weakness is the linear arrangement of the nodes: if one fails, the entire network goes down—in a fashion similar to Christmas tree lights connected in a series. Despite this risk, the Ethernet bus continues to be highly popular, as evidenced by the fact that Ethernet LANs have the largest installed base of any network standard.

Star Topology

The star topology shown in Figure 5.9 connects the individual network stations to a central node. It uses more cabling than the other topologies, resulting in increased cost. The central wiring concentrators also represent a higher cost than concentrators for other networks. However, star

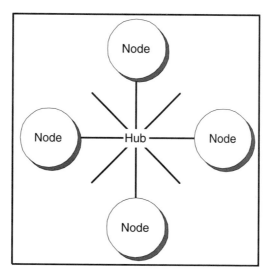

Figure 5.9 Star topology for a network.

topology offers some significant benefits over the others. For example, since each node on the network is individually wired, a defective cable or node only affects one workstation, allowing the rest of the network to continue operation. And, since all signals are routed through the central concentrator, the network can be monitored from that location, greatly contributing to network diagnostics and management.

The Token Ring standard, despite its name, uses a star topology. It gets its name from the fact that the central node uses a device called a Multistation Access Unit (MAU or MSAU) to create a logical ring in which all incoming lines are connected in the middle of the star. Communication is achieved with a special group of bits called a token, used to control access to the ring. The token circulates from station to station around the ring, until one that wants to transmit takes the token and transmits the signal. At the end of the transmission, the station must release the token so that other stations can access the ring.

Token Ring networks can use unshielded or shielded twisted-pair cable in a star topology. The transmission speeds are either 4 or 16 Mbps. The unshielded twisted-pair networks can support a maximum of 72 computers, with a maximum of 45 meters from a computer to the MAU/MSAU. The highest possible shielded twisted-pair distances are 100 meters, and they can attach 260 computers. In both cases, there can be no more than 33 hubs in a single ring.

RING TOPOLOGY

This topology, illustrated in Figure 5.10, consists of a loop of cable that connects all nodes on a network; the signals pass from node to node around the ring. As each node receives a message intended for another node, it simply repeats the message to the next node on the ring.

Individual LANs are not usually wired using the physical ring topology—rings are usually used over a large geographic area in which a star would be inefficient. Rings can be used to connect several sites within a city, or even several cities across a broader region. Ring networks are very good at providing fault tolerance, because they provide a backup signal path; if a break affects one of the ring segments, the signal can be routed back through the ring's backup unit. The advantages of ring technology are the redundant paths and the efficient use of cabling when covering a large geographic area. The main disadvantage is that there is no central area to monitor the network, and it has generally lower data throughput (the amount of data that can be transferred over a network in a given amount of time) relative to the others. An exception to this is the Fiber Distributed Data Interface (FDDI), which uses a ring variation. This networking standard uses fiber-optic cable to provide high-capacity, high-speed (100 Mbps) data transmission in Metropolitan or Wide Area Networks (MANs and WANs).

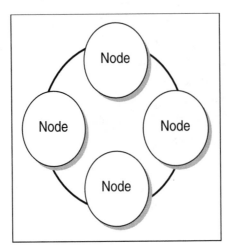

Figure 5.10   Ring topology for a network.

Internetworks in a Nutshell

Up until now we've been focusing on the individual LAN, but in most networked organizations today there are many LANs that are interconnected to form MANs and WANs. These internetworks are constructed by using *bridges* and *routers* to connect similar and dissimilar LANs, as well as alleviate bottleneck problems in network traffic. Bridges and routers can be specialized computers that run programs to provide the bridging and routing functions, or in the case of Windows NT, can be a conventional server whose OS has been configured to deliver these functions.

BRIDGES

Bridges are used to connect two separate physical networks to form a logical network. In the example in Figure 5.11, a bridge is used to connect a Token Ring and an Ethernet LAN. The bridge has two network adapter cards, one Token Ring, the other Ethernet. Using Figure 5.11 as an example, when the bridge receives a data packet from a station on the Ethernet LAN, it first determines if the destination is on the same physical network; if it is, the packet is routed to its destination. If, however, the recipient is on the Token Ring network, the bridge translates the packet header information into the appropriate format for transmission in a Token Ring environment. Because bridges operate at the data link layer (Level

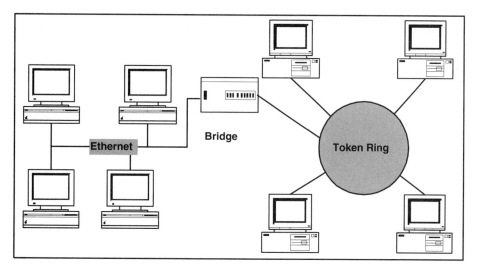

Figure 5.11 Using bridge technology to connect dissimilar LANs.

2) of the OSI model, they do not have access to the addressing information which is contained at the network layer (Level 3). This information is necessary for a device to handle intelligent data routing over a network. As a result, bridges are primarily effective for connecting a small number of LANs—they become less effective as the number of interconnected LANs and the corresponding need for routing grows.

ROUTERS

Since routers function at the network layer of the OSI model, they have access to the address information that is needed to carry out the routing function. A network route consists of addresses and paths that can be taken by a data packet. Routing algorithms are used to select the best path for a given data packet, and are used to assess numerous criteria, such as whether or not the destination can be reached, the number of hops a packet has to take, what the time delay will be to reach the destination, the status of the links along the path, and the available bandwidth.

The sophistication of router technology means that routers are more expensive and require more ongoing maintenance than bridges; since they do more in terms of data transmission, they are also usually slower. However, when large numbers of LANs are interconnected, they are the tool of choice for providing connectivity.

Network Design Considerations

In *Interconnections: Bridges and Routers,* author Radia Perlman, a leading designer of bridging and routing algorithms for Digital Equipment Corporation, set out seven characteristics for good network design. They are as follows:

- *Scope*—The network architecture should be as general as possible, in order to accommodate a wide range of applications and meet as many needs as possible.

- *Scalability*—The network should work well with both large and small networks.

- *Robustness*—Basically, the network should continue to operate if nodes or links fail, and it should provide:

- *Firewalls*—These are necessary for security reasons, and to contain the spread of disruptions, such as LAN broadcast storms (severe congestion on the network).

- *Self-Stabilization*—In the event of faulty hardware or undetected data errors, the network should return to normal operation within a reasonable amount of time, without human intervention.

- *Fault Detection*—The network should perform self-diagnostics to identify faulty or failing equipment.

- *Byzantine Robustness*—In the case of a node performing incorrectly, but not failing outright, the network should be able to continue functioning.

- *Autoconfigurability*—Networks should be able to run themselves as much as possible, making it easy to add pieces and manage the network.

- *Tweakability*—While networks should be autoconfiguring, network managers should be able to change the defaults to improve performance.

- *Determinism*—Identical conditions will yield identical results, making analysis easier through the ability to reproduce a given condition.

- *Migration*—Networks should provide the ability to add new features to a node without disrupting network operation.

General Network Considerations

The overall performance of a network depends on many factors, such as the network standard, topology, media, and number of nodes on the network. Of prime importance are the number and types of applications being run. If these require high bandwidth or distributed processing using multiple servers, there will be a significant impact on the network. A good example is the difference in network capacity required for two Internet applications, Telnet and FTP. Telnet, which enables remote connection, transmits a character at a time, meaning that the volume of data is very low, and the length of time the network is in use is long. FTP, on the other hand, uses a lot of bandwidth for a short period of time. Understanding the nature of the application and the characteristics of your network makes it possible to eliminate many of those unpleasant surprises that come with networked applications. There are numerous online resources on the sub-ject of networking. If you're interested in a broad, not-too-technical un-derstanding of networks, look into *Network Computing's Interactive Design Manual*, which can be accessed at the Network Computing Online site located at **http://techweb.cmp.com/nwc/current**.

Windows NT Server—The Network Operating System

Unlike a traditional Network Operating System such as Novell Netware, NT is a member of the new generation of NOSs (mind you, some network specialists will argue that NT represents the older generation, and Novell, the newer). These new NOSs have built-in networking functionality, but don't force their own protocols and resultant topologies onto the network—the OS can either stand on its own, or integrate with other networks. NT has the flexibility to incorporate additional protocols other than the na-tive peer-to-peer networking protocols, whereas Novell was designed with full-scale system integration in mind. In a Novell environment, all the com-puters on the network, in addition to the server, must run a version of the Novell software.

NT, then, provides very good integrated networking support, in addition to peer-to-peer client/server networking. All NT computers can act as cli-ents and servers, sharing files and printers with other computers. It's also very easy to add other networking software and hardware to an NT system, and it includes four transport protocols: IPX/SPX, TCP/IP, NetBIOS Frame (NBF) (the Windows NT version of NetBEUI that removes the 254 node limit), and the Data Link Control Protocol (DLC) which lets NT machines communicate over the network with IBM mainframe computers. Its interoperability with other networks is quite good, and includes Novell Netware networks, Unix networks, and SNA networks for IBM mainframe and mid-range computers. It permits distributed applications using Re-mote Procedure Calls (RPCs), and also supports NetBIOS sockets, the Windows network APIs, named pipes, and mail slots. Remote access is fa-cilitated by the Remote Access Service (RAS), which allows client PCs to dial into any Point-to-Point (PPP) or Serial Line Internet Protocol (SLIP) server. The Windows NT RAS servers support any remote clients using TCP/IP, IPX, or NetBEUI. Security is robust and solid, providing various levels of authentication and data encryption. (More detail on NT security mechanisms is provided in Chapter 8, "Protecting an Intranet.")

Windows NT Workstation—The Network Client

On the client side, NT supports any client that will run TCP/IP, as shown in Figure 5.12. You can have machines running MS-DOS, Windows 3.1, Windows for Workgroups, Windows 95, Windows NT, Macintosh, or Unix.

Optional Configuration—The Database Back End

Adding a database component to an intranet is optional, but if you're serious about leveraging the existing investment in Information Technology (IT), then doing so can provide significant payback through the use of existing data. Another reason to consider this option seriously is that it provides good proof of concept for your pilot intranet. In many of the

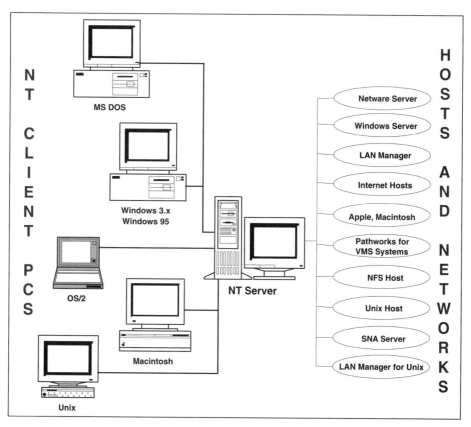

Figure 5.12 Windows NT Server support for heterogeneous hosts, networks, and clients.

newsgroups and articles we've read, a frequently-asked question is, "How do I sell this idea to management?" If you can show management how the proposed intranet can use existing databases to enhance the distribution of information through the organization, it will go a long way toward selling them on this idea.

Within any organization, there are a variety of database applications used to support business processes. They vary a great deal in size and complexity, from the single-user database to those that are mission-critical and enterprise-wide. These databases use their own Database Management System (DBMS) to provide users access to the data. There are two access standards used for interacting with the DMBS: Structured Query Language (SQL) and Open Database Connectivity (ODBC).

Each database type and its associated DBMS has its own processing requirements. For reasons of performance and security, complex, mission-critical databases are hosted on their own database servers.

The computing requirements of a given database application depend on several factors, one being the nature of the activity taking place—if it's data read from the database, less processing activity occurs than in an operation where records are being updated. Other factors are the frequency and types of searches conducted. For example, a complex search requiring multiple table joins in a relational database requires far more processing than a simple search based on a primary and secondary key.

The database your Web pages access to retrieve and display information can have either a direct or indirect impact on your intranet. A database residing on its own server will have a less direct impact; nonetheless, it will still affect network load and increase the amount of data-handling the Web server computer has to do. For this type of database, you must also consider the complexity of the routines or interfaces that are required to allow interaction between the server and the hypertext pages. The level of complexity and functionality, too, has an impact on the Web server's processing load.

Smaller database applications, particularly those using the ODBC access method, put a direct load on your server since they have to reside on the same computer as the Web server software. Consequently, there is going to be an increased demand on the CPU and a need for more storage capacity. As is the case with the distributed database applications we covered earlier, the server's processing requirements should be determined by the frequency and nature of the database accesses and by the complexity of the searches conducted against the database.

Despite the capacity issues that are presented by integrating Web pages with databases, this integration provides the opportunity to tap into a valuable resource by enhancing the quality and timeliness of the information you make available throughout the organization. By having some understanding of server and network performance issues, and by doing some capacity planning prior to building an intranet, your company will benefit from integrating traditional information technology and Web technology.

Windows NT Resources

There are a growing number of Windows NT resources on the Internet— the following are only a small sampling.

Newsgroups

The following newsgroups on the USENET are useful for gathering NT information and for making personal contacts (misery loves company).

comp.os.ms-windows.nt.admin.misc

comp.os.ms-windows.nt.admin.networking

comp.os.ms-windows.networking.windows

comp.os.ms-windows.networking.ras.

Internet Sites

In addition to the USENET, there are a wealth of sites on the Internet that provide information about Windows NT.

Windows NT Magazine
http://www.winnt.com

Microsoft
http://www.microsoft.com

Webwriter
http://www.webwriter.com/winnt.htm

Warehouse 32 Hot Sites for NT Information
http://www.warehouse32.co.uk/hotsites/hotsites.htm

Robelle Consulting Ltd., Windows NT Resources
http://wwwnt.robelle.com/winnt.html

Win32 Support BBS
http://www.vnet.net/users/daleross/

The One-Stop Windows NT Site
http://www.win95.com/NTpages.html

Windows NT InfoCenter at Digital
http://www.windowsnt.digital.com

CHAPTER

6

Information Content: The Data Sources

6

Information Content: The Data Sources

Information content for Web pages is provided either manually or electronically. The manual approach involves collecting information, organizing it, and typing or scanning it into the source files for hypertext pages. The electronic approach takes advantage of existing information collections by linking the pages to specific data stores, or collections. Using existing data to create new information views is one of the main ways to leverage your technology investment, and is the subject of this chapter. Every organization with a modest level of computerization already has a large collection of diverse, electronic information that can be used in an intranet-based system. In addition to examining these sources, we'll look at using data conversion, interface activities, and Web page retrieval techniques to update existing databases or populate new ones. Before proceeding further, however, we need to understand what is meant by *data* and *information*, and how we use these terms.

Existing Data Sources

The most common sources of data used in constructing Web pages are:

- Documents

- Spreadsheets

- Presentations

- Custom graphics

- Databases

Material from any of these sources can be included, either in its entirety or in selected portions, to deliver the required content. Since each of these kinds of data is stored in a different format, accessing and displaying the information is not a straightforward procedure for the page builder. First, we'll examine each type, along with the common format used to store it, and then go on to the methods employed to incorporate the data seamlessly into a hypertext page.

Is It Information or Data?

The U.S. Department of Defense Directive 5200.28 defines data as: "A representation of facts, concepts, information, or instructions in a manner suitable for communication, interpretation, or processing by humans or by an AIS [Automated Information System]."

A database professional, such as a Database Administrator or Developer, uses a much narrower definition which says that numbers and characters stored in electronic format have no meaning by themselves. After this "raw data" is processed and interpreted, it becomes information.

For the most part, we use data and information interchangeably, more in keeping with the DOD directive. Furthermore, the source data for a hypertext page may have existed as information in a previous incarnation; it is viewed as data from the perspective of the page creator. Figure 6.1 illustrates this idea.

Documents

There are two types of documents that we'll examine here: plain text and word processed text.

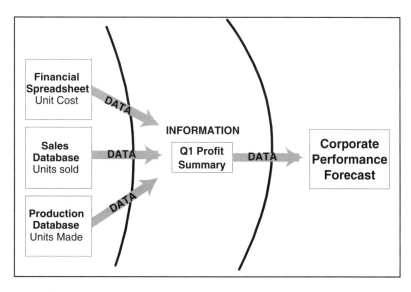

Figure 6.1 Data becomes information, which in turn becomes data.

PLAIN TEXT

Until the advent of the PC and word processing software, most documents consisted only of text and were stored in ASCII format, which contained no special characters like tabs or boldfaced letters. Formatting was limited to left justification. To achieve more sophisticated results, such as full justification, different typefaces, bolding, and so on, it was necessary to use a text-formatting software program such as SGML or Textform. The programmer manually placed formatting commands called tags in the text, and then the processor interpreted them and produced a formatted document. It was tedious work, but it had the advantage of being portable. The type of computer hardware or operating system used was irrelevant; text was text, and if the system had text-formatting software installed, a document could be formatted.

WORD PROCESSED TEXT

Word processing was developed to provide users with a tool for creating, editing, and viewing material, without the tedium and time consumption of text processing. Early word processors allowed the writer to construct documents with such basic formatting controls as underlining, boldfacing, justification, and adjusting typefaces. (Today, it is also possible to include custom graphics, clip art, or spreadsheet data.) The price of this productivity was portability—each word processing package stored documents in its own proprietary format. Until the 1990s, the writer/reader was forced to use the same software employed in creating a document to carry out tasks such as editing, viewing, or printing. In more recent years, the situation has improved; although the leading word processors still have their own unique formats, they now allow you to convert text from one format to another, or to save a document in a different format. Conversions and alternative format saves, however, are not 100-percent effective, particularly if text is formatted in tables. There is, of course, the option of saving the work as an ASCII file, but this may be counterproductive, since the formatting controls are lost.

Spreadsheets

The electronic spreadsheet came into being as a result of the introduction of the microcomputer. The idea behind spreadsheet software was to give users the ability to work with numbers electronically, in a fashion similar to working with the rows and columns of the paper-based accounting world. Rather than just manipulating text, the computer could be used to manipulate numbers.

The limitations we've described for word processing software apply to this tool as well—there are proprietary storage formats, limited portability, and less than fully-successful conversion to other file formats. Spreadsheets do, however, provide a degree of formatting control, plus the ability to create graphs based on the numeric data in the spreadsheet.

Presentations

Also referred to as "presentation graphics," this type of software is designed to create, edit, and show presentations based on the slide show paradigm. Presentation graphics software provides color, graphics, and the text-formatting controls we expect from a word processor. These packages enable the user to sequence pages, use simple animation, and control image display with techniques such as fade-in for online presentations using a PC. When online capability isn't available, the presenter can use the electronic images to create conventional slide masters for use on an overhead projector.

A wide range of data inclusions, conversions, and selective storage options are available—within the limits outlined for text processors and spreadsheets.

Custom Graphics

There are also specialized programs for creating custom graphics, each offering a variety of techniques (such as animation, perspective, and 3D) to manipulate images. As is the case with other document-handling software, individual packages store data in a proprietary format, and offer a range of conversion and storage options. However, a much greater degree of portability is possible in this medium, because the computer graphics industry has established several standards for image storage.

While several software developers have put forward their own proprietary standard, there are, in fact, three that can be considered industry standards. These are the Graphics Interchange Format (GIF), the Joint Photographic Group (JPG or JPEG), and the Tagged Image File Format (TIFF).

Sound and Motion

As in the case of graphics, certain standards have emerged for storing audio and video information in files. In terms of a cross-platform standard, the Sun Audio (AU) specification by Sun Microsystems is the broadest. The Musical Instrument Digital Interface (MIDI) extends the range of audio by providing a hardware specification and protocol for the exchange of information between computers, keyboards, controllers, synthesizers, and other electronic music devices.

In the realm of video, the broadest standard is set by, and named after, an ISO committee called the Moving Picture Experts Group (MPEG). With the recent porting of the Macintosh QuickTime video standard to Windows, this standard will enjoy broad usage as well.

Databases

A database provides a location for storing large volumes of information. Any data type can be stored—straight text, graphic, numeric, audio, video, and even hypertext documents—although most databases still consist primarily of text and numeric data. They are much like other files, such as spreadsheets and word-processed text, in that they constitute a repository whose contents can be manipulated. (Many spreadsheet users simply regard their spreadsheets as a database.) However, a true database provides a far greater level of functionality, and is distinguished by its ability to store particularly large volumes of data, to organize and index, and most significantly, to allow for the selective retrieval of its contents. This capacity for selective retrieval makes databases rich sources of data for Web page content, unlike those resources that provide an "all or nothing" approach. Admittedly, it is possible to extract portions of word processing documents and spreadsheets, but not without doing significant programming.

An integral part of a database is the Database Management System (DBMS), which provides a user interface and the tools to construct, index, populate, extract, update, and manipulate the database contents. Each DBMS uses a specific command language that allows the user to issue statements required to carry out particular operations, such as updating or searching for data. The two primary language standards are the Structured Query Language (SQL) and Open Database Connectivity (ODBC).

Portability Issues

File and document portability have been singled out several times as stumbling blocks to the exchange of material between software packages. The widely used word processors Word and WordPerfect provide an excellent illustration of the difficulty—a person using Word should be able to open a file, edit it, and save it in either format. As you've probably noticed, however, the level of compatibility between the different word processing packages is not ideal, particularly for special formatting. Portability also becomes an issue when sending output to a screen or printer. For example, to print a Word document, a computer must have printer drivers specific to both Word and the particular make and model of printer it's using. Two approaches have been put forward to address these portability issues: Rich Text Format (RTF) and Portable Document Format (PDF).

RTF

The RTF standard was developed by Microsoft in response to the problem of document portability. Documents saved in RTF can be read by different word processing and desktop publishing packages, including Word,

WordPerfect, Interleaf, and Adobe Illustrator, without losing any of the basic formatting controls in a file. It should be noted that this portability is really at the exchange level between various products, and doesn't adequately address the issues of displaying or printing at the output level.

There have been several attempts to achieve portability at the output, or presentation, level (printing or viewing a document on the screen). The most notable of these is the PDF.

PDF

Adobe Systems put forward the PDF approach as a means to transport existing documents over a network, and then to display or print them. The file containing a document is converted to PDF, while the original formatting—layout and font sizes—is preserved; these converted files can then be viewed using a PDF document reader. An Adobe product called Acrobat Amber has been developed to work with a Web browser for viewing PDF files, thereby making it possible to incorporate PDF documents into an intranet Web site.

Using the Data Sources

To take full advantage of your data sources, first it will be necessary to make a thorough assessment of existing information content and flow. Many times, organizations do not have an accurate picture of the potential resources that could provide useful content for Web pages. In addition to databases, any computer-generated data, including documents, spreadsheets, and graphics files, can be incorporated. During the evaluation process, you also need to gain an understanding of how the information is currently used, and how it could be used in new or different ways, in the context of an intranet.

Additionally, you must determine the information needs of your intended audience and the presentation format they are accustomed to working with. By marrying the results of the data source analysis and the information destination analysis, you will be more likely to realize the full potential of the intranet technology. (We will cover data source analysis and information destination analysis in more detail in Chapter 14.)

Once the data source assessment has been completed and you have selected the appropriate resources, there are three ways of using the information within the network: in its *original format*, by *converting* it to HTML source documents, or by building *interfaces* from the Web pages to the data source.

USING DATA IN ITS ORIGINAL FORMAT: HELPER APPLICATIONS AND PLUG-INS

When using data in its original format, the file containing the data will be retrieved by the browser and its entire contents will be shown as part of the hypertext page. Although this is by far the simplest method for using existing information, it is not without limitations—primarily, the inability of browsers to display different file types. Every browser is capable of displaying certain file contents, or MIME types, such as text, HTML, and GIFs; any additional types require an external program called a *helper application* to present the contents. These programs are installed on the user's PC, and the browser is configured so that it can associate certain file types with the appropriate helper application (this association is based on the extension of the file name, so that an image file using GIF, for example, would have .gif as the extension). A helper application can be any external program activated to deal with a given file type. For example, the Word program is started any time the browser encounters a file type identified as a Word document.

When a file is retrieved, the following sequence of events takes place:

1. The browser checks the file type of the incoming file.

2. The browser then checks its own configuration to see if it can display the file, or if a helper application is required.

3. If it can't display the file, and no helper application is available, the browser displays a prompt asking the user what to do next (such as save, configure, or cancel), as shown in Figure 6.2.

4. If the appropriate helper application is available, the application is launched, and the file loaded into it.

5. When the user is finished with the file, he closes the helper application and is returned to the browser window.

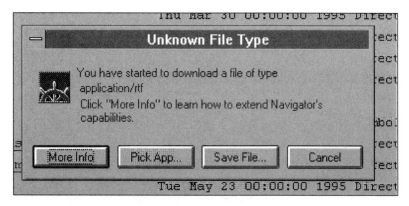

Figure 6.2 The browser's prompt when an unknown file type is encountered.

Netscape Communications, the developer of the Netscape Navigator browser, takes the helper application concept further through the use of *plug-ins*. Rather than launching external applications to deal with different file formats, a plug-in is a software module that extends Netscape's capabilities by providing helper application functionality within the browser.

In addition to basic file-viewing capability, plug-ins can:

- obtain data from URLs

- generate data for other plug-ins and the Netscape browser

- run another program

- enable applications to communicate with each other

A good example of a plug-in is Acrobat Amber, the Adobe product for viewing documents stored in the PDF format. (Figure 6.3 illustrates the use of this plug-in, which can be obtained from the Adobe site at **http:// www.adobe.com.**) After selecting a PDF file to view, the Amber plug-in is started; the document is still displayed in the Netscape viewing area, but the document-viewing controls provided by Amber now appear below the Netscape tool bar area.

You can obtain more functional and technical information, as well as a plug-in Software Developer's Kit (SDK), from the Netscape Communications Web site (**http://home.netscape.com/eng/mozilla/2.02/handbook/ plugins/index.html**).

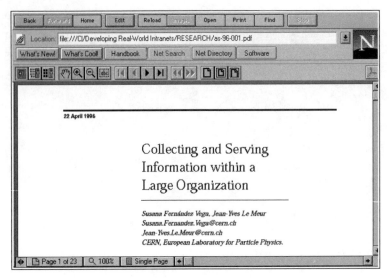

Figure 6.3 Using the Amber plug-in to view a PDF file.

DATA CONVERSION

Unless you decide to use source material in its entirety, as shown in Figure 6.3, the information will have to be converted to HTML format. In the case of small documents, this conversion can be done manually. The process is quite simple: After saving the original document as a text file, HTML tags can be added, using either a conventional editor or one of the many specialized HTML editors. In the case of larger files, using *conversion programs* makes more sense, because multiple documents can be converted at one time. Although some touching up is typically needed to achieve the desired formatting, converters do provide a less labor-intensive alternative to manual editing. (See Chapter 10 for an in-depth examination of editors and converters.) As you'll learn in Chapter 7, existing documents will likely need restructuring in order to be more effective and easier to view online as hypertext.

Conversion software is available for each of the major word processing programs, but at the present time the most efficient and feature-rich is RTFtoHTML, which converts files from RTF to HTML source files. The current version for the IBM world is run from the DOS command line, and includes the ability to generate a table of contents, create HTML head levels, and include/exclude inline graphics in converted documents.

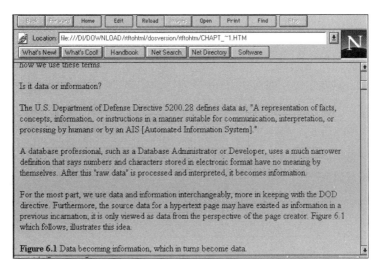

Figure 6.4 A Word document after conversion to HTML, using the RTFtoHTML program.

Figure 6.4 shows a portion of this chapter (created in Word 7.0 and saved as RTF) after it was converted to HTML by RTFtoHTML.

Chris Hector, a software tester at Cray Research and the program's developer, is currently working on a Windows version of RTFtoHTML that will handle HTML 3.0 tags, the generation of indexes with hypertext links, document splitting, and extensions to HTML developed for Netscape and Microsoft Internet Explorer. Chris's Home Page at **http://www.sunpack. com/RTF/** has information on the RTF specification, details on the features and operation of RTFtoHTML, and the most recent version of the software available for downloading.

In organizations where more than one type of PC word processor is in use, the best approach is to save all documents in RTF. There are two reasons for this: First, it provides the highest level of portability in a mixed software environment; second, it requires the use of only one conversion program, which results in HTML document consistency. It's also generally easier to support. Figure 6.5 shows how conversion of documents from multiple sources can be used to create a Web page.

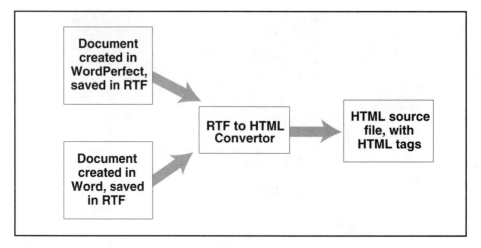

Figure 6.5   The multi-document conversion process within an organization.

INTERFACES TO THE DATA: GATEWAY PROGRAMS

If the source of data for the Web pages is a database, then the issue is not conversion, but gaining access to and retrieving data—all while working within the constraints of the database's DBMS. What is needed is a link between the hypertext page and the database via the Web server and the DBMS. This link is a program commonly referred to as a *script*, and it contains a series of statements that are executed when the script is activated. In the Web hypertext world, these scripts are based on a protocol called the Common Gateway Interface (CGI).

In the initial implementation of the World Wide Web, the content of hypertext pages was static. When a user activated a link, the target object (page) was retrieved from the specified server—a one-way transfer of information, with no content alteration at either end of the connection. CGI was developed to expand this capability, and can be viewed as an extension to HTTP. CGI facilitates bi-directional communications between applications and information servers, thereby enabling interactive hypertext applications.

A CGI program is a collection of instructions following the CGI standard that executes in real-time and outputs dynamic information.

The Parts of a CGI Script

In a paper presented at the Fourth International World Wide Web Conference in 1995 (Schoenfeldinger, Werner J., "WWW Meets Linda: Linda For Global WWW-Based Transaction Processing Systems"), the author describes CGI scripts and identifies the major parts of one of these programs:

CGI scripts are written to perform a certain user-defined task. The task can range from simple output-only scripts to sophisticated programs. Generally, we can identify three major parts in CGI scripts:

- Reading the data passed via the CGI and converting it into data structures suitable for further processing.

- Processing the data and computing the results. For example, database access or simple computations. This is the main task of the program.

- Formatting the results of the program to HTML and sending the results to standard output.

These programs can be written in any of the languages that can run on your system; in the case of Windows NT Server, these would include C/C++, Perl, and Visual Basic. All scripts reside on the server and are activated from the client side of the client/server link. After a CGI program is activated, data is stored on the server side in temporary storage areas called *environment variables*. These variables are used to hold a variety of information, such as the server's IP address, input provided by the user, a document, a document URL, and so on. Once data is stored in one of these variables, it is possible to perform calculations, as well as to send information to the client or to a database.

These gateway, or interface programs are identified within a hypertext page as reference links. The scripts are executed when their reference links are activated, either automatically or dynamically, based on input from the user. In the first case, the script is activated spontaneously when the Web client requests the page containing the script reference. This type of activation can be used to automatically display personalized messages based on the identity of the user, such as: "Hello Dan, you are not authorized to view this information." User-initiated activation can be achieved in either of two ways: by providing a hypertext link on the screen, which can be used to trigger the execution of a script, or by providing an electronic form that the user can fill in and submit to the Web server. Typically, the latter method is used to submit searches to a database on a network.

To illustrate how CGI works, we'll use the simple database query shown in Figure 6.6.

The following list illustrates a process that could use CGI to accept input when extracting information from an existing database. The process works equally well in reverse, using forms and CGI to add, delete, or update information in a database. This database could be an existing one, or a new one created for the express purpose of building a new information resource for your organization.

1. The user submits a search string using an online form at the client PC.

2. The user's input is sent as an HTTP request to the Web server.

3. The Web server activates the CGI script.

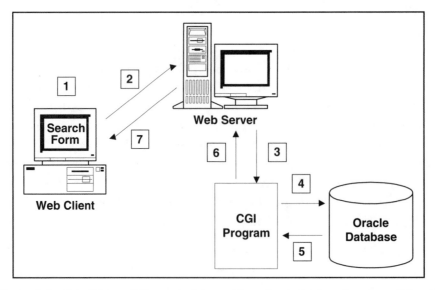

Figure 6.6 Submitting an SQL search statement to an Oracle database by using a CGI script.

4. The CGI script formats the search string into an SQL query statement, and sends it to the database.

5. The database returns the query results to the CGI script.

6. The CGI script formats these results in HTML and passes this information to the server.

7. The server sends the formatted results to the client.

FastCGI

It is accepted that CGI executables are generally not as fast as Web server APIs, however these APIs are vendor-specific, complex, language-dependent, and more difficult to maintain than CGI programs. In the case of Web sites that have a high volume of traffic, speed is a real issue. An extension to CGI, called FastCGI has been put forward by several vendors to address this performance issue. It will maintain the openness of the CGI standard while providing increased performance. In addition to maintaining CGI functionality, it adds the ability to execute CGI programs on a computer other than the server, perform modular authentication and authentication checks, and translate data from one type to another.

At this time, the developers promoting FastCGI have made application libraries (C, C++, Java, Perl, Tcl) and upgrade modules for free servers (NCSA, Apache) available at no cost. In support of FastCGI, Tim Berners-Lee stated: "CGI, whilst a common interface used by many servers, is intrinsically slow. The W3 Consortium is looking forward to the development of new open standards for this interface, and FastCGI is one promising proposal in the spirit of open standards." A clearinghouse for FastCGI information has been set up by Open Market and is located at **http://www.fastcgi.com**.

CGI Issues

The two main issues related to the use of CGI on your Web site are cost and security.

Cost

The cost of interface programming will be determined by the following factors:

- *User Access Requirements*—The way in which your users access the data will determine the complexity of the CGI scripts needed. If, for example, the user selects items from a predefined list, the scripts and database calls will be relatively straightforward. On the other hand, if the user can conduct ad hoc queries, and in turn, use the results to create and submit additional queries, the interface programming will be more complex.

- *Database Diversity*—Given diverse data sources—multiple, varied types, such as SQL- or ODBC-based databases—the interface programming is likely to be much more extensive than if all requests were made to a single database.

- *In-house Skills*—Are there, within the organization, programmers who already have, or could readily acquire, the skills needed to build these interfaces? If not, it will be necessary to bring in a contractual programmer to do this work for you.

Security

In spite of the fact that your intranet is an internal information system, don't be lulled into complacency in the area of security. Keep in mind the fact that an inexperienced or untrained user can unintentionally wreak havoc on the system. With regard to CGI, two items are important: watching who has access to the scripts, and monitoring user input. In order for CGI scripts to be used by the server, they must reside in a special directory on the server machine so the Web server software knows they're to be run when referenced. Since these programs are executables running on the system, access to existing CGI scripts, or the ability to create and run new ones, should be restricted to qualified individuals.

Another area to watch is the input section of a form; unless there are controls in place to limit the volume of input, a user could potentially dump the electronic version of *War and Peace* into your system. And, while certainly not dangerous, this could have a dramatic affect on system performance.

Additional information about CGI is available from the National Center for Supercomputing Applications (NCSA). NCSA provides an excellent overview, as well as detailed information about the CGI protocol, at its Web site: **http://hoohoo.ncsa.uiuc.edu/cgi/overview.html**.

7

Developing Web Pages

Producing basic hypertext pages using HTML is, in itself, very simple; creating a collection of well-designed pages, and then bringing them together to first form high quality electronic publications and, finally, a cohesive Web site, is another matter entirely. In this chapter we will examine the many broader issues associated with this process: document and page structure, planning and design activities, some HTML basics, and the hypermedia aspects of hypertext. Dynamic information updates and interactive pages will also be discussed.

Document Structure: The Paper Medium

To design well-constructed hypertext documents, it's necessary to start with a thorough understanding of how printed material is structured. To begin, let's examine a paper document, such as a book, in fairly extensive detail. A book is a container filled with information, and for a reader to progress through it and understand its contents, it must have an organized structure. The broadest level of this structure is the table of contents, which encapsulates a map of the book's sequencing, and gives the reader the option of accessing material non-selectively, according to its major structural elements, or selectively, based on interest. Similarly, the index provides a tool for accessing specific information throughout the book, but based on key words rather than structure.

The next level of structural division is provided by the chapters that divide the work into its major components. Each chapter (in most non-fiction works) is divided into major sections, and each of these sections, in turn, is divided into sub-sections and sub-sub-sections, according to the book's content and the level of detail it requires. (For example, a book like this one uses three levels of division within a chapter.) These chapter subdivisions are referred to as heading (sometimes head or header) levels, and can be indicated in several ways. In the document template for this manuscript, heading levels are indicated by using different typefaces and font sizes, as shown in the following example.

Heading One

Heading Two

HEADING THREE

Manuals and textbooks, on the other hand, tend to use a numbering system, similar to the following example, to identify sections and subsections within a chapter.

1 Heading One

    1.1 Heading Two

        1.1.1. Heading Three

Both of the preceding methods for providing structure are completely obvious; more subtle (but equally effective) structuring is provided by the actual document page and the paragraphs included on it. Do you recall being interrupted while reading a book? To make note of where you stopped, you may well have glanced at the number on the page you were reading, or inserted a bookmark at that point. You've probably also used a page number to reference a particular section of a document you wanted someone else to read. And, although they lack numbers, paragraphs also provide reference points, by dividing information into manageable blocks and making processing easier. Figure 7.1 shows the separation of a document into its structural components. It should be noted that the only physical divisions in a book are the actual pages; all other structural divisions are visual. The reason for making this distinction will become clear when we discuss the electronic publication.

Document Structure: The Electronic Medium

In addition to the paper-based concepts discussed above, there are aspects of HTML and its document structure that must also be taken into account when designing electronic publications. However, before looking at the structure of hypertext documents, it's necessary to digress for a moment to discuss terminology.

Two terms borrowed from the paper print world, page and document, are used somewhat differently in the context of electronic publishing. To avoid confusion, they are clarified in the following sidebar.

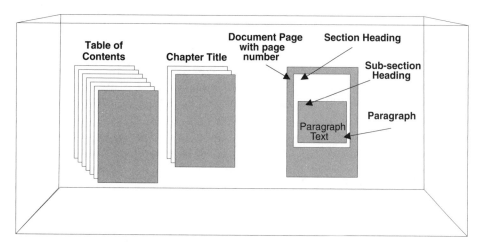

Figure 7.1   The book as a physical container, with visual cues providing structure.

The HTML Document Definition

At the HTML level, a Web document refers to a source file that contains information. Three paired HTML tags must be included within the file in order to meet the *minimum* requirements of a document definition. First is the **<HTML>**tag, which is used first to denote the beginning of a document, and then again, to indicate the end. The two other paired tags that are required are placed within these commands: the **<HEAD>** tags that mark a *document head* area, and the **<BODY>** tags that define the *document body*. When a file contains these tags in the specified order, it is, by HTML standards, a document.

Problems seem to arise with the use of the word *page*, probably because we immediately think of a printed page. In fact, in the electronic world, it is simply a synonymous term for document, and unlike a page in a book, a Web page may be of any length.

The term *file* also causes confusion. However, in the hypertext world, it also means the same as document (and page). Because an HTML file, by default, has the specified paired tags discussed above, it must be defined as a document. (Without the tags, it would simply be a text file.)

document = page = HTML source file

To further clarify the issue, we will use *publication* to describe a complete work on a specific topic. It follows, then, that a publication may be composed of many documents, or pages.

While HTML makes use of the paper-based concepts discussed earlier, there are also aspects specific to this electronic medium and its document structure that have a significant impact on the design, creation, and presentation of electronic publications. As the writer, you have the option of structuring your pages to contain one paragraph, a collection of paragraphs that form a larger section, or a chapter comprised of many sections. (In the case of small publications, the entire contents may be contained in one electronic container, or page.) Regardless of how you choose to structure the information, there is a starting point called the *home page,* which serves as the equivalent to a table of contents. Figure 7.2 shows how an electronic publication can be structured physically by using separate pages, and visually, by using HTML tags to set off paragraphs and sections.

By combining the best of both the paper and the hypertext media, your content creators will be able to develop effective, user-friendly electronic material for use within your organization.

The Nature of the Electronic Medium

Although very powerful and capable of providing many benefits, the electronic medium is not without limitations that have immediate and direct impact on the user. The first limitation, and probably the most consequential, is the viewing area of the PC monitor (the screen). This will determine how the writer organizes and displays information, as well as how easily the reader can progress through and process the content presented. In the paper-print world, a standard-sized 8 1/2 × 11 inch page provides a viewing area that displays between 32 and 36 lines of text, usually orga-

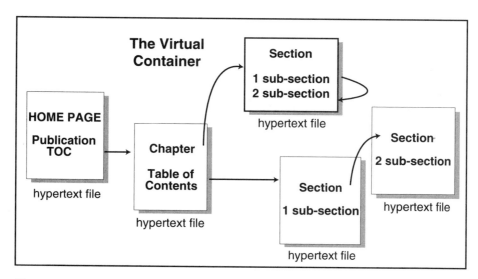

Figure 7.2   The electronic publication as a virtual container, with structure provided by separate containers and visual cues.

nized into several paragraphs. If the reader needs to refer to preceding text, the chances are good that it will appear on the same page; if not, he can very easily turn back to the previous page.

The same, however, cannot be said of the electronic viewing area available to computer users. The effective display area (using the Netscape browser) provides 18 lines of single-spaced text, less than half that of the paper page. On a given screen, there is less space available for referencing previous information, and maintaining visual reference points is difficult while scrolling through large quantities of information.

Another limiting factor in using the electronic medium is the amount of experience that the user has in navigating through electronic information. With the exception of computer professionals who work with PCs day after day, the majority of computer users in an office environment are not accustomed to staring at a monitor for extended periods of time. Content, monitor quality, image quality, contrast, color combinations, and so on, also figure in determining the ease with which users can read information on the screen. In addition, the average user is not particularly facile with moving backward and forward through large volumes of online information; it's all too easy to get lost in an electronic publication. In this medium, then, content presentation, structure, and sequencing are critical.

Publication Planning and Design

You can appreciate that while there are many similarities between the paper and electronic publishing media, the differences are significant enough to warrant serious planning and design prior to publication. It's not simply a matter of moving information from the paper container to the electronic container.

Planning

At least as much planning is required for an electronic publication as for a paper-based work. The publisher has to identify the content, determine an appropriate structure to deliver the information, and select the best layout to accommodate the needs and experience of the readers.

Given the fact that each planned publication will be one of many available on the intranet Web site, there must be an understanding of the entire business' document collection, and how all the publications are related. Once put into electronic format, this collection provides the foundation for your Web site. If it's well-structured—logically sequenced and cross-linked—the Web site document repository can have a significant, and sometimes dramatically positive, impact on business processes. The opposite is true as well: missing or unrelated information will not yield the expected benefits from electronic publishing. The importance of planning and organizing content is highlighted by Aetna Health Plan's intranet experience.

Content Organization: The Aetna Health Plan's Perspective

In assessing Aetna intranet activities to date, Gary Fendler, a key member of AHP's intranet team, identified *content organization* as the number-one issue AHP had to address. He believes that it's not good enough to simply know what information a company has; there also must be an understanding of how that information is used and organized. This knowledge, gained from interviewing key staff in the areas providing the information, is essential for content planning and document publishing. In Fendler's opinion, this activity is so important that he recommends bringing in outside experts if necessary.

Prior to starting actual page development, Fendler feels that it is essential for the intranet project team to construct page maps, or diagrams, that show document structure, page relationships, and the navigation logic of each document. This activity yields paybacks during page construction by eliminating time-consuming and frustrating document rebuilds that drive development costs higher.

Design: The Technical Considerations

Technical aspects such as LAN routing and server configurations are not the main thrust of publication design; however, you do need to consider some general technical issues when designing a publication. The most important technical point related to page development is capacity—it will be affected by, and in turn will affect, the publication. Since capacity is related to overall performance, it ultimately determines whether or not users will enjoy, and continue to use, your intranet. There is a widespread expectation of good response time from a computer system. (Generally, the appearance of information on the screen within three or four seconds after the Enter key has been pressed qualifies as good response time.)

In a networked environment, there are several elements related to the capacity/performance equation. From the perspective of the technical infrastructure, the determining factors are the user's workstation, the network, and the server. The capacity, or performance capabilities, of all three are affected by your publication's structure, content, and complexity.

STRUCTURE

Structure refers to the number of individual files used to divide the publication into its component parts. Take, for example, a printed publication that is 400 pages long and divided into 20 chapters. Stored as a single text file containing no pictures, it is approximately one megabyte in size. There are three options for presenting its content to the reader: as one file, one chapter at a time (20 files), or one page at a time (400 files).

One extreme is to store the publication in a single hypertext file, which means that the reader receives the entire publication when it's requested. On a 10 Mbps Ethernet LAN, running under ideal conditions, it would take close to one second to transfer the file from the Web server to the user's PC. Remember that the file contains no graphics, and the network load is such that the 10 Mbps transfer rate is actually attained—conditions that are rarely met in a production environment.

The other extreme is to have the reader request one page at a time. Since each of these smaller documents appears more quickly on the screen, this method appears, on the surface, to be a faster way to transfer the information. However, this isn't actually the case; transferring the entire publication as separate pages increases the number of requests sent to the server and, on a large network, results in degradation of server performance. The net effect is actually a slower transfer rate to the user.

The ideal situation is to split the publication into a reasonable number of files, each of which is a moderate size. Unfortunately, there is no formula or benchmark that can be used to define "reasonable"; you must determine this by testing page transfers on your own network under typical operating conditions. This testing is well worth the effort and will be appreciated by both the readers and your technical support team.

CONTENT

Content refers to the type of data contained in the pages, such as text, graphics, audio clips, or video clips. Each of these data types requires progressively more storage space, more bandwidth, and subsequently takes longer to transmit from one point to another. A text file that fills one screen in the Netscape browser viewing area uses less than 1 K of storage space, whereas a black-and-white line drawing such as Figure 7.3 (in GIF format), when sized to fit the same viewing area, requires 6.4 K. Depending on the nature of the non-textual data, differences in the size of storage requirements can be significantly greater, and will have an impact on individual page transfer rates, as well as overall network performance. (A high resolution, one-minute video clip, for example, is approximately 2.5 MB in size.)

Also related to content is the nature of the HTML language itself. Each image inserted in a page requires a separate retrieve call to the Web server, and each of these connections takes approximately .2 seconds. If, for example, you had a ten-item bulleted list on a page, and decided to use ten small (1K) happy-face images instead of conventional text bullets, the cost of retrieving the ten images alone would be two seconds. Admittedly, this may not seem significant on a 10 or 16 Mbps LAN, but if that LAN is delivering a variety of other applications and data to a few hundred users, these additional calls to the Web server may require rethinking.

COMPLEXITY

A publication based on the delivery of static information doesn't put a high demand on system resources, since it only involves communication between the client and the Web server. If, however, the data on the pages is updated dynamically from a database, additional hardware, software, and application program elements are involved. Using our example in

Chapter 6, where a user conducted searches against an Oracle database from a Web page, you have a situation where there is interaction between the reader's browser, the Web server, the CGI program, the DBMS, and the database. This data flow is bi-directional, and continuous, for as long as an individual conducts searches. Looking at Figure 7.3, you can see that there are several potential areas where a bottleneck in the flow of information can occur just within the main components. Taking the underlying hardware and software into consideration would complicate the process even further.

The final technical issues your design must take into account are the types of equipment used and the access your readers will have to the Web server. Users on the network require PCs that are adequately equipped to meet the performance demands of your application. If the publication's pages will use many graphics, or incorporate audio and video clips (sound cards, speakers, and high-performance video cards are required for the latter two), workstations must have sufficient CPU speed and memory capacity to process various types of multimedia information. Trying to get by with lesser configurations is counterproductive in the long term, because users faced with a less-than-adequate technical environment won't be bothered to access the Web site

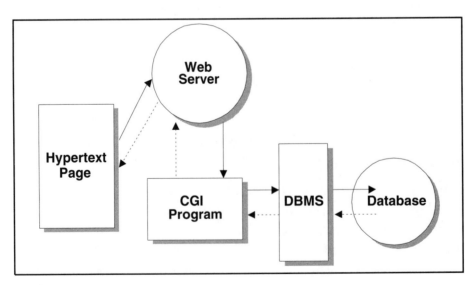

Figure 7.3   Information flow during the dynamic update of a Web page.

During the process of assessing equipment needs and network capacity, it's very easy to overlook the remote users in an organization. These are workers who, either from home or on the road, connect to the company's network via modem over public telephone lines. Unless you've recently gone out and purchased Pentium notebooks for these users, most of them are likely using 486s with 8 or 12 MB of RAM, with an internal 14.4 Kbps modem. Although perfectly adequate for most applications, this equipment is not going to meet the performance requirements of a graphics-intensive or multimedia application designed solely for network-attached, high-performance PCs. Another aspect of dialup access is telephone line quality, over which you have no control, and which varies within a given geographical area in response to such factors as the load on the telephone system or weather conditions.

Design: Publication Structure and the Pages

As we've noted, the structure of a publication is crucial, and each type of publication should be structured according to its objectives, contents, and readership. There are three basic approaches to structuring a Web publication: linear, hierarchical, and blended (both linear and hierarchical). The type you select depends on the way you want to guide or control the reader's movement through the material. The intent of this control is not to limit the user, but to insure that he or she is presented with information in the most logical and effective sequence for achieving the publication's objectives.

LINEAR STRUCTURE

A linear structure, as shown in Figure 7.4, lets the reader move through the publication in the same fashion as he does a book. It is intended to be sequential, and like a book, it allows a person to skip forward or backward. In terms of design, it is the easiest to develop, implement, and maintain. This structure can also provide alternate paths (pages shown with dashed lines in Figure 7.4), which allow the reader to break away from the main flow and take a different route to the end.

This style works well when the information must be presented sequentially in order to meet its objectives. For example, the author of a strategic planning document wants the reader to follow through the logic to see how

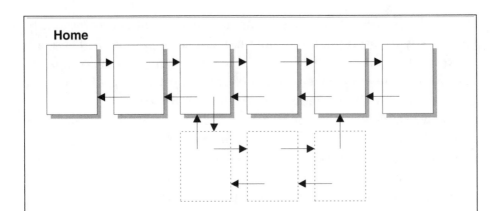

Figure 7.4   Using a linear structure to control movement through a Web publication.

the final conclusions and recommendations are reached. Instruction guides also make use of the sequential delivery of information in order to teach the reader how to do something.

HIERARCHICAL STRUCTURE

The hierarchical organization of material is the one we're most familiar with in online systems. This structure, shown in Figure 7.5, organizes material by providing general information at the top, and then lets the reader work down through the framework to access more detail at each of the lower levels. A hierarchically-organized publication is fairly easy to implement and maintain, and it is easy for readers to keep track of where they are in the material. The designer must watch out for two things that can make a publication based on this structure cumbersome and unpleasant to use: too many layers in the hierarchy and too many screens with branching choices. Both of these factors are annoying to users and will turn them away from your system.

The hierarchical structure illustrated in Figure 7.5 is particularly well-suited to online reference material or an online help manual.

BLENDED STRUCTURE

The blended structure combines linear and hierarchical flow to provide the most flexible of all structures in terms of user navigation. It is, however, the most difficult to design and maintain. Figure 7.6 shows how the hierarchical structure portrayed in Figure 7.5 incorporates linear flow

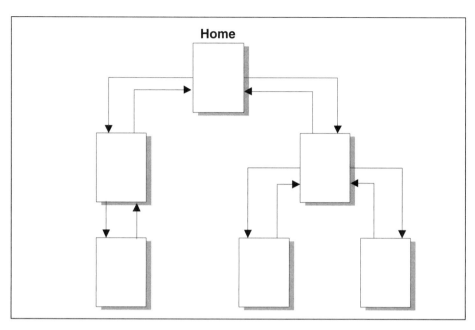

Figure 7.5   A Web publication organized in a hierarchical structure.

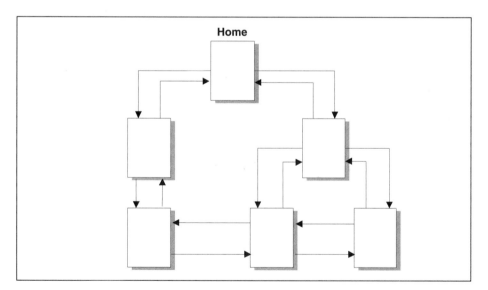

Figure 7.6   Blending the linear and hierarchical structure to achieve the greatest flexibility.

by using lateral links between pages. *The Encyclopedia Britannica* on the World Wide Web uses this type of structure, and contains more than 750,000 links—which gives you an idea of how complex these structures can become. If you're planning a large, complex publication using the blended structure approach, you should seriously consider implementing a search tool to help the reader locate and access specific content within the publication.

A policy or procedures manual would be a good place to implement the blended structure. Then, the reader has the benefit of working down through the hierarchy to access greater levels of detail, as well as the ability to access cross-referenced material through the lateral links provided.

 Regardless of the structure you use, identify key branch points in the publication and provide the means for the user to return to these points without having to work back one screen at a time. The reader should always be able to return to the home page from any point in the structure with one key press or mouse click.

The Pages

Your page design is going to be influenced by the content, the readers, and the nuances of this medium (which we've already discussed). The same principles of layout and design that apply in the print-based medium relate to Web pages as well, keeping in mind the viewing area limitations that exist. Your writers and designers need to be aware of and assess content, content organization, and page layout.

CONTENT

- Write for clarity, using simple sentence structure whenever possible.

- Write for the audience, using terminology and expressions they already know.

- Use a presentation style that the reader is familiar with. For example, a page containing financial information being delivered to an accounting department should use tables where appropriate.

- Use graphics judiciously where they can clarify meaning or add emphasis—otherwise, they can detract from content.

- When using images, use the *ALT* attribute of the image tag to provide descriptive text—this accommodates users who turn off their image display (usually because of a slow modem connection).

- Provide publication information somewhere on the home page (including the last revision date), and information on how to reach the author or another contact (contact information should include telephone number, as well as email address).

CONTENT ORGANIZATION

- Organize material logically, so that it scans well and is easy to follow.

- Try to avoid splitting topics across pages (each page should be as self-contained as possible).

- Use a list to provide a preview of subsequent material.

- Try to group related information visually.

PAGE LAYOUT

- Use headings to provide visual structure to the page.

- Don't overuse emphasis by employing too much italics, boldfacing, and uppercase text.

- Use white space to break up the text so that it is easier to read.

- Use a simple, but above all, consistent layout for the publication.

- Provide on-screen navigation links in addition to those provided by the browser, so users can return to previous sections or jump to the top of the page or publication.

- Where appropriate, provide the capability for readers to give online feedback.

There is a wealth of material about good hypertext page design and layout available on the World Wide Web. An excellent starting point for HTML programming in general is *A Beginner's Guide to HTML*, available from the National Center for Supercomputing Applications, and located at the following URL: **http://www.ncsa.uiuc.edu/General/Internet/ WWW/HTMLPrimer.html**.

HTML in a Nutshell

HTML, like a programming language or a natural language, uses certain conventions and has its own syntactical rules. It is fundamentally a text-processing language that takes the unformatted text in a source file and puts it into a simple format. At a minimum, with no format commands used, text in an HTML file is left-justified when viewed on the browser screen, extra spaces between words are eliminated (all words are separated by one space), and words spread over several lines in the original document are concatenated to form sentences. Figure 7.7 shows a text file without any tags, and then how it appears on the browser screen after formatting.

Tags

Each tag, or instruction, is enclosed in left (<) and right (>) angle brackets, and may be typed in mixed, lower- or uppercase. Most, but not all, of the tags are used in pairs, the first tag indicating the beginning of format control, and the second tag denoting the end of special formatting. For

Raw text in source file	Formatted text
At a minimum, with　　　　　no format commands used, this raw text is left-justified when viewed on the browser screen, any extra spaces are eliminated (all words are separated by one space), and words spread over several lines (you could have 　one word per line) are concatenated to form sentences. Figure 7.7 shows a raw text file with no tags, and how it appears on the browser screen after it is formatted.	At a minimum, with no format commands used, this raw text is left-justified when viewed on the browser screen, any extra spaces are eliminated (all words are separated by one space), and words spread over several lines (you could have one word per line) are concatenated to form sentences. Figure 7.7 shows a raw text file with no tags, and how it appears on the browser screen after it is formatted.

Figure 7.7　The browser renders basic text into formatted text.

example, the tag used to indicate centered text is the word **CENTER**. The start of the centered text would be marked by **<CENTER>**. The closing tag of the pair uses the same word, but **CENTER** is preceded by the forward slash (/), so that the end tag becomes **</CENTER>**.

HTML does not require any specific placement of tags, as long as the basic syntactical rules are followed:

- Angle brackets are used correctly

- Both tags in a paired set are present

- Nested structures are composed properly

- Usage restrictions are followed, since certain tags can only be used in designated portions of the defined document   .

The Current HTML Specification

The current published specification for HTML is Level 2.0, and is contained in RFC 1866, published in November 1995. The complete set of tags and their usage is provided in Appendix C.

But What About Tables, and Colors, and...?

There are numerous tags available to enrich your hypertext pages by providing capabilities such as varying font size, changing screen background color, arranging information in tables, and so on. These HTML extensions are not part of the HTML 2.0 specification but are supported by most of the popular browsers. Furthermore, the current draft HTML 3.2 specification includes most, if not all of these extensions.

The main push for, and development of, extensions came from Netscape Communications. It was apparent that their browser could provide much richer formatting than the current language specification provided, so their programming staff created new tags that the Netscape browser could interpret, format, and display in its viewing area. During the past year, other companies have begun supporting these extensions, and the Internet Engineering Task Force (IETF) is working at publishing a new HTML specification. Unfortunately, at the international level, the development, acceptance, and publishing of new standards is a time-consuming, lengthy process. This was evident during the work done on HTML 3.0, a specification which simply could not keep pace with developments in the computer industry. As a result, the HTML 3.0 working document has been closed, and the IETF has put forward a new draft specification (HTML 3.2), which hopefully can resolve the standards dilemma.

HTML Extensions

The main body of HTML extensions, provided by Netscape Communications, is divided into three sections that deal with: HTML Level 2.0, anticipated 3.0 specifications (now defunct), and proposed tags beyond Level 3.0 (which we denote as 3.0+). Detailed information about the Netscape HTML extensions is provided in the Appendix, and is also available from the Netscape Web site at: **http://home.netscape.com/assist/net_sites**.

Future HTML Specifications

As we indicated earlier, a working group of the IETF has been working on the HTML 3.2 specification, which they believe can incorporate many of the current extensions and meet the demand for future changes in the HyperText Markup Language. The first draft of the specification was released in April 1996, and is the result of collaborative work between the World Wide Web Consortium (W3C) and the vendor community (IBM, Microsoft, Netscape Communications, Novell, SoftQuad, Spyglass, and Sun Microsystems). A summary of the this new specification is available at **http://www.w3.org/pub/WWW/MarkUp/Wilbur/features.html**.

A significant feature of HTML 3.2 will be the use of style sheets (which have been a component of PC word processing software for several years now) to address the underlying weakness of HTML. This weakness lies in the fact that HTML is geared toward producing transportable, machine-readable text, as opposed to text styled for the convenience of readers. To date, the solution has been found in the collection of extensions provided by Netscape Communications and, more recently, by Microsoft, which supports style sheets. Style sheets provide a simple, workable alternative for handling features such as frames, shown in Figure 7.8. However, the consequence of proprietary extensions is that not all browsers support them.

Page creators will be able to use the basic HTML specification to deal with structure and content, and then employ style sheets to handle form and appearance. Since a style sheet is separate from the HTML code and content, it can be applied to many other hypertext documents, making it easier for authors to provide consistency throughout a Web site. The style sheet contains the basic style that is used throughout the site, and that can be embellished with HTML.

Style sheets are prepared with their own markup language, then associated with a given HTML file. When this file is displayed on the screen, its contents are formatted in accordance with the style sheet in use. There are currently two specifications for a style sheet language: the Document Style Semantics and Specification Language (DSSSL), and Cascading Style Sheets (CSS). DSSSL, although an ISO specification, has not been implemented

Figure 7.8 A Web page using frames to create three windows—one fixed, and two scrollable.

anywhere, while CSS has received support from Microsoft, Spyglass, and Netscape Communications. The working draft for style sheets was released by W3C in June 1996, and the HTML 3.2 draft includes a command for the use of style sheets (**<STYLE>**). More information on style sheets is available from W3C at: **http://www.w3.org/pub/WWW/Style**.

Publication Enhancement

Up to this point, we've been viewing the publication's pages primarily as static entities that will be displayed to a reader at his request. Hypertext, however, offers an opportunity to produce dynamic pages that can enhance the reader's information gathering and processing experiences. The main ways to achieve this are through the use of dynamic data updates on the page, reader interaction with the pages, and hypermedia—graphics, sound, and video.

Dynamic Information Updates

For some publications, such as policy manuals, information will naturally be relatively static, with content changing only at fixed times throughout the year, or as often as is required to reflect policy changes within the organization. Other publications, such as product catalogues and company performance reports (sales, production, and so on), which are not static by nature, can be more useful if updated dynamically. As we've seen, page contents can be updated from active databases through the use of CGI programs. In addition, Netscape supports extensions that allow dynamic updates from the client side (client pull), and from the server side (server push). On the client side, it is possible to have a screen refreshed continuously, while on the server side, screens can be updated whenever new information is available.

In making the decision to provide dynamic page updates, you should consider the following:

- The business requirement for dynamic updates—are they solving a problem, or enhancing information by providing more current data

- The specialized programming skills that will be needed

- Performance issues—the network, the server, and the DBMS/database

- The degree and complexity of ongoing maintenance

Interactive Pages

Interactive pages, through the use of conventional hypertext links, online forms, or hypertext-based applications, can also completely change the character of a publication or information system. The level of user interaction varies a great deal, from a simple office sign-out system, to a more complex system, such as a training manual. The degree of interaction is determined by the individual application, and the same concerns mentioned in the section on dynamic page updates apply to interactive pages. Figure 7.9 illustrates a simple form used to gather customer information at a Web site.

Hypermedia: Graphics, Sound, and Video

The term *hypermedia* describes the World Wide Web version of multimedia, and refers to the inclusion of static graphics images, audio files, and video files in a hypertext publication. Assuming the user's browser has the

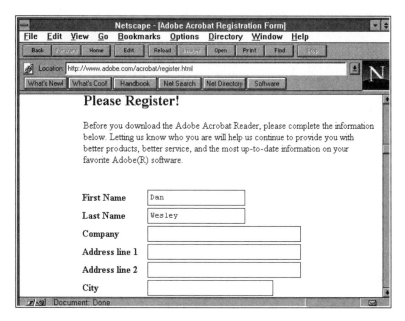

Figure 7.9   An online form used to collect customer information.

appropriate helper applications or plug-ins, the user can see and hear the objects that are included on the pages. The use of audio and video is still leading-edge technology, and packet-switching and bandwidth are major issues when dealing with these two data types. Even in a self-contained intranet that has the advantage of high data throughput on the LAN (relative to dialup connections), audio and video files are very large, and their impact on performance is a major consideration.

For the most part, corporate intranets use static images on their hypertext pages, either to accompany textual information, or to provide links to other information. These images or pictures (called artwork, in the traditional publishing world) can be photographs, screen snapshots, or line drawings. Artwork is really any representation of information stored in a graphics file data format.

The appearance of products like Shockwave, developed by Macromedia, an established firm in the multimedia software business, is extending the envelope of hypermedia. Shockwave consists of Shockwave plug-ins and Afterburner applications for the major browsers, which enable HTML page creators to deliver multimedia productions on a hypertext page. The Web site construction and management tools allow authors to customize and change the multimedia content, based on context and events. Content possibilities include animation, graphics, sound, and user interaction. Performance is enhanced by the Afterburner component, which optimizes and compresses material created with the Macromedia product set.

Pictures as Complementary Information

As in the case of paper documents, a picture can enhance or clarify information by providing a visual summary or extension of the text content. However, pictures should always serve a specific purpose, even if it's only to draw the reader's attention to a portion of the page. Appropriate image use is highly subjective, and should be dictated by the nature of the publication, its objectives, and its audience. A product catalogue, for example, would be expected to contain pictures of the products, whereas a year-end financial statement would likely only contain performance graphs as images. The following guidelines will help you use graphics in your pages.

Colors—To create and manipulate artwork, graphics software uses multiple colors drawn from a palette that includes pure black and white, shades of gray, and from 8 to 16 million hues. (Keep in mind that images are stored as areas of color, not colored spaces defined by lines.) Image type (a line drawing versus a photograph, for example) provides a guideline for determining the appropriate number of colors to use. Restricting variety is necessary for two reasons: final file size (again, because of bandwidth and performance), and the ability of the individual user's graphics card, and monitor, to display a large number of unique colors. Where possible, use 8 or 16 colors, but if more are essential, go to 256. The Bandwidth Conservation Society provides some good advice on graphics and color handling at its Web site **http://www.infohiway.com/ faster/original/crli2.html**.

Size—In situations where a picture fills the screen, or is larger than can be displayed without scrolling, consider using a smaller graphic called a thumbnail, with a link to the full-sized picture. This allows the reader to see both the text and the thumbnail; if he then wishes to see the enlarged picture, he can activate the link.

Quality—Images produced by scanning or digitizing a photograph are often of poor quality. Depending on the quality of the original, software can be used, within limits, to enhance these images. However, if an image can't be fixed, don't use it; using no picture is better than using a poor one.

Layout—If your pages are graphics-intensive and content is tightly tied to the pictures, contract the services of someone who is experienced in layout and graphics design. Quality is as important as content.

PICTURES AS LINKS

It is possible to use pictures as links to other parts of your publication. The simplest method is to include the image in the tag for a link. For example, you could create an icon of an upward-pointing arrow to indicate a link to the top of the current page. When the user clicks on this picture, she moves to the beginning of the page. Aids such as this make it easier (and faster) for a reader to move around in a document. The key, once again, is consistency—in the pictures used, and in the results of their activation.

A second, albeit slightly more complex, use of pictures for linking is the inclusion of image maps. An image can be divided into areas called *hot spots*, each of which is linked to a specific object. The user can position the cursor on a hot spot and, by clicking the mouse button, activate the link to the corresponding object. Figure 7.10 uses an image map to define hot spots. On the AltaVista logo picture these areas are: Advanced Search, Simple Search, Surprise, and Help. Clicking on any of the hot spots will retrieve a new page and display it on the screen.

Not all browsers and PCs are created equal; therefore, it's important that you test your graphics display on the type of equipment and browser your readers will be using. Since there is likely to be a wide range of PC types within your organization, test on the least robust equipment—use the Internet's lowest common denominator approach. It works!

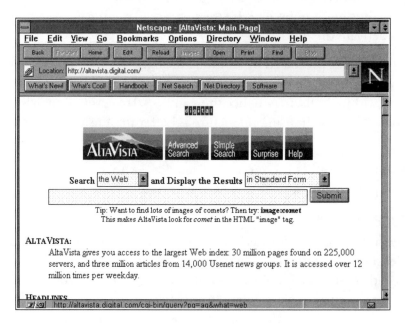

Figure 7.10   An example of an image map.

Since each of the major browsers handles the display of graphics differently, it's a good idea to set a browser standard for your organization. This will facilitate easier page design by programming for only one browser, and will provide more consistent content presentation for your readers.

VRML: The Shape of Things to Come

The Virtual Reality Modeling Language (VRML) is a specification for creating interactive, 3D simulation. Once the simulation is created, the user can navigate or manipulate a VRML image with a specialized browser. The latest specification is called Moving Worlds (VRML 2.0), and was put forward by Silicon Graphics and Netscape Communications with the intention of providing open, platform-independent 3D graphics. This specification uses Java (discussed in the next section) for creating motion and interaction, and allows third-party plug-ins to be used without modifications.

Enabling Technologies

While CGI programs are useful tools for providing links between Web pages and a variety of data sources, they are not really suitable for developing complex hypertext applications. One reason for this is their inability to easily maintain the environment variables' values as the user moves from page to page ("maintaining state"). Another reason is the relative inefficiency of CGI program performance—the programs are interpretive, rather than compiled, and are executed on the server. These problems are being resolved by the appearance of tools to develop *component* software that runs on the Web client.

Component Software

Sun Microsystems' Java programming language, which appeared in 1995, has already had a dramatic impact on hypertext applications through its use of software modules that can be loaded into the browser and executed, as opposed to scripts that are referenced and run outside the browser. David Chappell, a principal of Chappell and Associates (a Minneapolis consulting and training firm), and the author of a 1996 article called "Java

Applets vs. ActiveX Controls," for Network World Inc., describes this approach to Web applications by referring to components and containers. He says: "The fundamental notion is to create an application by plugging software components into some kind of container. The components may be specifically written for an application or, better yet, reused from some other project or purchased off the shelf." On the subject of containers, he says: "A Web browser, such as Netscape Communications Corp.'s Navigator or Microsoft's Internet Explorer, can also play the role of a container. And components can be loaded not just from the local disk or file server, but also from a Web server located on a corporate intranet or the Internet."

Java

Java is a programming language developed by Sun Microsystems to provide an alternative to C++, making it easier to write bug-free code and execute programs across a network. It has already become the de facto standard for programming Web applications. Most of the major vendors have announced support for it, including Oracle, and Microsoft (although Microsoft has proceeded with the development and implementation of its own functional equivalent, called ActiveX). Designed to be cross-platform, and to provide the extensive security features required in networked applications, Java is a tool you can use to increase the functionality of your intranet Web site by:

- Creating content handlers that can display the contents of a file without launching an external program

- Off-loading processing to the client CPU

- Enabling greater user interaction through the ability to capture information, such as keystrokes and mouse clicks

- Creating *applets*

Java Applets

On the World Wide Web, Java is best known for its ability to create the small applications called applets that are sent to the client's browser and executed there, rather than on the server. (Using David Chappell's convention, an applet is the software component that is run in a container.) The development of this technology has revolutionized Web page content by providing the ability to include such applications as: animation; real-time, active information screen updates, such as a stock ticker; real-time, dynamically updated graphing; and real-time transaction systems—for example, order entry.

Because applets are machine-independent, they can be electronically distributed throughout an organization and used on any available computer platform that can run Netscape or Microsoft Internet Explorer. Another advantage of these modules is that they can be used in different circumstances; for example, a graphing applet can be applied to different data sets on different screens. Applets are somewhat limited, in that they can only be programmed using Java.

ActiveX Controls

Microsoft's ActiveX controls are a repackaged version of Object Linking and Embedding (OLE) *and* OLE Control Extensions (OCX). Unlike Java applets, they can be written in any language (but are not platform-independent; they are targeted at systems running the Win32 interface). ActiveX components can run in many different containers (Visual Basic, for example) and, as a result, a large collection of these modules already exist, waiting to be plugged into Web applications. The other advantage (temporarily, at least) that ActiveX components provide is execution speed. As compiled binaries, they run faster than the Java applets, which must be interpreted when run on the client.

Once you've gotten past the planning and design aspects of Web pages, the world of hypertext is opened up to you. This medium can significantly enrich the information currently in use within your organization, as well as provide countless opportunities for increasing the effectiveness of corporate information-sharing.

Before proceeding further with an examination of an intranet's components, and the tools needed for intranet construction, we'll deal with computer security, which is the subject of the following chapter.

Protecting an Intranet

CHAPTER
8

Protecting an Intranet

Computer security is concerned with loss of, or damage to, both the hardware and software components of the computing environment. Protection of physical assets, including computer equipment, is standard operating procedure in all organizations, but is not within the scope of our subject. The focus of this chapter will be the safeguarding of data and applications. We'll examine the impact and cost of security intrusions, what can be damaged or stolen, how your systems and data can be compromised, and how this can be prevented. Most of the topics covered apply to networked systems in general, while others are specific to Internet- and Web-based technologies. We will highlight the Windows NT Network Operating System tools.

"We don't have to worry about security, our Web site isn't connected to the Internet," said an anonymous business owner. This common point of view is irresponsible at best and, at worst, it can be dangerous. The fact that a corporate intranet isn't connected to the Internet doesn't negate the necessity for good security practices. The reach of this internal information system, and the number of data sources it draws on to provide information, makes an intranet susceptible to any and all of the intrusions possible on an external network.

Unfortunately, activities related to computer security tend to fall to the bottom of the priority list in many organizations, which perceive security as a nuisance, rather than as a real value. As a result, the effort and resources dedicated to this activity are minimal, and don't get a high profile until something happens—either to the system itself, or to the organization's data. Security is given short shrift because it's complicated, expensive, time-consuming, and offers no visible payback in the normal course of business. In addition, security is inherently a centralized function, and broadly-distributed networks do not lend themselves to this kind of control. Yet, as distributed, networked business computing increases, the potential for damage to these computing assets increases as well.

In today's computing environment, security is not an option—it's essential for survival. It should be transparent to the user, and has to meet the following objectives:

- **Confidentiality**—The data being transmitted must be accessible only to the people who should have access to it.

- **Integrity**—The data cannot be corrupted or tampered with, since this invalidates the entire information architecture the organization uses to conduct business.

- **Availability**—Computing resources and data must be available to groups and individuals within the organization in a timely fashion, in order to allow them to carry out their tasks.

- **Validity**—Access to databases or computing resources must be given only to legitimate users in the organization.

What's at Risk

Damaged systems, corrupted data, or stolen information can cripple a company and, in extreme cases, put an organization out of business. Some consequences of failing to put adequate security measures in place are:

- **Financial Loss**—The recovery of corrupt data or the restoration of damaged systems can take days or weeks, resulting in monetary losses through disruption of business, plus the direct cost of recovery (data has to be reconstructed and system integrity has to be restored).

- **Loss of Confidence**—The users of the system, as well as the organization's customers, can lose confidence in the integrity of your system. In the case of customers, this can quickly translate to lost business.

- **Legal Implications**—In some situations, legal action might result. If your firm has a custodial role in data storage, processing, or transmission, you are liable for anything that happens to that data. Litigation may follow from an inability to fulfill contractual arrangements, when a product or service cannot be delivered as a consequence of security failure.

- **Loss of Life**—This may sound like exaggeration, but organizations involved in the health-care field depend on accurate and timely information for various aspects of patient/consumer care. The effect of corrupted or delayed information could even be loss of life.

The Cost of Security Failure

The National Computer Security Association (NCSA) estimated that in 1994, the projected cost of lost time and file reconstruction in the United States was close to $3 billion. This figure relates only to damages from computer viruses; it does not include the activities of hackers or other personal intrusions into computer systems.

Another 1990s survey, conducted by Price Waterhouse in the United Kingdom, estimated that if a highly-computerized business is offline for three days, it stands a 60-percent chance of going out of business. If its computer systems are out of operation for an entire month, the possibility of business failure increases to 90 percent.

Sources and Types of Security Threats

Damage to a system can come from either inside or outside the organization, and it can be unintentional or deliberate, as shown in Figure 8.1.

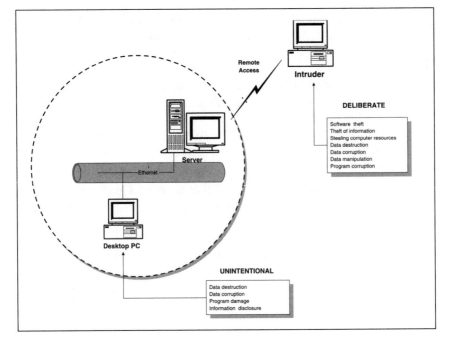

Figure 8.1 Sources and types of security threats to the computer system.

Unintentional Damage

Although they might be unintentional, there are certain activities that can result in the destruction or corruption of data, operational interruption, and inadvertent disclosure of sensitive information. This is usually the result of inexperienced or inadequately trained staff working with applications that don't have properly-installed safeguards.

A simple example that illustrates unintentional damage is the overwriting of a file on a Web server through the use of an online form. RFC 1867 allows a form to upload one or more files in addition to the form's data. When this ability is enabled in a form, the user can upload files to the server. This can be quite a useful feature, but with one major flaw: If the site administrator has set up the CGI processor to accept absolute path statements for file uploads, the file being uploaded can overwrite existing files on the server. Every activity involving the transfer of data to the server has the potential to cause this type of damage, so it's imperative that the site administrator ensures that only a carefully selected group of people have this type of access, and that those people are knowledgeable.

In a similar fashion, data can be destroyed through accidental deletion. If file and directory permissions aren't properly set in critical areas, entire portions of a hard drive can be deleted, and will need to be restored. These unplanned purges seem to result from employees' poor understanding of the consequences of the operating system commands available. System maintenance staff can prevent this type of damage by ensuring that if users do have access to commands such as Format, the appropriate protections are in place to prevent the deletion of critical directories and files.

The situations described in both the previous examples create an operational interruption. The first stage of the interruption is characterized by data or applications becoming unavailable to other users; the second occurs when data is restored, or an unstable application is repaired and tested. With luck, the length of time between damage and recovery is short. However, when data has become corrupted, but the system is still functioning, it may take several days or longer before the problem is even discovered. In this case, other systems and users will be using unreliable data, a situation which will have severe consequences for mission-critical systems.

Users can also compromise an information system by accidentally disclosing sensitive or critical information through remarks made in the presence of visitors or outside contractors. This type of security breach, unlike those already discussed, can't be prevented by system safeguards; personnel must be made aware of what information is confidential, and of the consequences of information leaks.

Deliberate Damage

Deliberate attacks on a system can be either active or passive. In the first case, data on the network is altered or destroyed, and evidence of the intrusion is visible. Passive attacks, on the other hand, are harder to detect, because data is not altered; the attacker's intent is simply to gather information by eavesdropping. Regardless of the nature of the incursion, the net effect is the same: your computing assets have been stolen or misused, destroyed or damaged.

Types of Attacks

An individual who breaks into a computer system does so with the intent of stealing information or programs, stealing computing resources, or disrupting the business. The computer system attacker, like the legitimate user, has an array of techniques and technology at his disposal; unfortunately, he uses them for illegal, destructive purposes.

Hackers, Crackers, Vandals, and Pirates

In the computer community, the term *hacker* describes a programmer who achieves the seemingly impossible—such as rewriting a program that formerly took 20,000 lines of code, but this time using only 10,000 lines of code and providing more functionality—with few tools other than ingenuity and programming talent. Hackers who use their talents to break into computer systems are called *password hackers, network hackers,* or *crackers.* A cracker who breaks into a system and alters programs or data is referred to as a *vandal,* while those who steal programs or information are *pirates.* Not all crackers, however, are bad—some are employed by companies to test computer security procedures and identify weak areas.

Unauthorized Access to the System

An attacker can gain access to your system in several ways, but the most common method is stealing the password that authenticates a legitimate user, then using that person's User ID to enter the system. Once he's in, the cracker has all the account privileges and access rights associated with the ID he's using. Some of the techniques employed for obtaining passwords are: using software to generate and try different combinations of letters and numerals; attaching a device called a sniffer to an incoming modem line, to capture passwords as they are used; or *piggybacking* on a legitimate connection. In the last case, the attacker waits until the connection is established, then bumps the user off the line and takes over the session. Two other techniques for gaining entry are the *trap door* and *back door.* A trap door is created during the development of a system; it lets the programmer enter the system to carry out service or maintenance tasks without being hindered by security controls. The back door allows the same kind of access, but is created unintentionally.

The magnitude of unauthorized access is illustrated by the "1996 Computer Crime and Security Survey," conducted by the Computer Security Institute (CSI). The survey results indicate that 42 percent of the respondents (drawn from U.S. corporations, government agencies, universities, and financial institutions) had experienced some form of intrusion or unauthorized use of their computer systems in the last 12 months. (You can obtain copies of this, and other recent surveys, by calling CSI at (415) 905-2626, sending email requests to prapalus@mfi.com, or accessing CSI's Web site at **http://www.gocsi.com**.)

Computer Viruses and Other Malicious Programs

In spite of public awareness, and readily available virus detection and removal software, the virus problem in North America continues to grow. This is born out by the National Computer Security Association (NCSA) 1996 Virus Prevalence Survey, whose findings show that:

- 98 percent of North American corporations and other large organizations have first hand experience with virus infections.

- As of early 1996, 90 percent of organizations with more than 500 PCs have a virus incident each month.

- The chance of having a virus incident is about 1 chance per 100 PCs per month.

VIRUSES

A computer virus is a program that has been written solely for the purpose of causing damage to a computer system by infecting other software. Viruses are designed to attach themselves to a legitimate program, and to remain inactive until that program is run. Once activated, they can alter data, cause programs to perform incorrectly, or make data inaccessible; they may also replicate or modify themselves. While there are more than 500 core viruses (and upward of 3,000 variations), they are classified under four main categories: file infectors, system infectors, cluster infectors, and multipartite viruses.

- **File Infectors**—These viruses attach themselves to either executable (EXE) files, or other files that contain executable code. (A good example of the latter is the virus being transmitted through MS Word macros—not supplied by Microsoft—as this book is being written; it is triggered only when the macro is executed.) There are several different types of file infector viruses, each of which behaves differently and has a different approach to spreading the infection:

    - **Companion**—Creates a new infected program that resembles the legitimate program.

    - **Direct Action**—Chooses one or more different programs to infect each time the host program is run.

    - **Resident**—Is placed in computer memory the first time the host program is executed, then infects all other programs as they are run. Some will affect a program that is opened, but not run; these are called *fast infectors.*

    - **Slow Infector**—Infects files as they are created or altered.

    - **Sparse Infector**—Infects files in an apparently random fashion. However, the timing is based on some criteria set by the virus' author.

- **System Infectors**—This type is also known as a *boot record infector,* since it invades the executable code in the system region of the hard drive.

- **Cluster Infectors**—Also called file system viruses, these programs corrupt directory table entries; this results in the virus being loaded before the legitimate program the user selects is loaded.

- **Multipartite Viruses**—These viruses are usually called *boot-and-file viruses,* since they attack both file and boot records.

Figure 8.2 shows the main ways that computer viruses are brought into an organization, as indicated by the results of the NCSA Virus Prevalence Survey.

Malicious Programs

Unlike viruses, this software is designed to infect computer memory, tying up processing cycles so that other programs are unable to use the system, or causing programs to malfunction. The best example of this type of at-

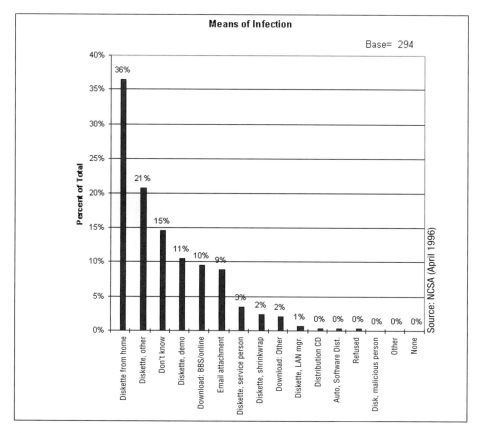

Figure 8.2 Different means of virus propagation in an organization.

tack is called a *worm*; the most famous is the Internet Worm, released on the Internet in 1988, and infecting an estimated 10,000 computers. This worm caused CPU resources to be used up, thereby degrading system performance noticeably.

There are also *time* and *logic* bombs—methods used to defer the triggering of a virus or another malicious program. By delaying activation until a certain date, or until specified conditions are met, they make finding unwanted programs on the computer system more difficult for technical staff. It's interesting to note that some software vendors use time and logic bombs to ensure that their customers cannot break license agreements or duplicate software programs. Another method used is the *Trojan Horse*, which, as the name implies, is a technique for sneaking unwanted programs into a computer system. This program, undetectable by virus-detection software, contains a virus, worm, or trap door, and is hidden in an innocuous routine.

Areas of Vulnerability

As illustrated in Figure 8.3, any part of the computer network is susceptible to various forms of attack. However, some areas are particularly vulnerable, including the individual PC, the Web server, and the physical network itself.

The PC

The microcomputer is threatened primarily by unauthorized access, destruction or alteration of data (either through intervention or electroni-

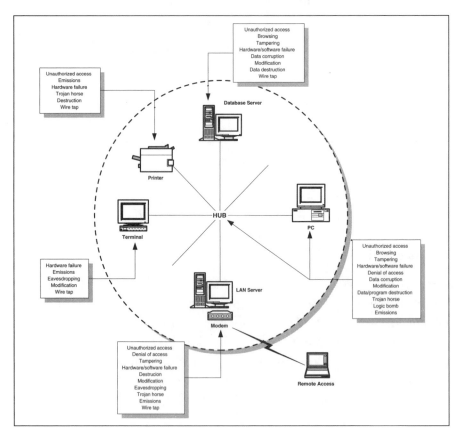

Figure 8.3 Network component exposures to different types of attack.

cally, using software programs), and browsing with the intent to steal information or programs. The level of exposure to these dangers is higher in two specific situations: during equipment reallocation and disposal, and through the use of portable (notebook) computers.

EQUIPMENT REALLOCATION AND DISPOSAL

It is normal, within any organization, to move equipment around in response to computing needs, or to make better use of machines through redeployment. This, in itself, is good management of resources; poor management, on the other hand, is reflected in a lack of predetermined procedures to regulate these activities.

For example, assume that a high-performance machine (such as a Pentium Pro) is needed to speed up program testing being done by a contractor on a specific development project. A Pentium Pro is underutilized in the Finance group, and can be freed up for use elsewhere. Technical Support is contacted, and instructions are given to move and set up the PC in the contractor's work area. In this situation, it isn't unusual to find that the new user of this equipment has full access to the company's financial data, which was stored on the hard drive. In all likelihood, no one would have bothered to remove the data, let alone use a cleaning program to ensure that it could not be reconstructed by a skilled PC user.

With very little effort, procedures and appropriate tools can be put in place to prevent this type of exposure. Data removal is particularly important when equipment is declared surplus and sent out for disposal. It isn't uncommon to read about such equipment appearing on the street with sensitive data on the hard drive—often including information related to financial or legal matters. Although it's difficult to assign a dollar value to this type of disclosure, the embarrassment to a company, or possible personal damage, can be significant.

NOTEBOOK COMPUTERS

Notebook computers are a valuable tool for organizations that need to provide computing capability for an increasingly mobile workforce. With a notebook and a modem, employees are able to access the corporate network at any time of the day or night, 7 days a week, 365 days a year.

Assuming the availability of a phone line, staff can retrieve and deposit information, as well as perform computing tasks required for their job. The downside of mobile computing is an increased level of security risk. Because they are highly portable, notebooks are easy to steal, resulting in an immediate financial loss from stolen equipment and software, the loss of data, and the consequences of having information fall into the wrong hands.

Also, mobile workers are more likely than employees in a conventional work environment to come into contact with diskettes infected with computer virus programs. Virus detection procedures tend to be more rigorously followed (or at least, enforced with more vigor) in the office than on the road. Part of any virus eradication strategy is isolating the source to ensure that the virus has, in fact, been completely removed from the entire computer system. In the case of notebooks, determining the source is usually difficult, and frequently impossible.

Finally, a notebook used for dialup access to the network will contain communications software that provides dialing directories and login scripts (predefined prompts and replies used for logging on to a system) to connect to a specified computer. Users should enter the telephone number and go through the login process manually; instead, they often automate the procedure to save time. Worse yet, all too many of these mobile users store their passwords in the automated login script. If the notebook is stolen, the thief has everything required to connect to the host computer and gain access to the system.

The Web Server

Any server on your intranet is a good target, but those directly supporting remote access by modem connection provide the most obvious entry point for illegal access to the network. While the loss of a PC, or a peripheral such as a printer, causes some disruption, the loss of a server causes a severe interruption in, and loss of, computing services, either for a short period of time (a few hours), or an extended one (several days). In addition to the length of downtime, you must also consider the role of the server on your intranet. If, for example, there is only one server for the network, the disruption will be more widespread, affecting every user on the system. Such a possibility lends a great deal of support to the argument for having multiple Web servers supporting your intranet. Unlike networked PCs, which are limited in their ability to distribute software on the LAN, a server is a prime target for a virus or rogue software attack, because it provides a single point of distribution for these programs to infect all the computers on the local network. If the contaminated server happens to be connected with others, it can spread the virus to the other networks as well.

The Physical Network

The physical network—the cabling—is a good target for passive attacks on your organization. Since most cabling is tucked out of sight for aesthetic reasons, it provides an ideal location for undetected wiretaps. Another technique for attacking the network is for intruders to add more nodes, thereby allowing them to analyze traffic at their leisure.

Security Standards

There are numerous national and international bodies contributing to the development of standards related to computer security. These standards fall into five functional categories:

1. Encryption

2. Authentication

3. Emissions Control (electromagnetic emissions)

4. Policy and Procedure

5. Trusted Systems (design of systems according to formally-specified security levels)

Table 8.1 summarizes the security standards-setting bodies, and the security functions that each deals with. These standards form the basis for security measures and tools.

Table 8.1   International and National Standards Setters

Acronym	Name	Standards
NIST	National Institute of Standards and Technology	Encryption, Authentication, Policy and Procedure
FTSC	Federal Telecommunications Standards Committee	Encryption, Policy and Procedure
ANSI	American National Standards Institute	Encryption and Authentication
NSA	National Security Agency	Encryption, Authentication, Emissions, Policy and Procedure, and Trusted Systems
IEEE	Institute of Electrical and Electronic Engineers	Encryption and Authentication
ISO	International Standards Organization	Encryption, Authentication, and Trusted Systems
IAB	Internet Architecture Board	Encryption and Authentication
IBM	International Business Machines	Encryption
RSA	Rivest-Shamir-Adelman	Authentication
CSSPAB	Computers Systems Security and Privacy Advisory Board	Policy and Procedure

Note: This table does not include President Clinton's administration, which is not a standards body, but is putting forward standards in the areas of Encryption and Authentication (such as Clipper and Capstone, which we will discuss later), and Policy and Procedure.

Security Measures and Tools

As computer systems have become more complex, and the methods of compromising them more sophisticated, the tool set for protecting a company's computing assets has changed as well.

Virus Detection and Removal

Anti-virus software is designed to detect and remove viruses on storage media, including diskettes and hard drives, using a variety of techniques such as monitoring activity for unusual program behavior, checking files for contamination (integrity checking), and looking for virus signatures (a unique sequence of bits that can identify certain viruses). The better anti-virus software packages do all three types of scanning, because some viruses can hide or change their signatures, legitimate programs can set off false alarms during activity monitoring, and integrity checking won't find memory-resident viruses. Select a product that is updated regularly, and make sure it's kept current—new viruses are appearing daily. Virus scanning software should be used on workstations, on the server, during boot-up, and while the system is running.

Do not depend on a single product to handle all your virus detection needs. Experience has shown that even the best programs can miss a particular virus; installing two programs increases the odds of successfully dealing with all attacks on your system.

Since your intranet users will be using a browser, the recently-released WebScan from McAfee is worth investigating and testing. It works with the browser (support is provided for Mosaic, Netscape, and Microsoft Internet Explorer), and examines all incoming files, including archived and compressed files, before they are stored on the hard drive. If a virus is detected, it notifies you and gives you two options: save the file for later cleaning, or delete it immediately. WebScan will also examine email attachments, and can be configured to send a notification to your system mail administrator if an infected mail message is received.

Workstation Access Control

Within an organization, access to workstations and applications can be controlled using both hardware and software techniques. One approach requires that a token, such as a magnetic card, be swiped through a scanner before permitting a user access to the workstation. When work has been completed and the user has logged off, the workstation automatically disables itself. Software approaches consist of limiting access to files, applications, hardware, and peripherals, as well as using other authentication techniques in addition to passwords. Windows NT, for example, uses a security subsystem to set user permissions for local and global groups within a domain, and permits multiple domains with levels of trust between them, such as shared resources and access privileges.

An approach that works very well in distributed systems is a software program called Kerberos, which was designed to accommodate two realities: users require access to different applications, and they move from PC to PC. The Kerberos system has every user log in to a security server first. Only after their user and access privileges are authenticated are they allowed to complete the login process. In addition to providing this security function, Kerberos uses encrypted transmissions to prevent analysis of information by unauthorized people.

Remote Access Control

One of the prime targets on your system will be dialup access. However, by using a selection of hardware, software, and good practices, it is possible to drastically reduce the risk of intrusion at this entry point.

CALLBACK

The callback technique does not allow a remote user to have access to the system on the first call. Instead, after the connection is made, the host computer breaks the contact and calls back to the modem that placed the call. Some approaches require the user to submit a special code that identifies his telephone number; the weakness of this particular method is that the number, like a password, can be captured and used by a cracker. A much safer callback system is one where the host places the call to a predefined telephone number stored in a database.

PORT PROTECTION DEVICES

A more secure alternative to a callback system is a Port Protection Device (PPD), which is installed on the host end of the communications link, as shown in Figure 8.4, and uses a Data Encryption Standard (DES) challenge-response system (DESes are discussed in more detail in the section on encryption). When a user initiates a call, she submits a password to software on her PC, which, in turn, sends it via modem to the PPD. The PPD validates the User ID and sends a DES-encrypted, one-time password challenge back to the user's PC. If the workstation software answers the challenge correctly, login is allowed to continue.

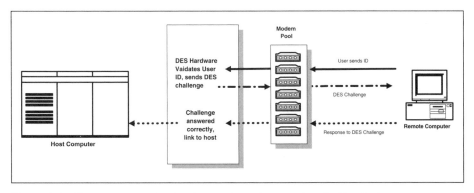

Figure 8.4 Remote access to a host computer using a port protection device.

Password Encryption

Any system that has a significant amount of dialup access should provide password encryption. Rather than transmitting a plain-text password for authentication (which can, of course, be easily captured and used by a cracker), the password should be encrypted before transmission, then decrypted by the host computer.

Dynamic Passwords

The dynamic (or random) password technique ensures that passwords are changed each time the system is used, and that there is no pattern to their creation. The host computer and dialup user employ a random password generator in synch with each other. In some cases, as an additional safeguard, the password is valid for only 60 seconds; even if it is captured, anyone trying to break into the system won't have time to make use of it. Some modems provide all three of the previously-described techniques. Windows NT, for example, supplies callback and password encryption as part of its Remote Access Server (RAS). In addition, RAS can support authentication devices/software and dynamic password generation.

Authentication

Passwords are used to identify an individual to a computer system; authentication is used to prove the individual's identity—first, when gaining access to a computer, and later, if necessary, to establish electronic communication.

ACCESS AUTHENTICATION

The National Security Agency/National Computer Security Center sets out three types of authentication:

- **Authentication by Knowledge**—An individual has private information, known only to himself, that can be used to confirm his identify, such as his family information or Personal Identification Number (PIN).

- **Authentication by Ownership**—A person can possess physical or electronic keys, identity badges, or magnetic strip cards.

- **Authentication by Characteristic**—Each user has unique distinguishing characteristics, such as fingerprints, retinal patterns, or DNA patterns.

A fairly common technique in a callback environment is the use of a PIN to confirm the identity of the person requesting access to the system.

COMMUNICATIONS AUTHENTICATION

In communications, the purpose of authentication is to protect both the sender and the recipient of messages or documents. (It should be noted that authentication-only techniques merely provide validation, and do not protect contents.) Authentication software is used to prove that the sender of a file is, in fact, the originator, and that the receiver is the intended recipient. It also confirms delivery, and proves that no one has tampered with the file.

The process involves the attachment of a digital signature to the end of the file. One of the most widely used methods is the RSA Public-Key Technique (patented by RSA Data Security, Inc.), which uses two private keys—the sender's and the recipient's—based on prime numbers. When the two numbers are multiplied by one another, the result is the public key, a number that can only readily be factored back by using the two original private keys, thereby authenticating the message. Figure 8.5 shows how this system works. To date, the largest public key that has been successfully factored back was a 129-digit number—this took approximately eight months, using 1,600 computers in 24 countries. (RSA recommends using a minimum of 150 digits!) An alternate approach, called the Digital Signature

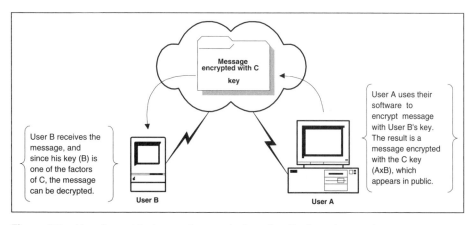

Figure 8.5   How the public-key system works to authenticate and encrypt messages.

Standard (DSS), was developed in 1994 by the National Security Agency and is approved by the United States government. The attractiveness of RSA over DSS is that, in addition to providing authentication, the RSA technique also has encryption capability.

Encryption

Encryption uses mathematical algorithms to make file contents indecipherable; only someone with valid access and the proper formulas can decrypt the file, returning it to its original form. As noted in the preceding section, the RSA public-key technique provides encryption as well as authentication. Another encryption standard is the Data Encryption Standard (DES) developed by IBM for the U.S. government, and published in 1977. DES uses a single-key approach, but since there are about 76 quadrillion keys available, the likelihood of an attacker finding the correct one is extremely small.

The anticipated replacement for DES is Skipjack, whose algorithm produces a key that takes three times longer to break than one generated by DES (based on today's technology). Furthermore, the Skipjack algorithm is embedded in silicon, a measure meant to ensure its confidentiality. The Clipper chip promoted by the Clinton administration uses Skipjack. An enhanced Clipper chipset called Capstone combines the ease of the public-key approach with data source and data integrity authentication. The current debate centered around the government-supported Clipper and Capstone initiatives stems from the fact that the Clinton administration proposes to hold everyone's private key in escrow. In addition to being opposed by civil liberties groups, Clipper and Capstone are opposed by the banking community because they don't meet any international or banking standards.

Other encryption standards and tools include:

- **Privacy Enhanced Mail (PEM)**—This standard for encryption on the Internet uses RSA and DES algorithms.

- **Pretty Good Privacy (PGP)**—PGP uses an approach similar to RSA, and offers authentication, data integrity checking, and encryption.

 If you intend to use encryption, and will be sending communications across international borders, find out if you might violate any national laws. Some countries have made it illegal to send encrypted data across their borders; in others, it is illegal to encrypt anything within the country.

Generally, normal data traffic on a network is not encrypted, because it affects system performance by slowing down transfer rates. However, encryption of data should be considered on your Web server if users are inputting or retrieving highly sensitive information, such as financial records. In these situations, access can be controlled by the use of passwords, which can be encrypted as well. For encryption on the Web server to work, both the Web server and the browser must be able to encrypt/decrypt the data being transferred. The major Web server software products and browsers, such as Netscape Navigator and Microsoft Internet Explorer, support one or both of two standards for secure transactions: the Secure Sockets Layer (SSL), and Secure-HTTP (S-HTTP). Both protocols are based on public-key cryptography for data encryption:

- **Secure Sockets Layer**—This protocol, which uses the RSA data security algorithm, was developed by Netscape Communications for their Commerce Server and the Netscape browser.

- **Secure-HTTP**—Developed by Enterprise Integration Technologies (EIT), this protocol has been incorporated in Secure NCSA HTTPD (Hypertext Transport Protocol Daemon) servers.

Newer server software (and updated server software) supports both of the above protocols, as do most browsers.

Good Computing Practices

The practices I've listed here should generally be followed in any computing environment. In the case of policies and procedures, currency should be maintained and reviews should be carried out on a regular basis to ensure that the procedures are adequate and relevant.

- **Physical Security**—Equipment that users do not require direct access to should be physically isolated; for example, other than technical staff, no one should have access to servers on the network.

- **Audit**—The NOS provides logs of events on the network; use these to monitor access activities in order to detect attempted intrusions, such as the number of unsuccessful login attempts for any given User ID.

- **Passwords**—Follow industry-recommended guidelines for passwords— make sure passwords are of good quality, are changed on a regular basis, and are not stored in plain-text files.

 Make certain users have unique passwords for each of the accounts they access. When dealing with multiple accounts, people are tempted to use the same password for all of them. This may make password administration easier, but it makes unauthorized access to several systems easier, as well.

- **Program Sharing**—Develop a policy that details the extent to which personal software tools can be used, and shared, on the organization's PCs.

- **Mobile Equipment**—Set out procedures and sanctions regarding the acceptable use of notebook computers, including encrypted data, hard-coded routines, and passwords in automated dialup software.

- **Virus Detection and Removal**—Set policies and procedures relating to anti-virus activities, such as frequency of testing and steps to take if a virus is detected.

- **Level of Employee Access**—Determine and monitor the levels of employee access to equipment and information, including server access and sensitive or critical information.

- **Monitoring**—When warranted, carry out monitoring of appropriate and required levels of employee activity; for example, repeated attempts to access certain information or areas, or unusual amounts of after-hours activity.

- **Acceptable Use Policy**—Establish a policy of acceptable use for communications, equipment, and behavior, such as communications content and personal use and treatment of company assets.

- **Termination**—Establish a termination policy regarding the computer environment, and set procedures to follow when an employee leaves the company, such as removal of system access privileges.

- **User Privileges**—Provide users with only the appropriate set of privileges for the work they are required to do; this might mean limiting access to files and directories, as well as to the NOS command set.

- **Backup Procedures**—Establish appropriate and timely backup procedures for the computing environment, including incremental and full backups, on an established schedule for the servers and workstations.

- **Recovery Testing**—Conduct test restorations from the backups to ensure that you can, in fact, restore your system if necessary.

- **Backup Security**—Make sure backups are stored off site, and that access to the backup media (tapes, diskettes) is restricted to authorized personnel only.

Windows NT Security Features

Windows NT Server provides a broad range of security mechanisms, ranging from file security to remote access. Table 8.2 provides a summary of the features that we will examine in more detail in this section.

Table 8.2   Windows NT Server Security Features

Feature	Function Provided
Domain security	Security for network access points
Security Descriptors, Identifiers, and Access Control Lists	File system security
Simple Network Management Protocol support	Authentication traps
Remote access permission	User validation
Remote access authentication	User authentication
Callback	Security for remote access
Security hosts	Layered network access
Auditing	Audit trail for network access
Disconnect	Response to intrusions by unauthorized users
Network access restrictions	Access control for remote clients
Encryption	Data transmission security

- **Domain Security**—As part of the Windows NT Domain (workgroup) schema, all Remote Access Servers (RAS) have identical copies of the user account database, ensuring that there are identical security restrictions for each site that has remote access to the network.

- **Security Descriptors (SD), Identifiers (SID), and Access Control Lists (ACL)**—These mechanisms are used for controlling file and directory access, as well as the level of permissions granted for any given file. They are also used to provide a system audit trail related to file usage—for example, a list of the users who have accessed specific files.

- **Simple Network Management Protocol (SNMP) support**—Windows NT provides full support for SNMP security features, allowing the network administrator to:

  - Configure authentication traps, which are messages sent to the server when a request for services fails authentication.

- Set accepted community, or host, names from which the server will accept requests.

- Set accepted community names from which incoming packets will be accepted.

- Select which of the server's services are to be reported on through SNMP—for example, email and IP gateway services.

- **Remote Access Permission**—An NT user account can be given or denied permission for remote access to the network.

- **Remote Access Authentication**—In addition to requiring valid remote access user accounts, remote users can be required to pass through an authentication procedure.

- **Callback**—RAS permits the configuration of callback, or dial-back, mode for individual user accounts. When dial-back is enabled, the user is not connected to the network immediately. RAS breaks the connection and calls the remote user back at either a telephone number supplied by the caller, or a preset telephone number that has been established for the user.

- **Security Hosts**—These third-party authentication devices sit between the remote client and the RAS server, and verify that callers from remote clients are authorized to connect to the server.

- **Auditing**—RAS generates audit information concerning all remote connections, such as failed logins, number of attempts, and so on.

- **Disconnect**—At any time, the network administrator can disconnect individual remote sessions without shutting down RAS or affecting other users.

- **Network Access Restrictions**—RAS can be configured to limit access to specific services or protocols on the server, or to specific portions of the network itself.

- **Encryption**—Passwords transferred during validation or authentication activities can be encrypted using the Challenge-Handshake Authentication Protocol (CHAP). Any data passed through remote connections can also be encrypted.

Security Payback: Cost vs. Loss

Unlike an investment in equipment, a visible and tangible asset, your security investment (which is intangible and invisible to most employees) is not generally perceived as providing any payback. A higher level of management support for security can be obtained by a Risk Assessment/Consequences Review. This activity will also help identify any potential security weaknesses in your system.

Risk Assessment

The purpose of a risk assessment is to identify security weaknesses and the likelihood of such an intrusion occurring. There is, of course, the potential for a security breach on any computer system. However, to determine the probability in real terms, it is necessary to examine both your computing environment and the people using it.

THE COMPUTER ENVIRONMENT

Your computer environment—an intranet, LAN, or WAN, for example—will determine the number of potential access points available to an intruder. The nature of software distribution (automated from a central site vs. manually from several locations), the level and quality of network administrative tools in use, and the percentage of staff requiring remote access are also areas that need to be reviewed. You will also need to consider the nature of the applications used, and their attractiveness as targets for damage or theft.

THE PEOPLE

People attack systems; therefore, an assessment of the employees working for the company and using the computer system is essential. Always remember that whether an attack is unintentional or deliberate, it can come from inside the organization as easily as from the outside. If there's a high employee turnover, you need to understand why people leave, and examine how well new staff are screened and trained. A high turnover rate can suggest poor morale, resulting in disgruntled current and former employees. If this is the case, the potential for an attack on the system is much higher than in an office with a stable employee base. Also, with more and more computer functions being outsourced, the use of contractors continues to grow. These workers have no particular loyalty to the organization, but often have access to sensitive or critical information.

Consequences of Attack

Assuming someone breaks into your system, what would the consequences be? Say, for example, that the attacker obtains sensitive information; would there be legal or business implications? What are the real costs of the breach—how badly would system downtime affect production schedules, and what would it cost to restore and stabilize the system? Could the system, in fact, be successfully and totally restored to its state prior to the intrusion? Placing a value on tangible assets is fairly straightforward; assigning costs to the intangibles is not easy, and requires experience. If your organization lacks the experience, time, or staff to conduct this kind of analysis, an investment in an independent study will prove worthwhile. In addition to providing the expertise you need, an external review can be more discerning and objective.

Security Awareness

As I mentioned earlier, unintentional acts can be as destructive as intentional security breaches. These acts can result in corrupted or destroyed data, leaked information, and exposure of the computer system to attack. Employees must understand that even an apparently trivial joke virus can disrupt business activity and cost the company money in lost productivity and recovery expenses. Over time, these attacks affect profitability, and, ultimately, a company's ability to stay in business. Most people are incredibly naive about both security and the consequences of not having proper safeguards in place. (And, yes, people do still write their passwords on a yellow sticky note and put it on their monitors.) Regularly scheduled information sessions are essential for ensuring that security awareness is maintained, and that staff are up-to-date on the latest issues.

The Security Audit

An audit of existing security policies, procedures, and practices should be undertaken on a regular basis. The following questions need to be addressed:

- Are the existing policies, procedures, and practices effective? If not, how can they be improved?

- Are the existing policies and procedures up-to-date?

- Are security practices followed diligently?

- Are the existing security practices adequate?

The security audit should focus on critical areas, and strive toward identifying areas of improvement, rather than attaching blame. Handled in this fashion, maintaining security will not be a prolonged, painful exercise people wish to avoid, but one that they are willing to participate in fully.

Online Security Resources

Purdue University
http://www.cs.purdue.edu/homes/spaf/spafs-hotlist.html

JANET (Joint Academic Network)
http://www.ja.net/newsfiles/janinfo/cert/cert.html

Raptor Systems Security Library
http://www.raptor.com/library/library.html

U.S. Department of Energy, CSTC (Computer Security Technology Center)
http://ciac.llnl.gov/cstc/CSTCIntroduction.html#computer

CERT (Computer Emergency Response Team) Coordination Center
http://www.cert.org

PART

3

The Intranet Developer's Tools

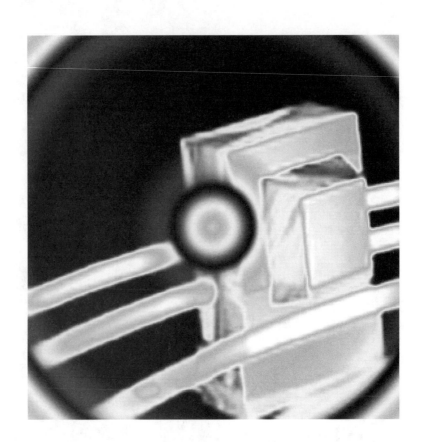

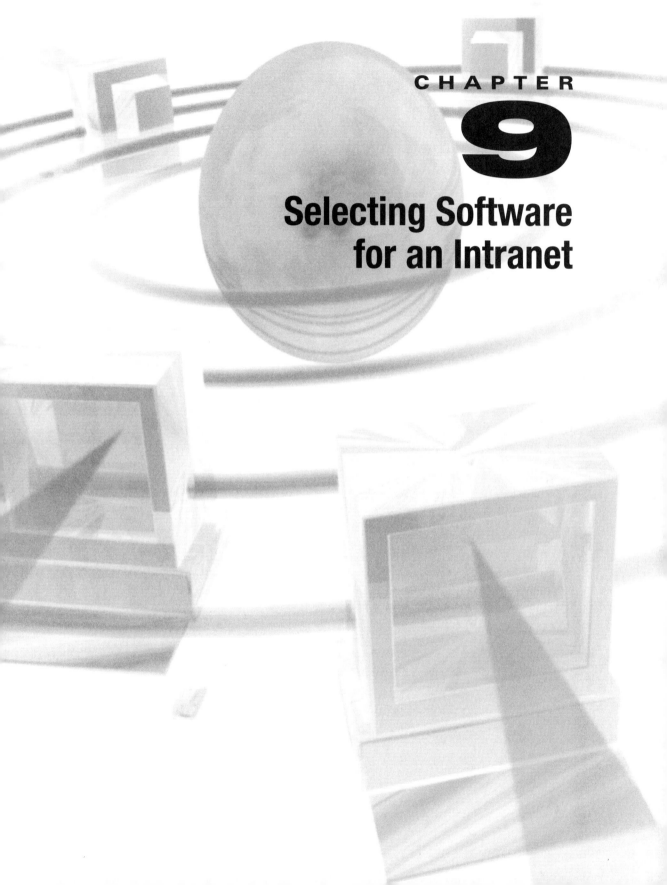

Selecting Software
for an Intranet

Selecting Software
for an Intranet

During the construction, operation, and maintenance of an intranet, you will need a variety of software products for specific tasks related to each phase of the intranet's operation. The number and sophistication of these software products will depend on the size, scope, and complexity of your intranet. There are two approaches to product selection: *mix-and-match* and *end-to-end*; both have advantages, disadvantages, and consequences. The route you choose to take should be based on many factors, but cost and functionality are two of the most obvious. By having detailed knowledge of these factors, you will be able to select the approach that is best for your organization, and be better equipped to handle the deluge of product announcements appearing daily.

The Intranet Marketplace

While you might view trend analyses and prognostications with some skepticism, it is safe to conclude that the *intranet* is not a passing fad. All the major players in the computer industry take the intranet concept, with all of its associated hardware, software, books, magazines, and seminars, very seriously. Intranets have the potential to impact office computing to an extent equal to, if not greater than, the introduction of the IBM personal computer. At a worldwide press conference in June 1996, Microsoft CEO Bill Gates said, "Intranets will have an immediate and dramatic impact on businesses over the next few years—but this is just the beginning." The activities of the two main rivals in this segment of the marketplace are a good indicator of how seriously the intranet product business is being treated.

NETSCAPE COMMUNICATIONS

Netscape Communications announced, and provided online, a 44-page strategy document called "The Netscape Intranet Vision and Product Roadmap," which is available at **http://home.netscape.com/comprod/ at_work/white_paper/intranet/vision.html**. The document also provides links to a full suite of products you can use for creating and deploying intranet applications.

MICROSOFT

Microsoft announced and set up its Intranet Resource Center at **http:// www.microsoft.com/intranet/**. At the same time, they announced a significant revamp of the Microsoft Office product suite. Called Office 97, this collection of desktop applications uses Web technology to make it easier for users to create, analyze, and publish on intranets. They also announced Microsoft Outlook, a new product for collaborative computing on intranets. Finally, in keeping with the white paper fever sweeping the computer industry, they have made "Microsoft's Intranet Strategy" available online.

Everyone Wants Your Business

The gold fever spawned by intranets is second only to the Internet/World Wide Web phenomenon of 1995. One research group places the current market for internal Web servers at $476 million, and another research firm predicts this market will grow to $1 billion by the year 2000. Yet another trend analyst estimates that 80 percent of Netscape Communications' revenue is generated by products used for intranets—not for the Internet.

The Existing Infrastructure

The most important aspect of software selection is knowing what your existing infrastructure consists of—not just the hardware and software, but the human resources, as well. This infrastructure, while not the sole determining factor in software selection, plays a major role in selecting one of the two possible approaches mentioned earlier. The various contributing factors to software selection are illustrated in Figure 9.1.

The tools your system may require for intranet activities are divided into the following general categories:

- Page Creation—Editors, converters, graphics and multimedia tools

- Page Display—Browsers, viewers, helper applications, and plug-ins

- Information Search and Retrieval—Indexing tools and search engines

- Information Delivery—Email, list servers, Gopher servers, and Web servers

- Data and Application Interfaces

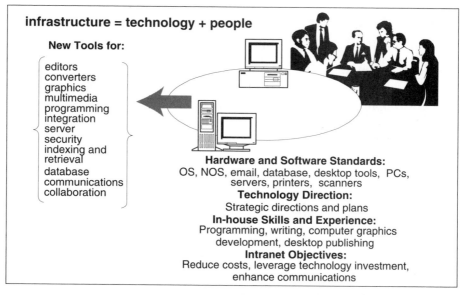

Figure 9.1   How existing infrastructure determines the best approach to software selection.

- General-purpose Programming

- Specialized Programming

In subsequent chapters, we'll take a detailed look at representative tools for each of the above categories, focusing on those currently available for the Windows environment.

Technology Resources

Your organization, assuming it's networked, already has many standards in place. At the hardware level, there is network topology, cabling, a network interface card, a PC workstation, and a LAN server. The corresponding software standards will be the NOS and workstation/server OS. It is at the applications level that existing standards play a strong role in software selection. Any intranet application must, at a minimum, coexist with the organization's applications, particularly any databases that will provide data to the Web pages. For example, if you are choosing off-the-shelf WWW/ DBMS gateway software, and your corporate databases all use SQL, it's essential that you select the software that provides the best level of support for your SQL standard.

Human Resources

The human component of the infrastructure is as important as the technology, yet is often overlooked. People in your organization will need the skills to work with new tools—tools for development, maintenance, and use of the application. It is important, then, to know the level of applicable in-house skills and experience when determining software requirements and pricing the alternatives. If the necessary skills are lacking, you have a training issue, which is going to impact your decision in a number of areas, including:

- *Cost*—Can the training be handled in-house, or will special arrangements need to be made for providing training for the technical support team, the developers, and the users?

- *Development time*—The level of product-specific staff skills will have a direct impact on how quickly the application can be developed, tested, and implemented. If deadlines are critical, there also may be a cost implication if outside consulting resources are needed.

- *Application usage*—The speed and ease with which staff can use the application interface (the browser in this case) will have an effect on how quickly and effectively the application is used.

Let's assume, for example, that you've decided to take full advantage of HTML's capabilities and want to incorporate graphics, sound, and video in a system that will provide online training for staff. It is, in essence, a multimedia application, and specialized skills will be required. Table 9.1 is an extract from a skills inventory checklist we will be using in Chapter 14, which deals with intranet construction. The table sets out the following items:

- *Activity*—The specific activity to be undertaken

- *Skills Required*—The typical skills that would be required

- *Products Used*—The specific products the staff member has used for the activity

- *Experience*—The amount of experience using a given product, either in years of usage, or as applied to a similar application

- *Skill Assessment*—The staff member's personal assessment of his skill level (beginner, intermediate, or advanced)

Table 9.1 has been partially filled out using the multimedia training system as an example, but does not include basic infrastructure skills such as installing and configuring Web server software.

Table 9.1 Sample Staff Skills Inventory

Activity	Skills Required	Products Used	Experience (years, systems built)	Skill Assessment
Custom graphics	Ability to create graphics using a software program	Corel Draw, Paint Shop Pro	2 years	Intermediate
Computer generated audio and video clips	Ability to create audio and video clips using software	none	none	none

(Continued)

Table 9.1   Sample Staff Skills Inventory (Continued)

Activity	Skills Required	Products Used	Experience (years, systems built)	Skill Assessment
HTML programming	Create HTML source programs	various editors	3 years	Advanced
CGI programming	Create CGI scripts to interface with database	Perl	1 year	Beginner
Page layout and design	Ability to layout computer screens	None	None	None

A checklist like the one in Table 9.1 is a useful tool in determining the staff resources that you have available for an intranet project, and will help plan for (and budget) additional training or outside consulting that may be required.

The Mix-and-Match Approach

The mix-and-match approach simply means using different tools from different vendors, according to the individual needs and situations that have to be dealt with during the course of building your intranet. Figure 9.2 illustrates this approach. Each user has a different browser for viewing pages; the developer has selected his tools of choice for creating pages and database gateway interfaces; the Web server uses server software from one company and another firm's product for providing document indexing and retrieval capability; and data is provided to the application from databases representing two different database standards.

Product selection is based primarily on the functional requirements of the application. The fundamental characteristics of this approach are:

- *Multi-vendor*—By default, you will end up with a cross-section of products from several vendors. It is important to consider the fact that the mix-and-match approach inevitably increases the support burden on

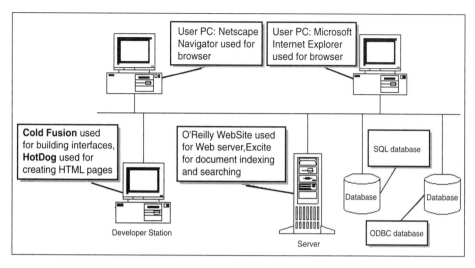

Figure 9.2   A multi-product, multi-vendor intranet environment.

the systems group, and necessitates more staff training, either for the support staff or the users.

- *Openness*—Vendors specializing in a narrow range of products strive to meet the needs of the broadest market possible, and to develop software that adheres to the open-systems philosophy. While they support widely adopted and non-proprietary standards, integration with existing proprietary technology within the company can be difficult to achieve. The consequence of this is often a lower level of integration between the various products that comprise the system.

- *Flexibility*—Implementing a selection of non-proprietary, specialized products provides a high degree of flexibility, and as new or increased functionality is required, it is easy to replace one component of the product suite.

- *Lowest cost*—The lowest total cost is a result of an interesting phenomenon in the intranet product sector. Much of the new software is being introduced by small start-up companies looking to establish market share. Since these companies are not burdened by the operational overhead of firms such as Microsoft, nor are they competing for Research and Development dollars between several product lines, it is possible for them to offer low-cost products.

Among the advantages of the mix-and-match approach is the nature of the products themselves—most of them are reasonably priced, perform well, offer high levels of functionality, are of high quality, and are readily available. By and large, intranet-related products are developed by small companies; the large, established vendors are hampered by corporate bureaucracy, broad product lines, and the inability to respond quickly to market demands. The smaller companies are also able to bring their software to market very quickly, and were the first to exploit the distribution potential of the Internet.

Depending on the particular products you select, there are some key factors you should consider: stability, support, and coexistence.

- *Stability*—The intranet segment of the computer software market is very volatile, with a high product and vendor turnover rate. For small companies with their entire businesses tied to one product, product failure can mean business failure. The risk, then, is investing in a product whose developer may not be in business six months from now.

- *Support*—A secondary concern, but one that may be crucial given the nature of your intranet application, is support. If the application is mission critical, then you need solid vendor support when it's required. Many start-up companies do not have an extensive support infrastructure available.

- *Coexistence*—This refers to relationships between vendors, and can be a significant issue when you are caught in the finger-pointing crossfire. The familiar refrain, "It's not our software, it's the other company's," creates more problems than it solves.

The End-to-End Approach

In direct opposition to mix-and-match is the end-to-end approach, where all the products used for the intranet application are supplied by one vendor. Figure 9.3 illustrates this solution, with all the products, from the client through to the database, being provided by one vendor, in this case Microsoft.

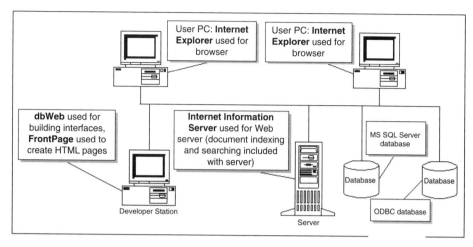

Figure 9.3 A multi-product, single vendor intranet environment.

Using the end-to-end approach, product selection is vendor-based and highly dependent on the products that are currently in place. (End-to-end products are different from bundled solutions, covered in Chapter 13, because a vendor provides a total solution that typically includes all the hardware, software, and training required to implement and operate an intranet.) The main characteristics of the end-to-end approach are:

- *Single vendor*—There are many companies that may not have a formal policy regarding dealing with multiple vendors, but informally maintain a single-vendor philosophy. Sometimes this just makes good business sense, in that it removes the element of finger-pointing, provides a single point of contact, and generally makes it easier to support a complex computing environment.

- *Proprietary*—End-to-end solutions are proprietary, but since one vendor controls the code for all products, there are the benefits of overall system performance gains and a high level of integration between the products. They do, however, limit the ability to add third-party components, thereby reducing flexibility.

- *Inflexible*—A proprietary set of products limits flexibility by locking you into a specific vendor's product line. This can result in major expense and inconvenience if it becomes necessary to replace components that have been discontinued or no longer provide the needed capacity and performance.

- *Higher cost*—End-to-end solutions do tend to cost more, not necessarily at the time of purchase, but for ongoing vendor support and licensing. The latter can dramatically increase a product's cost, particularly when it becomes necessary to increase the number of concurrent user licenses—multi-user database products are a very good example of this. This higher cost, though, is often offset significantly by reduced support and training costs within the organization.

As was the case with mix-and-match, the end-to-end approach has advantages and disadvantages. It is, without doubt, more expensive in the long run, but the requirements of the application, not the bottom line, should drive any cost/benefit assessment. The two biggest weaknesses of end-to-end are its proprietary nature and the sluggishness with which products and product enhancements are brought to market.

In the final analysis, you must decide which approach is best for meeting your intranet objectives, providing the best fit with your current technology, and building on the existing infrastructure. Focus on the business objectives of your intranet and try to build on the infrastructure in place. Don't get hung up on technology—there are new products showing up daily, and there's always someone willing to sell you a solution to the problem you didn't know you had.

In subsequent chapters we'll be taking an in-depth look at the various products used in constructing an intranet, and examining another option for acquiring the tools that you may need—the bundled solution.

10

Working with
Web Pages

10

Working with Web Pages

Web pages are the core of your intranet—the delivery medium for your information system and the interface with your readers. In this chapter, we will focus on building and viewing these pages, with particular emphasis on their creation and the tools required for this process. Basic hypertext composition, the preparation of inline graphics, testing, and some of the more esoteric elements of Web page construction, such as sound and video, will be considered. We will also examine browsers, hypertext viewers, and the helper applications and plug-ins needed to round out browser functionality.

Creating Web Pages: The Process and the Tools

Although the steps required prior to actual page creation are dealt with in some detail in Chapter 14 (and an HTML primer is provided in the Appendix), a brief overview of the information at this point will aid in understanding the material in this chapter. These preliminary tasks define:

- *Objectives and Audience*—The objectives for the publication are established and the target audience is

215

identified, thereby determining information content, how it is to be presented, and how readers will navigate through it.

- *Information Content*—The data that provides the content is identified, along with its sources. Issues related to data ownership, security, or access are also addressed at this time.

- *Data Inclusion*—The method to be used for converting material to hypertext source files is determined: manually by typing, scanned in, through conversion of existing material, or by programming database interfaces.

- *Publication Structure*—A storyboard, or map, of the entire publication is set out to show how the screens are related, and how the user will navigate through the material.

- *Layout and On-Screen Formatting*—Screen layout standards and formatting approaches are established to ensure presentation consistency.

Authoring Tools

The purpose of an authoring tool, or HTML editor, is to work with hypertext source data (text and graphics) electronically, in much the same way that you create a report or memo in a word processor. With an HTML editor, you enter tags into the file to control how the information will appear on a browser screen, to provide links to other pages, or to add objects such as graphics to the page. The available authoring tools range from the very basic (analogous to MS Write) to highly sophisticated programs that resemble PC desktop publishing software packages. While any text editor can be used to create HTML source files, these specialized authoring tools make the task easier, faster, and less prone to error. Based on features and functions, we've defined three categories for examining representative tools: the basic editor, the editor/word processor, and the hypertext publisher.

BASIC EDITORS

Basic editors are the least feature-rich of the authoring tools; they enable the user to add tags to documents either manually, or by using pull-down menus or buttons on a toolbar. In addition, several of these editors provide templates for creating more complex document structures, such as forms or tables. This class of tools assumes that the user has a good knowledge of HTML document structure and tag syntax. At a minimum, basic editors provide support for HTML 2.0, and most include support for the Netscape HTML extensions. Document previewing is handled by your browser of choice, which is configured to work with the particular editor you are using. When the preview mode is activated, the browser is started and the file being edited is loaded into it. These editors cost little (most are freeware or shareware), take up only a small amount of space on your hard drive (HTML Notepad, fully installed, occupies 251 K), and don't require high-performance PCs. One limitation to keep in mind is that some have a size limit on the file being edited; HTML Notepad, for example, has a 32 K ceiling.

Editor/Word Processors

Tools in this class provide the features and levels of functionality we have come to expect from our experiences with word processing packages such as WordPerfect or MS Word. In addition to the functions provided by the basic editor, numerous additional features are present. These may include drag-and-drop editing, sophisticated templates for creating complex structures, support for all the HTML extensions, a certain level of built-in document conversion (text to HTML, and HTML to text), HTML syntax checking, a spell checker, and/or a thesaurus. Some, like HotDog, also support the creation of multiply-linked pages, and include a find-and-replace capability that encompasses an entire Web site and greatly enhances the ability to maintain files and links. Programs in this classification occupy more space on the hard drive, and need a more robust PC than the basic editors do. The 32-bit version of HotDog Pro from Sausage Software, for example, takes up 3.5 MB of drive space, and requires a machine capable of running Windows 95.

Workstation requirements aside, the biggest weakness of some of these packages is the proprietary elements that have crept in. For instance, when saving source files, the HoTMetaL editor inserts a special code that identifies the source files as its creation; if any editing is done with another product, the files become corrupted. Not only is this a nuisance, but it also runs counter to the ideal of document portability, which is why the Web protocols were originally developed. This is not a reason to reject one of these tools out-of-hand, but should certainly be considered if your page authors are using different tools for collaborative projects.

WORD PROCESSOR ADD-ONS

Existing PC word processing packages with hypertext editing add-on modules are an option for hypertext page creation that allows writers to continue working with familiar tools. For the WordPerfect world, a product called Internet Publisher is available from Novell. Word users have two options: WebAuthor, from Quarterdeck Corporation, or Internet Assistant, from Microsoft. Based on the reviews, and from talking to users of these tools, the general consensus seems to be that these packages are limited in functionality and are really geared to the novice user. Of the three, WebAuthor is the most helpful, since it provides dialog boxes to guide the user through different tagging activities, such as table creation.

HYPERTEXT PUBLISHERS

These tools have moved authoring capability beyond the level of word processing into the realm of hypertext desktop publishing. Their feature sets include image manipulation, drag-and-drop editing, What You See Is What You Get (WYSIWYG) editing, image map creation, and link management.

FrontPage, from Microsoft, enables the user to set up a local Web site environment that makes it possible to test forms, image maps, and CGI scripts—processes that normally require the use of an operational Web server. As a result, all testing can be done locally, before the publication is moved into a production environment, helping ease the burden on the LAN support team during development. FrontPage also has site management tools that make it possible to display a diagram of the entire publication that shows all the files and links, including any missing or defective links. This product stands at the high end of its particular class, but other vendors are working on, or have, products with similar feature sets. GNNPress, from Global Network Navigator, provides rich WYSIWYG editing, a built-in Web browser, and the ability to create local MiniWebs that can be administered from the editor. Its features include link maintenance, file version control, and the ability to set file access permissions.

Unfortunately, proprietary features are also an issue with the hypertext publishers. FrontPage, for example, has proprietary extensions for its image maps and CGI scripts (which employ FrontPage server extensions rather than the standard CGI script processor used by most servers).

Editor Functions and Features

Table 10.1 provides an overview of the functions and features that are available with various authoring software packages. The functions vary between software packages.

Table 10.1   Authoring Tool Functions and Features

Function/Feature	Description
Basic editing	Ability to key in or import text and add HTML tags
Templates	Availability of templates for complex constructs, such as forms
Rules checking	Validates HTML syntax in document
Conversion capability	Text to HTML, HTML to text
Link maintenance	Ability to test hypertext links
Spell checker	Provides spelling check
Thesaurus	Thesaurus incorporated with editor
Page preview	Pages can be previewed during edit session, either with built-in or external browser
Image manipulation	Converts GIFs to transparent GIFs
Web page update	Allows direct page update without using file transfer, to migrate revised pages to the server
Netscape extensions	Supports Netscape HTML extensions, including font sizes, tables, and background colors
Microsoft extensions	Supports Microsoft HTML extensions, such as marquees
Image maps	Facilitates creation of image maps
Direct editing	Allows direct editing of HTML source code
Customizable toolbar	User can customize editor toolbar to suit individual needs
Hot keys/short cuts	User can use hot keys or short cuts to execute commands

The Tools at Work

The following sections show how different levels of authoring tools can make page and site construction easier, particularly for a new developer. To illustrate how some representative authoring tools are used, we will construct a simple publication consisting of seven pages, including a home page. These sample pages will use the most common HTML tags to show how different levels of tools are used to handle required coding. Figure 10.1 shows the map of our publication, and includes file names for each page.

THE BASIC EDITOR

We used HTML NotePad from Cranial Software (**http://www.u-net.com/ virtua/code/**) to create our sample home page, shown in Figure 10.2. The source code is shown in Listing 10.1. (The purpose for including this listing, and those that follow, is primarily to illustrate progressively more complex HTML constructs. However, those who would like to understand more about the code can refer to a complete list of HTML tags in Appendix C.)

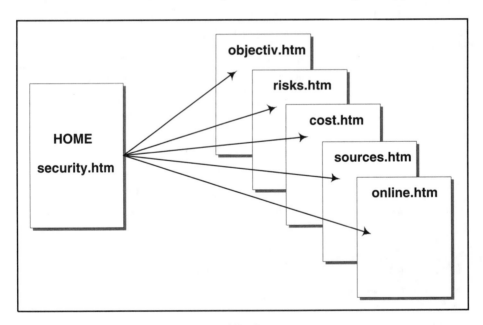

Figure 10.1 The site map for a sample publication.

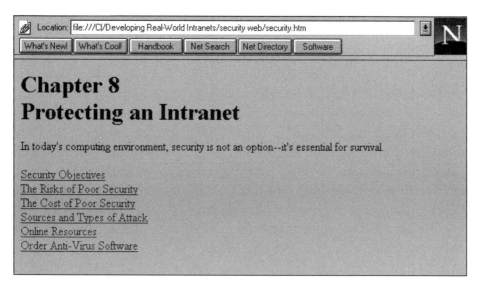

Figure 10.2 Sample home page viewed with Netscape Navigator.

Listing 10.1 HTML Code for SECURITY.HTM

```
<HTML>
<HEAD>
<TITLE>Chapter 8 - Protecting an Intranet</TITLE>
</HEAD>
<BODY>
<H1>Chapter 8<BR>
Protecting an Intranet</H1>

In today's computing environment, security is not an option--it's
                          essential for survival.<P>

<A HREF="file:///c:/developing real-world intranets/security web/
                     objectiv.htm">Security Objectives</A><BR>
<A HREF="file:///c:/developing real-world intranets/security web/
                     risks.htm">The Risks of Poor Security</
                     A><BR>
<A HREF="file:///c:/developing real-world intranets/security web/
                     cost.htm">The Cost of Poor Security</A><BR>
<A HREF="file:///c:/developing real-world intranets/security web/
                     sources.htm">Sources and Types of Attack</
                     A><BR>
<A HREF="file:///c:/developing real-world intranets/security web/
                     online.htm">Online Resources</A><BR>
```

```
<A HREF="file:///c:/developing real-world intranets/security web/
                    secform.htm">Order Anti-Virus Software
                    </A><BR>

</BODY>
</HTML>
```

As you can see, the HTML tags required to generate our home page are not particularly complicated; some, however, such as the tags specifying an anchor and a hypertext reference to a specific file (**<A HREF="file:///c:/ developing real-world intranets/security web/objectiv.htm">Security Objectives</A>**), lend themselves all too easily to typographical errors. Figure 10.3 shows how a more robust editor, HTML Assistant Pro 2, makes coding much easier, and in the process decreases the risk of error.

This editor provides a drop-down menu for specifying the object's URL, and the standard Windows browse button helps locate and identify the specific file and path statement required for the link reference. Nevertheless, while features such as these facilitate less manual coding, the user still has to understand basic HTML document structure and the correct syntax for the tags.

EDITOR/WORD PROCESSOR

Tools in this class provide a higher level of functionality and ease of use when it is necessary to build complex HTML constructs, such as forms and tables. Figure 10.4 illustrates a table, and Listing 10.2 contains the source code used to create it.

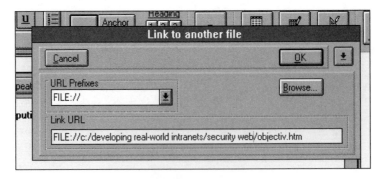

Figure 10.3   Adding link references with HTML Assistant Pro 2.

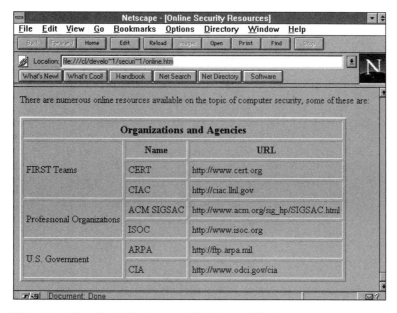

Figure 10.4   A multi-celled table viewed with Netscape Navigator.

Listing 10.2   HTML Code for ONLINE.HTM

```
<!DOCTYPE HTML PUBLIC "-//SQ//DTD HTML 2.0 HoTMetaL + extensions//EN">
<HTML>
<HEAD>
<TITLE>Online Security Resources</TITLE>
</HEAD>
<BODY>
<H1>Security Resources</H1>
<P>There are numerous online resources available on the topic of computer
security, some of these are:</P>
<TABLE BORDER="2" CELLPADDING="4" CELLSPACING="4"><TR><TD COLSTART="1"
                          COLSPAN="3" ALIGN="CENTER">
                          <B><BIG>Organizations and Agencies</BIG></
                          B></TD></TR>
<TR><TD COLSTART="1" ROWSPAN="3" VALIGN="MIDDLE">FIRST Teams</TD><TD
                          COLSTART="2" ALIGN="CENTER"><B>Name</B></
                          TD><TD COLSTART="3" ALIGN="CENTER"><B>URL</
                          B></TD></TR>
<TR><TD COLSTART="2">CERT</TD><TD COLSTART="3"><A HREF="http://
                          www.cert.org"> http://www.cert.org </A></
                          TD></TR>
<TR><TD COLSTART="2">CIAC</TD><TD COLSTART="3"><A HREF="http://
                          ciac.llnl.gov"> http://ciac.llnl.gov </A></
```

```
                                           TD></TR>
<TR><TD COLSTART="1" ROWSPAN="2" VALIGN="MIDDLE">Professional
                                           Organizations</TD><TD COLSTART="2">ACM
                                           SIGSAC</TD><TD COLSTART="3"><A HREF=
                                           "http://www.acm.org/sig_hp/SIGSAC.html">
                                           http://www.acm.org/sig_hp/SIGSAC.html </
                                           A></TD></TR>
<TR><TD COLSTART="2">ISOC</TD><TD COLSTART="3"><A HREF="http://
                                           www.isoc.org"> http://www.isoc.org </A></
                                           TD></TR>
<TR><TD COLSTART="1" ROWSPAN="2" VALIGN="MIDDLE">U.S. Government</TD><TD
COLSTART="2">ARPA</TD><TD COLSTART="3"><A HREF="http://ftp.arpa.mil">
                                           http://ftp.arpa.mil </A></TD></TR>
                                           <TR><TDCOLSTART="2">CIA</TD><TD
                                           COLSTART="3"><A HREF="http://www.odci.gov/
                                           cia"> http://www.odci.gov/cia </A></TD></
                                           TR>
</TABLE>
</BODY>
</HTML>
```

The code required to generate our sample table could have been keyed in with a basic editor program, but as you can see, the tags required for row, column, and cell specifications are extensive, and prone to easily over-looked typographical errors. These errors can be found and corrected, of course, but the task is very time consuming. The tools in the editor/word processor category make table creation a great deal easier, and some, like HoTMetaL, which was used to create this particular table, have a syntax checker to catch errors and identify them for you. Figures 10.5 and 10.6 illustrate two steps in the table creation process using HoTMetaL.

Figure 10.5 shows the table after the initial layout has been defined—that is, the number of rows and columns specified, the cells across a row joined to form one cell, and the cells down a column joined to form single cells. Text has been entered, but with no justification or special formatting. The next step is to carry out any special formatting, as shown in Figure 10.6.

Once a given table cell has been selected, a cell properties dialog box is activated, and can be used to specify the positioning of text.

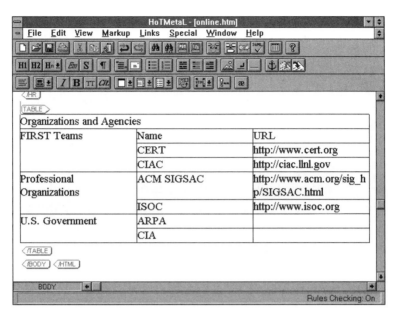

Figure 10.5 The initial table, with some data entered.

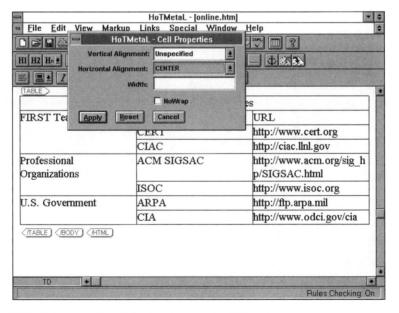

Figure 10.6 Using an editor dialog box to control cell format.

HYPERTEXT PUBLISHER

Another complex structure used in HTML pages is the online form, which has to be designed and coded not only with appearance in mind, but also with regard to the input that will be received from the user. This input must be stored in variables, so that the information can be passed on, either to the server's CGI handler or to an email server. Figure 10.7 illustrates an online form that was created using Microsoft's FrontPage.

The code required to produce this online form is shown in Listing 10.3, and was entirely generated by FrontPage, which, like HoTMetaL, uses a Form Wizard (dialog boxes) to walk the author through the creation process. (It should be noted that I spend very little time coding HTML forms—yet this example took me only 15 minutes, and this was the first time I had used the FrontPage editor.—DW) With the current selection of authoring tools in the Hypertext Publisher category, a new author can get up to speed and be producing high-quality pages in a very short period of time.

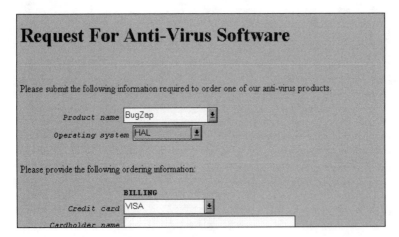

Figure 10.7   An online form created with FrontPage 1.1.

Listing 10.3   An Online Form Generated by FrontPage

```
<!DOCTYPE HTML PUBLIC "-//IETF//DTD HTML//EN">
<html>
<head>
<title>Software Order Form</title>
<meta name="GENERATOR" content="Microsoft FrontPage 1.1">
</head>
<body>
<h1>Request For Anti-Virus Software</h1>
<hr>
<form action="--VERMEER-SELF--" method="POST">
<!--VERMEER BOT=SaveResults U-File="formrslt.htm" S-Format="HTML/DL"
   B-Label-Fields="TRUE" -->
<p>Please submit the following information required to order one of our
                            anti-virus products.</p>
<blockquote>
<pre><em>     Product name </em><select name="Product_ProductName" size=1>
<option selected>BugZap</option>
<option>McAffee WebScan</option>
<option>F-Prot Professional</option>
</select>
<em>  Operating system </em><select name="Operating" size=1>
<option selected>HAL</option>
<option>Windows 95</option>
<option>Windows NT</option>
</select>
</pre>
</blockquote>
<p>Please provide the following ordering information:</p>
<blockquote>
<pre><em>                    </em><strong>BILLING</strong>
<em>     Credit card </em><select name="Ordering_CardType" size=1>
<option selected>VISA</option>
<option>MasterCard</option>
<option>American Express</option>
<option>Diner's Club</option>
<option>Discover</option>
</select>
<em> Cardholder name </em><input type=text size=35 maxlength=256
                            name="Ordering_CardHolderName">
<em>    Card number </em><input type=text size=20 maxlength=20
                            name="Ordering_CardNumber">
<em> Expiration date </em><input type=text size=5 maxlength=5
                            name="Ordering_CardExpiration">
```

```
<em>                </em><strong>SHIPPING</strong>
<em>  Street address </em><input type=text size=35 maxlength=256
                          name="Ordering_StreetAddress">
<em> Address (cont.) </em><input type=text size=35 maxlength=256
                          name="Ordering_Address2">
<em>            City </em><input type=text size=35 maxlength=256
                          name="Ordering_City">
<em>  State/Province </em><input type=text size=35 maxlength=256
                          name="Ordering_State">
<em> Zip/Postal code </em><input type=text size=12 maxlength=12
                          name="Ordering_ZipCode">
<em>         Country </em><input type=text size=25 maxlength=256
                          name="Ordering_Country">
</pre>
</blockquote>
<p>Please provide your name:</p>
<blockquote>
<pre><em>            Name </em><input type=text size=35 maxlength=256
                          name="Personal_FullName">
</pre>
</blockquote>
<p>Enter your email address in the space provided below.</p>
<blockquote>
<p><input type=text size=42 maxlength=7 name="address"> <br>
</p>
</blockquote>
<p><input type=submit value="Submit Form"> <input type=reset value="Reset
                          Form"> </p>
</form>
<hr>
<h5>Copyright information goes here.<br>
Last revised: <!--VERMEER BOT=TimeStamp S-Type="EDITED" S-Format="%B %d,
                          %Y" --></h5>
</body>
</html>
```

The representative tools we've looked at make HTML programming progressively easier, less prone to error, and faster. In addition to standard HTML programming, you may want to enhance your pages by including image maps and graphics. Tools are also available to aid in these specialized tasks.

Specialty Tools For HTML Constructs

Specialty tools are beginning to appear in the marketplace to aid authors in the creation of specific HTML constructs. One such product, recently made available by the Software Division of O'Reilly Publishing, is PolyForm, a software package that handles all aspects of form production, including the construction of CGI scripts for bidirectional communications between the server and the client.

This product seems to be particularly well-suited to working with a multiple form structure, where processing is dependent on one form receiving input from another. PolyForm allows users to either create their own material, or to use pre-existing forms that come with the software. The prebuilt forms can be used as is or tailored to fit the author's specific needs. Unlike some other products, PolyForm does not generate proprietary CGI routines and will, therefore, work with most of the common Web server software that is available for the Windows environment.

If your Web site is going to rely heavily on special constructs, you should seriously consider specialty software packages; they can shorten the learning curve for developers, cut down the amount of time required for coding, and eliminate most of the errors that creep into HTML documents.

Selecting an Authoring Tool

As you can see, the number of available authoring tools is somewhat overwhelming, and their diversity, features, and functions cover the entire spectrum. A tool such as HTML Notepad (shareware that can be registered for $30) provides bare-bones tag insertion, while the version of HoTMetaL that we used to create the sample table provides virtually every tool an author could possibly use (except the ability to set up a local Web server for development and testing). The problem with the availability of all these options is that the selection of appropriate editor software can become fairly complicated. Keeping the following points in mind when choosing an editor will help to alleviate the confusion somewhat:

- The level of HTML expertise and existing skills of the people who will be using the software to create hypertext pages

- The resources available for training

- The amount of lead time available to spend on developing staff skills to the point where quality pages can be created in production quantity

- Given the predominant types of HTML constructs to be included in the Web pages, the functions and features you will require of the software

Cost is another factor that you need to take into consideration when choosing an authoring tool. Unfortunately, we can be of little help to you in this area, since specifying product prices is like nailing Jello to a tree. Prices range from tools that are free (like GNNPress), to high-end products that fall in the $150 to $250 price range.For example, Microsoft FrontPage started out in the $650 price range at the beginning of this year, dropped to under $500 in eight weeks, and is now being sold as an MS Office upgrade for less than $100.

Two of the best resources for researching information on editors are the product reviews in trade magazines like Internet World and online sites such as Stroud's Consummate Winsock Applications List (**http://cwsapps.cu-online.com**). Fortunately, the majority of commercial products are available for test periods, and can be downloaded from the vendors' Web sites. Many of the new products, or new releases of existing products, are also provided for use during the beta-testing period.

 Before testing a given authoring package, plan a dummy page or select some difficult HTML constructs (such as forms with pull-down selection areas and checkboxes) that you'd like to build. Then start the program and see how long it takes you to accomplish your predefined tasks—without using any documentation or online help. The results, and the speed and ease with which they were achieved, are a true indicator of an "intuitive interface."

Setting Authoring Tool Standards

The discussions related to the issue of desktop software standards continue unabated, and it would be unrealistic to think that authoring tool software will avoid becoming part of this debate. Software standards are, by and large, a corporate issue, and your organization's policy on standards in general will determine whether or not you set a policy for authoring tools.

If, however, your standards policy is fairly flexible, there are some things to consider before you allow employees to select the software they prefer. Among these considerations are training, support, and portability, the latter of which is by far the most important issue. Typically, HTML source files will be created and edited by several people; therefore, it is imperative that the files can be easily transported among these people. Set out guidelines to ensure that all of the authoring software in use stores these files in a compatible file format. The last thing you want to be spending time on is converting files because someone will only use his favorite editor, which saves HTML source files in a proprietary format.

The authoring tool software category is the area where most of the new Web-related products are appearing. Table 10.2 lists several of the authoring tools that are currently available (as of July 1996), but is by no means comprehensive.

Converters

Document conversion is employed to capitalize on an existing repository of electronic documents—which may be in many different file formats— by converting them to usable hypertext files that can be easily accessed at your Web site, as depicted in Figure 10.8.

If it is desirable or necessary to use conversion, there are several tools available for converting existing files to the hypertext format. An important fact you must keep in mind regarding the conversion of *any* electronic file to another file format is that, most of the time, conversions are not 100-percent accurate ("clean"). Having said that, let's look at some of the

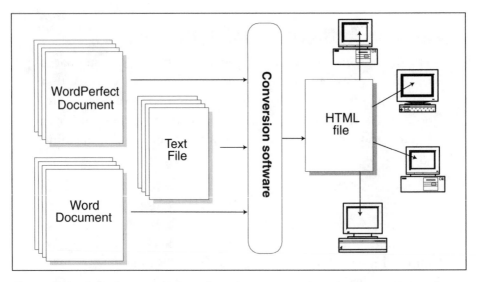

Figure 10.8 Capitalizing on existing information resources through document conversion.

Table 10.2 **Authoring Tools for Developing Web Pages**

Name	Source	Internet Location	Commercial, Freeware, Shareware, Etc.	Evaluation Copy Available?
<Live Markup> PRO Beta 22	Mediatech, Inc.	ftp://ftp.mediatec. com/pub/mediatech/ lv16b22g.exe	Commercial	Yes
HotDog 16-bit 2.53	Sausage Software	Ftp://ftp.enterprise. net/pub/mirror/ winsock-1/HTML/ hotdog25.exe	Commercial	Yes
HTMLed Professional 1.1b	Internet Software Technologies	http://www.eucanet. com/htp11b-e.zip	Commercial	No
InContext Spider 1.1	InContext Systems	ftp://incontext.ca/ pub/icspider/ setup-e.exe	Commercial	Yes
HTML Assistant Pro 2.00	Brooklyn North Software Works	ftp://ftp.cs.dal.ca/ htmlasst/htmlasst.exe	Crippleware *	Yes
HTML Writer 0.9 Beta 4	Kris Nosak	ftp://ftp.coast.net/ SimTel/win3/ internet/hw9b4all.zip	Donation-ware	Yes

(*Continued*)

Table 10.2   Authoring Tools for Developing Web Pages (Continued)

Name	Source	Internet Location	Commercial, Freeware, Shareware,Etc.	Evaluation Copy Available?
GNNPress 1.1 (Formerly Navipress)	Global Network Navigator (AOL)	http://www.gnhost. com/publish/ upgrade/gnnp11.exe	Freeware	Yes
HoTMetaL 2.0	SoftQuad, Inc.	ftp://ftp2.sq.com/ pub/products/ hotmetal/windows/ hmfree2.exe	Freeware	Yes
Internet Assistant for Windows 3.x 1.00z	Microsoft Corpor- ation	ftp://ftp.microsoft. com/deskapps/word /winword-public/ia/ wordia.exe	Freeware	Yes
Internet Publisher 6.1	Novell, Inc.	ftp://ftp.word perfect.com/pub/ wpapps/intpub/ wpipzip.exe	Freeware	Yes
SuperPad 1.3	Douglas Boling	ftp://ftp.zdnet.com/ pcmag/1995/0411/ spad.zip	Freeware	Yes
Web Wizard 16-bit 1.2	ARTA Media Group	ftp://ftp.halcyon. com/local/we bwizard/webwiz16.zip	Freeware	Yes
HTML NotePad 1.19	Cranial Software	http://www.u-net. com/virtua/code/ htmlnote/htmln119.zip	Shareware	Yes
HTMLed 16-bit 1.5	Internet Software Technologies	http://www.ist.ca/ htmled/htmled16.zip	Shareware	Yes
WebEdit 16-bit 1.4c	Nesbitt Software	http://www.nesbitt. com/webedit.zip	Shareware	Yes
Web Author 2.0	Quarter- deck	ftp://ftp.qdeck. com/pub/demo/ warval2.exe	Trialware	Yes

* Crippleware is a term used to describe evaluation software that is not fully functional.

conversion options available in the Windows world, where most of the existing word processing documents have been created with either WordPerfect, Word, or AmiPro.

As is the case with editors, conversion software programs cover the full spectrum of cost, functionality, and sophistication. At the low end are programs that are really nothing more than a set of macros written for a given word processor. When these products are used, the word processor becomes a quasi-HTML editor/converter, and the macros attempt to convert the existing document codes, such as paragraph breaks and headings, into the corresponding HTML tags. The quality of the program used will determine the accuracy of the conversion.

Moving up the scale, there are dedicated conversion utilities, stand-alone programs that are run against existing files to output new files containing hypertext markup tags. This class of conversion software is split into two categories: single-format conversion and multiple-format conversion. The former are built to handle only one input file format (Wp2Html, for example, converts WordPerfect documents into HTML files); the latter handle a broader range of source files. Some, like HTML Transit from InfoAccess, provide direct translation of Word, WordPerfect, AmiPro, FrameMaker, Interleaf, RTF, and ASCII files.

Figure 10.9 shows part of a Word document as it would appear using a word processor's Print Preview feature. (The drawing in the page was created using a product called Visio, and pasted into the Word document.)

Figure 10.10 shows the resulting file after it's run through HTML Transit to convert it into an HTML source file, without any additional editing.

The various conversion packages currently available are capable of dealing with most of the word processing documents likely to be found in an office environment. However, keep in mind that larger documents should be divided into smaller segments to take full advantage of the hypertext medium, and that conversions are not perfect. In most cases, some hands-on editing will still be required. Several of the current file conversion and filtering software programs are listed in Table 10.3.

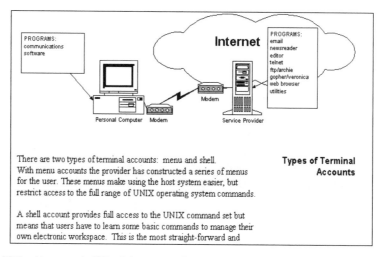

Figure 10.9   Unconverted Word document displayed using Print Preview.

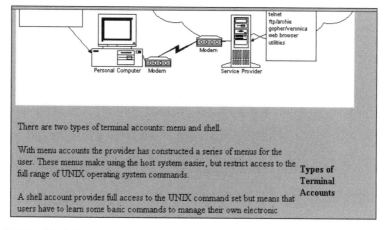

Figure 10.10   Word document converted to HTML and displayed in Netscape Navigator.

When converting large word processing documents that will have to be divided into smaller HTML files, consider splitting the files with the word processor prior to conversion. This is usually quicker and easier than picking your way through text and HTML tags.

Table 10.3   Document Conversion and Filtering Programs

Name	Source	Internet Location	Commercial, Freeware, or Shareware	Evaluation Copy Available?
BeyondPress	Astrobyte	http://www.astrobyte.com	Commercial	Yes
Cyberleaf	Interleaf	http://www.ileaf.com	Commercial	No
WebMaker	Harlequin Group	http://www.harlequin.co.uk	Commercial	Yes
WebWizard	NICE Technologies	nicetech@netcom.com	Commercial	Yes
Excel-to-Web	Baarns Publishing	http://www.baarns.com	Freeware	Yes
WEBIT	MultiMedia Xperts	http://www.he.net	Freeware	Yes
HTML Author	Grahame Cooper	http://www.salford.ac.uk	Shareware	Yes
RTFtoHTML	Chris Hector	http://www.sunpack.com	Shareware	Yes

Special Tools for Working with Content

A number of special tools are required to work with different areas of your Web site, particularly when dealing with images. The following sections deal with the specialized tools you should consider when you begin developing Web pages.

Image Acquisition

For some publications, particularly training manuals and how-to guides, computer screen snapshots (*screen captures* or *screen grabs*) provide a helpful aid for illustrating the material. The most familiar, and primitive, method for capturing the image of the screen being viewed is to hold down the Ctrl key and press Print Screen. The captured image contains everything displayed on the screen, and is stored in the Windows clipboard. At this point, it can be printed, pasted into a word processing document, or saved in a file for later editing. Specialized programs called screen grabbers, which are included in programs such as PaintShop Pro and HALO Desktop Imager provide a refined approach, making it possible to select specific portions of the screen for capture, and eliminating the need for later resizing or cropping.

Image Manipulation

In addition to text, there are files in other formats that you may want to include in your Web pages, notably graphics. The images can come from a variety of sources: they may have been created by artists using drawing packages; they may be pictures stored in electronic format through scanning; or they could be graphics digitized from photographs. To use them on a page, some manipulation is usually required—color adjustment, contrast changes, masking, cropping, resizing, and so on. While these adjustments can be made with the high-end graphics programs used to create images, far less expensive and cumbersome products, such as PaintShop Pro, are available to handle these tasks.

RESIZING AND CROPPING

Resizing or cropping is often necessary when incorporating a graphic into a page. Resizing can be used when an image is too large to fit well, either by itself or in combination with text, or to create *thumbnails*, a small version of a larger image. Thumbnails are often displayed in place of full-size images in order to save space on the screen and to eliminate retrieval of unnecessary graphics. If the reader needs to see the larger image, a hypertext link can be activated to retrieve it. Cropping is simply a method of cutting away the parts of an image that detract from the overall effect, while retaining the portion that is desirable.

ENHANCEMENTS

You may require image enhancements for images created by scanning, or that result from converting one graphics file type to another. These processes can result in graphics that have poor resolution, color balance, or contrast (too much or too little). Within limits, these pictures can be enhanced to provide better quality when viewed on the screen.

Some images are of such poor quality that, even with enhancements, there's little gain in quality—*don't* use them. Using no picture at all is better than using a poor one.

Image Maps

Image maps, as you may recall, provide the user with the ability to activate links by clicking directly on a picture that has been divided into hot spots. Hypertext tags are used to associate each of the defined areas (the hot spots) with other pages or objects on the network. The boundaries of these hot spots are specified in the source file through the use of screen coordinates, and typing in the numbers is, at best, a tedious process. There are editors available now that ease the burden of this particular aspect of HTML authoring. They work in the following manner:

1. The picture to be mapped is loaded into the editor.

2. The mouse is used to draw the outline (polygon, circle, or square) of a hot spot on the picture.

3. A URL is automatically associated with the hot spot.

One mapping product is Map This, and Figure 10.11 illustrates how easily image maps can be created with it. Other image mapping products work in much the same way. In the figure, the area marked out is indicated by an oval covered with cross-hatching; the accompanying dialog box lets the user specify a URL to be associated with this area.

Image Management

In a very short period of time, a large assortment of graphics images, such as icons and clip art, can accumulate. Keeping track of them, and remembering what is in each file, rapidly becomes impossible. Loading the individual files into a graphics program to determine the contents is a time-consuming task that can be eliminated with the use of specialized software. These programs can be used to scan a collection of graphics files and produce thumbnails for on-screen viewing. Two excellent pack-

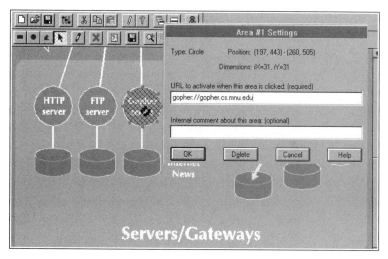

Figure 10.11 Using Map This to mark an area on the image and associate a URL with the area.

ness, the gains in functionality and performance of the tools used for viewing hypertext—the Web browsers—are unparalleled by any other category of PC desktop software used today. Equally as significant as these changes is the speed with which new or enhanced products are being brought to the marketplace.

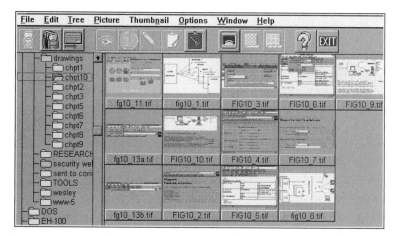

Figure 10.12 Using ThumbsPlus to create thumbnail images of graphics files.

Table 10.4 Software Tools for Working with Images

Name	Source	Internet Location	Commercial, Freeware, or Shareware	Evaluation Copy Available?
Asymetrix 3D/FX	Asymetrix Corp.	http://www.asymetrix.com	Commercial	No
CorelDraw 6.0	Corel Corporation	http://www.corel.com	Commercial	No
Executable	Execustaff Composition Service	http://www.execustaff.com	Commercial	No
FrameMaker	Adobe	http://www.adobe.com	Commercial	No
HiJaak 95	Quarterdeck	http://www.qdeck.com	Commercial	No
Mindshare	Silicon Graphics	http://www.sgi.com	Commercial	No
Transverter Pro	TechPool Software	http://www.techpool.com	Commercial	No
True Space	Caligari Corporation	http://www.caligari.com	Commercial	No
Visual Reality	Visual Software Inc.	http://netweb.com	Commercial	No
WebFORCE	Silicon Graphics	http://www.sgi.com	Commercial	No
WebImage	Group42	http://www.group42.com	Commercial	Yes
Fractal Viewer	Iterated Systems, Inc.	http://webber.iterated	Freeware	Yes
GraphX Viewer	Group42	http://www.group42.com	Freeware	Yes
Lview Pro	Leonardo Hadda Loureiro	http://world.std.com	Freeware	Yes

(Continued)

Table 10.4   Software Tools for Working with Images (Continued)

Name	Source	Internet Location	Commercial, Freeware, or Shareware	Evaluation Copy Available?
Map THIS!	ULead Systems	http://www.ulead.com	Freeware	Yes
ACDSee	ACD Systems, Ltd	http://ww.com	Shareware	Yes
Graphics Workshop	Alchemy Mindworks	http://www.mindworks.com	Shareware	Yes
HyperSnap	Greg Kochaniak	http://www.nb.net	Shareware	Yes
Image View 95	EarthWare	http://www.ewl.com	Shareware	Yes
JasCapture	JASC, Inc.	http://www.jasc.com	Shareware	Yes
Paint Shop Pro	JASC Inc.	http://www.jasc.com	Shareware	Yes
Thumbs Plus Inc.	Cerious Software,	http://www.cerious.com	Shareware	Yes
VuePrint 16-bit	Ed Hamrick	http://www.hamrick.com	Shareware	Yes

ages of this type are ThumbsPlus and PaintShop Pro. Figure 10.12 provides an example of the thumbnails created by ThumbsPlus when it scanned the sub-directory containing the artwork for this chapter. A cross-section of the various tools for working with images is provided in Table 10.4.

Viewing Web Pages

As the Internet, and the World Wide Web in particular, has moved into the forefront of the computer industry and public (consumer) conscious-

Don't Blink—You'll Miss the Changes

The original draft of Chapter 7, which was sent to our editor ten days before we wrote this, originally stated that Netscape Navigator was the only browser that provided support for Java applets. Since then, both Oracle and Microsoft have announced that the new releases of their browsers support both Java applets and ActiveX controls. Don't blink!

This continuous upgrade activity is a syndrome of today's computing environment, and it can wreak havoc with in-house software support, product maintenance, and training activities. Consequently, you should select a browser with a view toward standardizing on a single product, and staying with it as it evolves—or at least for as long as it continues to meet your operational needs.

Browsers

The function of a browser is to display hypertext documents on the computer screen and to enable the reader to manipulate the contents as required. The browser should provide, at a minimum, the following features:

- It should have the capability to display the selection of MIME types that are generally accepted as standard for any browser: ASCII, HTML, and GIF.

- The user should be able to scroll forward or backward through the material displayed (the current page) by using the directional arrow keys, the Page Up/Page Down keys, or the scroll buttons.

- It should be possible for the user to activate any hypertext links shown on the screen, whether they are text, icons, or image maps.

- Once pages have been retrieved, the reader should be able to navigate through them by using the browser interface as well as the links contained in the document.

- It should possess the capability to save any page displayed as a file on the user's PC, or to print that page at a printer the client PC can access.

- The browser should be capable of maintaining a list of pages viewed during that session. This is called a *hot list*, and it allows readers to go directly to a specific page in the list, rather than navigating back and forth through all of the pages that have been retrieved.

- Each user should be able to create and maintain a personal bookmark file of frequently accessed pages, making it easier and faster to access items of special interest.

While most browsers provide these capabilities, the differences lie in how these basic functions are implemented, and what additional features have been added. Take, for example, the browser's toolbar, which provides icons or drop-down menus that the user can activate to access available functions. Figure 10.13 provides a comparison between the default toolbars of Netscape Navigator Gold (V2.02) and Microsoft Internet Explorer (V3.0b).

Notice that the toolbars shown in the example provide access to many of the same functions, but that there are subtle differences in how the two toolbars implement these functions. Navigator has an additional row of buttons below the line showing the URL information for the currently-viewed page ("Location" on the Navigator toolbar; "Address" on Explorer) that provides links to pages at Netscape's Web site—for example, the "Net Search" button retrieves a page displaying various search engines. Microsoft provides a similar function, but without the use of an additional row of buttons—instead they have a Search button directly on the main toolbar. Both browsers also allow the user to store the locations of Web pages they want to revisit but, once again, each product takes a different approach to doing so—Netscape uses the "Bookmark" metaphor, whereas Microsoft uses "Favorites." The difference in design results from the fact that the Microsoft product is designed to be consistent with the Windows 95 desktop, and the browser therefore has the same iconic/functional characteristics.

Extended Functions

You can expect to find many additional features in the browsers that are currently available. Some of these features are:

- Support for HTML 3.0, as drafted

- Support for Netscape and Microsoft HTML extensions

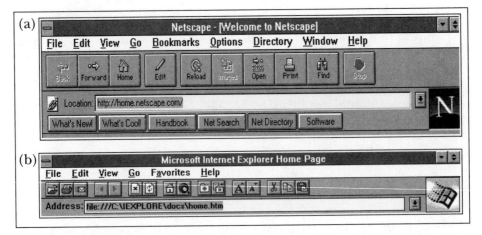

Figure 10.13   A comparison of the Netscape Navigator Gold 2.02 and Internet Explorer 3.0 toolbars.

- The ability to display inline JPG images

- The ability to display incoming images as they are transferred

- The ability to transfer multiple images simultaneously

- The ability to view the source code for the displayed page

- User-initiated page annotation

- Email capability with full MIME support

- User-customizable disk caching

- Customizable fonts for page display in the viewing area

There are other features available as well, but they relate more to browser use on the Internet (for example, the provision of PPP support, dialing directories, and newsreader capability), and as such, are not within the scope of this book.

Browser Selection

There are, of course, many factors that will influence your selection of the browser software to be used on your organization's intranet. However, assuming that company policy does not necessitate strict compliance with the end-to-end approach for product acquisition, the single most important criterion for browser selection is the information content of your Web site's publications.

If the pages are made up primarily of text and static graphics, then virtually any of the current crop of browsers will provide the functionality that is required. On the other hand, if your publications are multimedia in nature, the browser's capabilities must be far broader, and may have to include browser and plug-in support for audio and video files, as well as Java applets and ActiveX controls.

Another important consideration is security, which is also related to information content. For handling confidential or highly sensitive information, it may be necessary to run Web server software that supports either the SSL or S-HTTP standard, in which case the browser must also support one or both of these standards.

In the final analysis, the differences between the major browsers are not great, and as we've already seen, they are subject to very rapid change. The following guidelines will prove helpful in selecting one of these tools as the Web client software for your intranet.

- *Cost*—The size of the user base that needs to be provided with browsers will significantly affect cost, unless your company selects Microsoft's Internet Explorer, which, at present, is provided at no cost on the Microsoft Web site. If another browser is your product of choice, then it will be necessary to obtain a license for each user on your system or to negotiate a site license with the vendor, either of which can be a major expense.

- *Content*—If, in the early stages of your intranet project, the data types used are primarily text or graphics, almost any browser will suffice. However, as your Web site grows (and it will), the likelihood of a content shift to more interactive, multimedia pages will increase. The browser you select, then, should either have multimedia capability, or there should be some indication that the product will evolve to accommodate changing requirements. By circumventing a major software replacement through long-term planning, your company can protect its investment in software and employee training.

- *Employee Skills*—Try to select a browser that will enable you to leverage existing skills within the organization, thereby reducing training and support requirements. It's worthwhile to conduct a survey to see who has already acquired some Web-surfing experience, as well as to find out what browser they use.

Browser software is one case where establishing and enforcing a company-wide standard should be considered mandatory. Individual products display images and hypertext pages slightly differently, and support different HTML extensions; without a standard, your page creators will be swamped, writing multiple versions of each publication to accommodate the idiosyncratic behavior of various browser programs. The various browsers that are available for you to choose from are listed in Table 10.5.

For examples of how browsers differ in the way they handle text, graphics, and HTML tags, visit the ThreeToad WWW Browser Comparison site, located at **http://www.threetoad.com/main/Browser.html**.

There is a large selection of tools for creating and viewing HTML pages, tools whose functionality ranges from a bare-bones minimum to the very sophisticated, and that are priced to fit any budget. In Chapter 11 we'll expand our Web tool set by examining several of the general-purpose and specialized programming tools used in Web site construction.

Table 10.5   Web Browsers

Name	Source	Internet Location	Commercial, Shareware, or Freeware	Evaluation Copy Available?
Cyberjack 7.0	Delrina	http://www.delrina.com	Commercial	Yes
CyberSuite	Ipswitch Inc.	http://www.ipswitch.com	Commercial	Yes
Emmisary	Wollon-gong	http://www.twg.com	Commercial	Yes
Enhanced Mosaic	Spyglass	http://www.spyglass.com	Commercial	Yes
Internet Chameleon	Net-Manage, Inc. com	http://www.netmanage.com	Commercial	Yes

(Continued)

Table 10.5 Web Browsers

Name	Source	Internet Location	Commercial, Shareware, or Freeware	Evaluation Copy Available?
Internet Explorer	Microsoft	http://www.windows.microsoft.com/windows	Commercial	Yes
Internet Suite	Quarterdeck	http://www.qdeck.com	Commercial	No
Netscape Navigator	Netscape	http://home.netscape.com	Commercial	Yes
NetCruiser 2.0	Netcom	http://www.itl.co.uk/www/netcomm	Free to Netcom customers	No
Pipeline Browser	PSINet	http://www.pipeline.com	Freeware	Yes
America Online Browser	America Online	http://www.blue.aol.com	Included in AOL subscription	No
SlipKnot	MicroMind	info@micromind.com	Shareware	Yes
WinWeb and MacWeb	TradeWave	info@tradewave.com	Shareware	Yes

General-purpose and Specialized Programming Tools

General-purpose and Specialized Programming Tools

As with other applications (for example, accounting systems or database inventory systems), hypertext information systems usually require additional programming languages to construct and support the systems, particularly if any form of user interaction, or an interface to databases, is required. There are numerous programming tools available, which we've separated into two broad categories: general-purpose and specialized. We'll touch briefly on the general-purpose languages, but the focal points for intranet Web page applications are specialized tools such as Perl, Java, and ActiveX. Recently, tools for automating interface development have appeared as well, making this aspect of Web page development easier and faster.

General-purpose Programming Tools

General-purpose programming covers the languages typically used for PC application development. They are the bread-and-butter tools for developing a variety of stand-alone applications, or the interfaces needed in the client/server environment, and their strength lies in their ability to develop large, sophisticated applications that can handle virtually any type of data and information processing. Further, they are compiled languages, which means that the executable programs run faster than those of an interpreted language, whose code is processed each time it is run. Representative general-purpose languages in this category are C and C++. Their main disadvantage is their complexity (relative to languages such as Perl and Java, which are covered later in the chapter) and, as a result, it takes longer for new programmers to develop the skills required for production programming. In addition, the length of time needed to develop applications using these tools is greater. Although it's not a compiler language, Visual Basic is included as a general-purpose programming tool because it is the mainstay of the Microsoft Office applications environment, and heavily used for the development of GUI applications for the Windows environment.

With the appearance of newer tools that facilitate faster development through ease of use, developers are becoming less reliant on these older languages (age often being measured in months in the computer industry) for creating the various interfaces and routines used for Web page applications. Nonetheless, a brief review will provide some context for understanding why a language like Java could revolutionize Web page programming in the short space of a year.

Basic (Beginner's All-purpose Symbolic Instruction Code)

Basic goes back to 1963, when it was developed at Dartmouth College in Canada to provide an easy-to-learn, easy-to-use tool for student programming. Basic is an interactive, interpreted language that has since appeared on mainframes, minicomputers, and of course, the microcomputer. With the appearance of the PC, Basic was included as an integral part of the operating system (MS-DOS), and became a commonplace microcomputer programming language.

Visual Basic

Despite its name, Visual Basic is not a Visual Programming Language (VPL); rather, it is a textual programming language that uses a graphical GUI builder to make application development easier. The developer uses visual tools to design a screen consisting of objects that the user can manipulate—for example, an icon of a bullet that is activated with a mouse click (an *event*). Each event is associated with specific Basic code fragments that are executed when user input triggers the event (event-driven programming).

C

The C programming language dates back to the early 1970s, when it was created for use on PDP-11 computers at AT&T Bell Laboratories. It was broadly distributed with Unix in the 1980s, and has become the tool of choice for systems and applications programmers. In addition to being flexible, efficient, and portable, it is a powerful language that supports low-level interaction with the computer operating system and hardware. Depending on who you talk to, C may be described as either simple or complex.

C++

A superset of C, developed in 1986, this language also came out of Bell Laboratories. C++ was one of the earlier object-oriented programming (OOP) languages, the first being Simula-67, which was introduced about 1970. Since C++ appeared, the object paradigm has been applied to programming, systems development (including analysis and design), databases, and client/server technology.

OOP?

The term *object-oriented programming* describes a software environment in which a program consists of a collection of discrete objects, each of which is a self-contained collection of data structures and routines. Using an object-oriented (OO) approach results in objects that can be reused or shared by other programs.

An object's functionality is defined by the *methods* (procedures and functions) set out by its *class* (type definition). An object's methods are used to manipulate its *instance variables* (data), which are private, unless explicitly made available to other classes. Objects interact with each other by exchanging *messages* that

> name a method to be invoked, and may contain other arguments (similar to a procedure call). The named method determines the behavior of the object that receives the message.
>
> Conceptually, OOP requires a significantly different mindset than structured programming, and, as a result, many organizations have been slow to make the transition. However, its supporters cite the use of objects, which make more rapid development of complex applications possible, as one of its greatest strengths.

Specialized Programming Tools

With the tremendous growth of the Internet and the World Wide Web pushing the limits of hypertext applications and their functions, new tools were needed to provide the features demanded by users. As we've seen, the basic hypertext document model is static, unless CGI scripts, or programs, are used to dynamically transfer information between the client and the server. The main tools for interface programmers are Perl and Java, although others are now available—newer products such as JavaScript, ActiveX, and VBScript are rapidly establishing themselves as mainstream programming tools for Web environments.

Perl (Practical Extraction and Report Language)

Perl was developed as a general-purpose programming language that could be used to efficiently scan files containing large amounts of text, and to produce easily-formatted reports. Syntactically, it is a free-form language noted for its global variables and functions, neither of which need to be declared in advance. It is well-suited for writing one-up programs quickly, using far less code than would be needed by an equivalent C program. Since its creation, Perl's functionality has expanded to include file manipulation, system process manipulation, and interprocess communications over networks. It is also a highly portable language that can run under several operating systems, and on different computer architectures, including Intel/Windows NT. (There have been several ports of Perl to the NT environment, including one from Microsoft, which is in the Windows NT Resource Kit.) The current level of the language, version 5.002, features support for OOP.

Initially, this workhorse of the Unix world and the Internet was the only alternative to C as a language for handling CGI scripting. In spite of the appearance of newer and more powerful tools, this language—a software Swiss Army knife—continues to be very popular with systems and applications programmers, largely because of the vast collection of Perl routines freely available on the Internet.

REXX (Restructured Extended Executer)

REXX is a programming language designed by Michael Cowlishaw of IBM UK Laboratories in the early 1980s. It is a procedural programming language that has strong character and arithmetic manipulation features, as well as comprehensive debugging tools. Originally intended for use as a system utility in the IBM mainframe VM environment, REXX's strengths in file, data, and system process manipulation has led to its being ported to most of the other major computer environments. An ANSI standard, REXX is portable across a variety of platforms, ranging from the desktop PC to the mainframe, and across several operating systems, such as MVS/VM, VMS, Unix, OS/2, Macintosh, and DOS/Windows. From a programmer's perspective, REXX offers several features that make it an easy language to use, such as: easy readability, a minimum of special escape characters, mandatory notation and punctuation, reserved words, and variable type declarations (the language has only one data type—the character string). Paradoxically, its syntactical simplicity is offset by powerful control statements, as well as internal and external procedures. It is an interpreted language; however, there are compiled versions available. REXX is available as shareware or as commercial software, and like Perl, is a valuable tool for CGI scripting.

Java

The Java language is a simplified version of C++ that resulted from specific software programming requirements in the consumer electronics industry. Foremost among these requirements were the need for secure execution of code across a network and an alternative to the C and C++ programming languages, which were not well-suited to consumer electronics software development. The electronics programs were chip-specific, and each time a chip was changed, the code had to be recompiled to use the new software libraries that had been developed for the new chip. The Java design team was able to build a more suitable language from the ground up, based on the following criteria:

- It was to be an *efficient and reusable* language.

- It had to be *highly secure.*

- Both the language source code and binary form were to be *cross-platform.*

- The language had to promote the development of *bug-free code.*

The "The Java Language Environment: A White Paper," written by Java's developers James Gosling and Henry McGilton, is available at **http://java.sun.com/whitePaper/java-whitepaper-1.html**.

The Java design philosophy, and its resulting implementation, meet all of the stated requirements very well.

- *Efficient and Reusable*—Of all the broadly-distributed OOP languages, Java has the strongest object orientation. It has strong data typing, and most objects are defined (except simple types, like numbers and Boolean values). Efficiency gains are achieved by the elimination of all high-level programming language features that are not absolutely necessary; pointer arithmetic, structures, and multidimensional arrays are not included. Java also adds multi-threading, and automates memory allocation through the use of a program called a "garbage collector," which automatically frees up memory that is not in use.

- *Highly Secure*—To reduce the risk of bugs, the language eliminates the pointers that provide access to arbitrary addresses in memory, and enforces strict array bounds. Java also has a stringent set of rules used to verify both source code and the byte code produced by compilation.

- *Cross-platform*—Being strongly typed, Java is architecturally neutral; that is, types do not vary between platforms, as is the case with other languages. To achieve true cross-platform capability for Java source code and compiled binaries, the Java compiler produces an intermediate byte code that can be transferred to another platform, where it is interpreted and executed by the Java Virtual Machine, or Java VM, which is modeled on a very efficient but small CPU. The VM runs the compiled byte code as if it were machine language, converting the pseudo-machine code to actual hardware calls, by working with whatever OS the Java VM is resident on.

- *Bug-free Code*—There are many aspects of the Java language that lend themselves to creating a programming environment where application bugs occur less frequently; among them are: static and strong typing, enforcement of strict array bounds, the absence of undefined constructs, and the elimination of unsafe constructs. The fact that the language is concise, and that proficiency can be developed quickly, also contributes to the production of bug-free programs.

Figure 11.1 shows the sequence of events that take place in delivering a Java application to a client workstation, as well as how security is implemented in the application.

THE USES OF JAVA

Java provides the means to create small applications called *applets*, that are run on the client, rather than the server, side of a network. Applets contain code (or code and data) which, when executed on the PC, facilitate

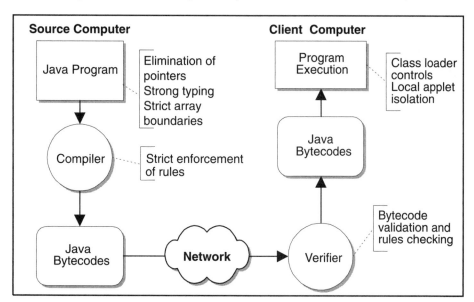

Figure 11.1   The delivery of secure Java applications to the desktop.

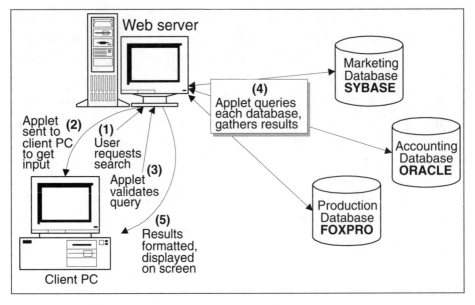

Figure 11.2   Using Java applets to search multiple databases.

dynamic, and bi-directional, data exchange between the client and the server. For example, as illustrated in Figure 11.2, an applet can be used to search multiple databases within the organization.

Because it is architecturally neutral, Java is ideally suited for building the processing and communications components of client interfaces that are needed for client/server applications. By merging World Wide Web protocols and Java, it is now possible to build *non-proprietary*, expandable, and extensible client/server applications, and to create distributed, object-oriented applications that can function independently of a given desktop architecture.

In terms of its potential applications, Java can be used in several ways, namely:

- Application prototyping
- Developing object-oriented client/server applications
- Database access—that is, data retrieval and updates
- Online transaction processing

Within the preceding categories, Java can be used in the construction of virtually any type of application, ranging from interactive simulations to the creation of live interfaces with stock market price information.

Hot Java

The following press releases illustrate the extent to which Java is impacting all aspects of the computer industry.

PC Week Online (May 23, 1996)—"The next course for Java is telephony. Sun Microsystems Inc., creator of the Java programming language, announced today it has teamed up with Northern Telecom to develop Java-powered telephone handsets that will enable users to surf the Internet."

Business Wire (April 29, 1996)—"IBM today announced that the next version of OS/2(a) [alpha version] Warp, code-named Merlin, will integrate Sun Microsystem's Java(b) [beta] programming language when Merlin ships in the second half of this year. In addition to incorporating a Java-enabled Web browser into Merlin, IBM will integrate Java into the operating system, allowing it to natively run Java applications and Internet applets independent of a Web browser."

PRNewswire (May 20, 1996)—"Corel Corporation (TSE: COS; Nasdaq-NNM: COSFF), an award-winning developer and marketer of productivity applications, graphics, and multimedia software, announced today at an Oracle press conference that its Corel Barista publishing technology will allow users to create Java-based content for the Network Computer. The NC is Oracle's implementation of easy-to-use, low-cost computing devices based upon open Internet standards."

JavaScript

Netscape Communications' JavaScript is a scripting language that lets Web page developers tie together HTML pages, Netscape plug-ins, and Java applets. This language, which is based on Netscape's LiveScript (an HTML scripting language), provides an object-based, cross-platform vehicle for creating interactive Web pages. While there are many similarities between JavaScript and Java, there are also key differences; Table 11.1 compares these two products.

The easiest way to distinguish between Java and JavaScript is to remember that Java is used to *create* objects and applets, whereas JavaScript is used to *control* the behavior of objects and applets.

JavaScript is capable of recognizing and responding to user actions; for instance, it can be used to carry out an instruction (such as to display a pop-up window or execute an applet) in response to a mouse click. Similarly, you can open or exit a page to invoke changes. This feature makes the language well-suited to programming routines that can be executed locally before network transmission occurs—for example, validating input on forms.

Syntactically, JavaScript is similar to Java, and supports Java's flow control, expression syntax, and types (Boolean, numeric, and string). It differs from Java in that it is an interpreted language, executed when called by the Netscape interpreter, and can be run from any page without requiring special file access privileges. As a scripting language, it's fairly secure, since no writes to a user's hard drive are permitted.

Table 11.1 A Comparison of JavaScript and Java Language Attributes

JavaScript	Java
Code integrated with, and embedded in, HTML source file	Code (applets) separate from HTML source code
Interpreted and executed on client	Compiled on server; executed on client
Object-based; the code uses built-in, extensible objects, but no classes or inheritance	Object-oriented; applications have classes with inheritance
Loose typing; variable data types are not declared	Strong typing; variable data types must be declared
Dynamic binding; objective references are checked at run time	Static binding; object references are checked at compile time
Automatic write to hard drive not allowed	Automatic write to hard drive not allowed

ActiveX

ActiveX is a repackaging of Microsoft's OLE and OCX, the intent being to provide the same capability as Java for interactive Web page development. It enables Windows and Web page developers to take advantage of the more than 1,000 OLE/OCX controls that have been developed for Windows applications, and which are supported by a wide variety of programming languages, including Delphi, Visual C++, and Borland C+.

Visual Basic Scripting Edition (VBScript)

VBScript, a subset of Microsoft's Visual Basic language, is implemented as an interpreter for Web browsers and other applications that use ActiveX, OLE, and Java applets. It differs from Visual Basic in that it does not use strict types, nor does it support file I/O or direct access to the operating system. Used with Internet Explorer, VBScript provides the functional equivalent to JavaScript and the Netscape browser.

ActiveX vs. Java

Although there are some similarities between ActiveX and Java, the differences are important to anyone building object-oriented client/server applications in an internetworked environment. Both can run over a network, and support an object-oriented feature called inheritance (the ability of an object to inherit functionality from its parent object), but Java applets are platform-independent, whereas ActiveX controls are not. One of the most important features for distributed applications is security, and only Java applets execute in a protected environment on the PC. Finally, ActiveX controls are not bi-directional; information travels in one direction only, from the server to the client. Java applets, on the other hand, are bi-directional, and can, for example, send messages to multiple servers on the network during a database search.

More Java

The Java language has generated a flurry of new development activities in the software industry, notably the creation of tools that make Java application development easier and faster.

It is an accepted fact that interpreted code, by nature, executes far slower than compiled code, and Java is no exception. Although Java applets execute significantly faster than scripted programs, they still run much slower than equivalent C++ binaries (up to 20 times slower, by some reckoning). For all that Java source code is compiled to create byte codes, these run-time programs are *interpreted* during execution on the Java VM.

Techniques for improving performance have been put forward by several vendors as part of an overall Java Integrated Development Environment (IDE). Three of these are discussed below.

SYMANTEC CAFE

Cafe is a 32-bit IDE for creating applets and embedding them in Web pages; it is also used to develop stand-alone applications for Java-supported environments. This creation and debugging environment includes tools for managing source code files, editing classes and class relationships, visual design, debugging, and source code parsing/editing, to name a few. Symantec has addressed the speed issue by providing a faster byte code compiler and an enhanced Java Virtual Machine. Symantec Cafe is available from the Symantec Web site at **http://www.symantec.com.**

BORLAND LATTE

Borland's entry into the Java IDE is called Latte, and is based on the Rapid Application Development (RAD) concepts and techniques used for the Delphi visual design environment. Latte will provide a visual design environment, high-performance compilers, database connectivity features, and a complete set of tools for code design, development, and testing. Borland is also currently testing a product called *App*Accelerator, which they call a Java just-in-time compiler, to address application performance issues. *App*Accelerator uses two techniques to increase performance: it translates byte code to native machine code, and it only translates the methods in a Java class as they are used. (Using native machine code increases performance at the cost of some portability, since the just-in-time compiler must be installed on the computer that will be compiling the byte code.) By using these two methods, Borland anticipates speed gains up to ten times faster for Java applets. The planned release date for Latte is fall 1996, and more information is available from the Borland Web site at **http://www.borland.com**.

SUN MICROSYSTEMS JAVA WORKSHOP

Sun's IDE, Java WorkShop, is now available from its Web site at **http://www.sun.com**. Java WorkShop's tool set features: a project manager, a visual design tool, a source code viewer and editor, a code compiler, a code debugger, an applet tester, and a Web publication tool. There has been no mention of specific Sun products related to the issue of applet execution speeds, but Java has been working with the Borland team to facilitate the development and testing of *App*Accelerator.

In the following chapter, we'll look at other products that can be used to automate Java-based Web page/database interface development, as well as at Web application builders that are broader in scope.

The Data: Interfaces, Delivery, and Indexing Tools

12

The Data: Interfaces, Delivery, and Indexing Tools

We've examined the tools for authoring and viewing hypertext pages in some detail, and touched briefly on the subject of connecting Web pages to various data sources. In this chapter, we will expand on the issues and options related to interface building, and look at some of the products that are now available for automating this process. We'll also examine Web server software, whose primary role is delivering Web pages to the users' workstations on request. (Since collaborative or workgroup computing involves file and document sharing, these programs are covered, along with the Web servers.) The final topic covered is information search-and-retrieval software, tools that make it possible for your users to find information easily and quickly.

Linking Web Pages to Data Sources

There are two ways to connect Web pages to databases: purchase off-the-shelf products that provide interfaces, or build them yourself. The use of third-party products will shorten the development process, whereas the custom-built interfaces provide greater flexibility in dealing with the particular gateway needs within your organization.

Pre-built Interfaces

The products that provide Web database integration are divided into the following broad categories:

- Proprietary gateways provided by a vendor to link the Web pages to their own database server

- Third-party gateways that support multiple relational DBMSs and ODBC databases

- Text and document databases for storing Web pages

- Database application development tools with Web page access functions

- Web servers and browsers that are database-aware

As with anything else related to the Internet, the area of Web/database integration is a rapid-growth area, with many products appearing weekly. A representative example is provided in each of these categories in this chapter.

PROPRIETARY GATEWAY

Oracle was among the first companies to provide a gateway to its database. It took the form of the Oracle World Wide Web Interface Kit, which consisted of five modules developed by Oracle users. While not an Oracle product per se, it was available as freeware on the Internet and was sanctioned by the company. The kit provided the foundation for a new product family called the Oracle WebSystem, consisting of client and server components designed to interact with the Oracle 7 DBMS.

IBM was quick to get into this area as well, providing the DB2 World Wide Web Connection for its DB2 users. Their gateway consists of a CGI program and macro files that map form fields to placeholders in an SQL statement.

THIRD-PARTY GATEWAY

One of the first products to appear in this category was Cold Fusion from Allaire. Cold Fusion uses its own set of markup tags called Database Markup Language (DBML), which contain SQL queries and instructions that are embedded in the hypertext page. No CGI programming is needed since the product uses one generic CGI executable that interprets the DBML tags, and interacts with the Web and database servers.

TEXT/DOCUMENT DATABASE

The industry leader in this area, Lotus Notes, was upgraded to include a module called InterNotes Web publisher, which is a program that converts Notes documents and databases into HTML. It structures files in accordance with the view of document information provided by Notes, and lets users browse the HTML pages following the same path that a Notes user would see.

WEB-AWARE APPLICATION DEVELOPMENT TOOL

Micorim has a product called R:WEB, which provides a Web-aware front end that interfaces with the company's R:BASE relational database package, and uses a forms-based approach for data entry and query-building. When an R:WEB link is activated, and the database is accessed, the user sees an R:BASE form as an HTML form on the screen.

DATABASE-AWARE SERVERS AND BROWSERS

Microsoft's Internet Information Server illustrates the growing trend toward database awareness in the server marketplace. A component called the Internet Database Connector (IDC) connects to SQL and ODBC-compliant databases such as Microsoft Access, Oracle7, Informix, and Sybase.

Building Your Own Gateway Interfaces: CGI

Common Gateway Interface scripts are heavily used to provide the essential link between Web pages, servers, and the information contained in your organization's databases. By using the CGI environment variables, it's possible to pass data back and forth between the user's client program (the browser) and the database via the DBMS. In addition to knowing the programming language used for writing CGI programs (for example, Perl, C, or C++), the script programmer also has to know the ins and outs of HTML, CGI, and HTTP and have a thorough understanding of the DBMS being used and the structure of the database's contents. He needs to ensure that the CGI program restructures the information passed from the client into the appropriate format for the DBMS, and that the database output is processed and reformatted for display on the client's Web page. Figure 12.1 illustrates the page-to-database relationship and the elements within each that the programmer must deal with.

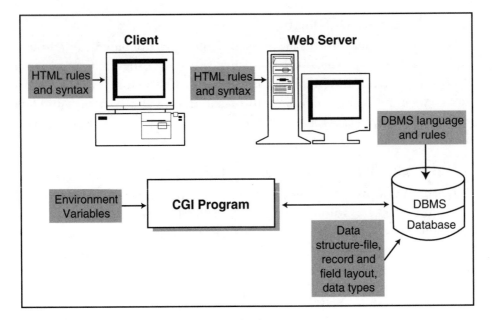

Figure 12.1 Interfacing a Web page with a database.

Gateway Architecture

Gateway architecture refers to the method used to connect databases to Web pages—that is, whether the required extensions (code that extends the function of programs such as Web server software) are provided on the server side or the client side.

THE SERVER-SIDE EXTENSIONS

Server-side extensions either use CGI or APIs to provide linkage. Using CGI, two techniques can be used. The first involves running the database application program as a CGI executable itself, with the application process being forked (duplicated) for every database request; with the second technique, the database application runs as a daemon process, and the CGI program is used to dispatch requests rather than accessing the DBMS.

In the case of APIs, the database application can be implemented with either the extensible API, or proprietary server method. In the case of extensible API, the application uses the extensible API of the Web server and the API of the particular DBMS being used. The application is dynamically linked with the server process, but the server itself has no knowledge of a specific DBMS. With a proprietary server, the extensible API of the server is also used, but the API from the database is used to link the application with the server process.

THE CLIENT-SIDE EXTENSIONS

Client-side extensions are either handled using an external viewer, or by browser extensions. In the first case, the application is launched by the Web server, and runs on the client side without any server support. The second type of client-side operation uses a browser extension (which understands the particular DBMS being used) to fetch and interpret information from the server where the database application typically resides.

Listing 12.1 contains a CGI program contributed by Serge Lezhnin, a student at Ural State Technical University in Ekaterinburg, Russia, and serves to illustrate the type of programming that can be required for CGI scripts. This particular program searches the site it's installed on, and locates all the text files (based on the filename extension) stored on the computer.

Listing 12.1   A CGI program written in C++

```
// Search
// Copyright Serge Lezhnin (c) 1996
// E-Mail: Serge_L@sges1.gs.pssr.e-burg.su
// HTTP://serg.gs.pssr.e-burg.su/
// Version 96.04.24
// Changes:
//   - Changing code to use updated CGIUTIL
//   - Adding support for .conf file
// Version 96.04.04
#include "..\cgiutil\cgiutil.h"
// Search string in form must have name "search"

// Search .conf file name
#define NAME_OF_CONF  "Search.conf"
// URL to root (where you want to begin searching)
#define URL_TO_ROOT   "URL_TO_ROOT"
// Path to root (where you want to begin searching)
#define PATH_TO_ROOT  "PATH_TO_ROOT"

// Length of the file search buffer
#define SEARCH_BUF_LEN 1024
```

```
// This function checks extention of the file name
BOOL CheckExtention(CString& path, CStringArray& exts)
{
   int idx=path.ReverseFind('.');
   if (idx<0) return FALSE;
   CString ext(path.Right(path.GetLength()-idx-1));
   ext.MakeUpper();
   for (idx=0; idx<exts.GetSize(); idx++)
    if (ext==(exts.GetAt(idx))) return TRUE;
   return FALSE;
};


// This functions searches file for searchStr
BOOL SearchFile(CString& fileName, CString& searchStr)
{
   CFile sfile;
   char buffer[SEARCH_BUF_LEN];
   UINT nread;
   if (!sfile.Open((LPCTSTR)fileName,CFile::modeRead)) return FALSE;
   nread=sfile.Read(buffer,SEARCH_BUF_LEN);
   do
   {
    CString bufstr(buffer,nread);
    bufstr.MakeUpper();
    if (bufstr.Find((LPCTSTR)searchStr)>=0) return TRUE;
    nread=sfile.Read(buffer,SEARCH_BUF_LEN);
   } while (nread==SEARCH_BUF_LEN);
   return FALSE;
};


// This function write out link to found document
void AddRef(CString& filename, CStringPairs& PI)
{
   CString url(filename);
   CString ptr(PI.Value(PATH_TO_ROOT));
   int idx;
   // cutting disk spec (PATH_TO_ROOT)
   if (url.GetLength()<=ptr.GetLength()) url="";
   else url=url.Right(url.GetLength()-ptr.GetLength());
// while (url[0]==ptr[idx]&&url.GetLength())
// {
//   url=url.Right(url.GetLength()-1);
//   idx++;
// };
```

```
  // transforming '\' to '/'
  for (idx=0; idx<url.GetLength(); idx++)
   if (url[idx]=='\\') url.SetAt(idx,'/');
  // adding html tags
  CString urlname=PI.Value(URL_TO_ROOT)+url;
  url="<br><a href=\""+urlname+"\">"+urlname+"</a>";
// printf((LPCTSTR)url);
  cout<<url;
};


// This function perform search
void Searching(CString& path, CStringArray& exts, CString& searchStr,
 CStringPairs& PI)
{
  if (path.GetLength()&&path[path.GetLength()-1]!='\\') path+='\\';
  WIN32_FIND_DATA findata;
  HANDLE findhand=FindFirstFile((LPCTSTR)(path+"*"),&findata);
  BOOL bFound=FALSE;
  if (findhand!=INVALID_HANDLE_VALUE) bFound=TRUE;

  // main loop
  while (bFound)
  {
   // Check if it's a directory
   if (findata.dwFileAttributes&FILE_ATTRIBUTE_DIRECTORY)
   {
    // Recursive call to this func
    CString subpath(findata.cFileName);
    if (subpath!="."&&subpath!="..")
    {
     subpath=path+subpath;
     Searching(subpath,exts,searchStr,PI);
    }
   }
   else
   {
    if (CheckExtention(CString(findata.cFileName),exts))
    {
     CString sfname(path);
     sfname+=findata.cFileName;
     if (SearchFile(sfname,searchStr))
     {
      AddRef(sfname,PI);
     }
    }
   }
```

```
      bFound=FindNextFile(findhand,&findata);
    }
    FindClose(findhand);
};
int main()
{
    CString sinput;

    // Getting input:
    //sinput=GetServerInput();

    // Transforming input parameters:
    CStringPairs PI;
    GetServerInput(PI);
    AddConfiguration(PI,CString(NAME_OF_CONF));

    CString searchString(PI.Value("search"));
    if (!searchString.GetLength())
    {
     HTMLBegin("Empty search string!");
     cout<<"<a href=\""<<PI.Value(URL_TO_ROOT)<<"\">Back to root
  document</a><br>\n";
     HTMLEnd();
     return 0;
    }

    CStringArray extentions;
    extentions.Add(CString("HTM"));
    extentions.Add(CString("HTML"));
    extentions.Add(CString("TXT"));
    extentions.Add(CString("TEXT"));
    extentions.Add(CString("DOC"));

    HTMLBegin("Found documents");

    searchString.MakeUpper();
    Searching(CString(PI.Value(PATH_TO_ROOT)),extentions,searchString,PI);

    cout<<"<hr><a href=\""<<PI.Value(URL_TO_ROOT)<<"\">Back to root
  document</a><br>\n";
    HTMLEnd();

    return 0;
};
```

Given this example, you can better appreciate the increased complexity of the programming required when CGI programs are used to prepare database queries and format the results for display on the client's Web page. This is why the appearance of tools to automate interface programming have been very well received—they can shorten the development cycle, reduce the number of program bugs, and build application components that require less maintenance in the long run.

Automating Interface and Application Programming

Tools for developing Web database interfaces range from those that handle CGI script generation to ones that provide a sophisticated development environment and are designed to automate screen production, build gateway interfaces, and produce any other routines that a complex Web application may require.

The early attempts at automating interface development were really nothing more than collections of scripts and templates, which could be modified by a programmer to meet the requirements of the particular interface he was building. During the past year, the number and types of options available to interface programmers have increased dramatically, and now we're seeing GUI software with point-and-click and drag-and-drop programming. The products in this category are evolving quickly from simple interface builders to full-blown development environments for Web applications.

Cold Fusion, from Allaire, was a pioneer product in this category of software, and provides all the functions needed to make an interface developer's life easier. Since its inception, this product's functionality has increased to the point where it can no longer be considered an interface builder, but is, in fact, one of the new breed of products used for building Web applications. Cold Fusion provides a good benchmark for ease of use, as well as the level of functionality you should expect from any program marketed as an application-development tool for Web sites.

In addition to the base product, Cold Fusion 1.5, there are several other add-ons available that can handle most of the development activities you'll encounter while building a Web application. These companion products, called Cold Fusion Fuel Packs, are:

- *Web Application Wizards*—These are a set of visual tools that walk the developer through all the steps required to build data entry or drill-down search applications. (There are some examples of this in action a little later in this chapter.)

- *Cold Fusion Java Graphlets*—This collection of Java applets has been developed to provide graphing capability for displaying information from databases. This is done by extracting raw data from the database, processing it through an applet, and then creating a graph that is displayed on the user's page.

- *Internet Server API Module*—The ISAPI module replaces the CGI on servers which support API, such as Microsoft Internet Server or Process Software's Purveyor. By eliminating the need to call an executable through CGI, the server can work directly with the Cold Fusion service, increasing performance.

- *Cold Fusion Database Component Framework (DCF)*—This set of Java elements is used to build applets that interact with databases through Cold Fusion.

- *Data-Driven VRML*—Based on the VRML standard, this module enables developers to create 3D representations of data from the databases that are linked with the Web pages.

The following screens illustrate some of the tools provided by Cold Fusion for developing database gateway interfaces. From the main screen of the Cold Fusion Administrator, shown in Figure 12.2, you can handle all the tasks associated with the databases that your application will use. (Cold Fusion can handle calls using either the SQL or ODBC standard.)

From this starting point, the developer can reference the data sources to be used, and control general access to a database. It's also possible to define database permissions such as full access, or allow only limited operations (Select, Insert, Update, Delete, or Run Stored Procedures) for the

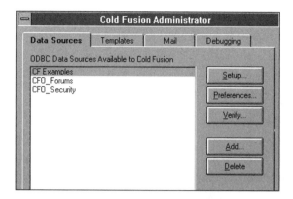

Figure 12.2 The main screen of the Cold Fusion Administrator.

individual users. Options for Template usage, Mail, and Debugging (shown in Figure 12.3) are also available.

The debugging feature in Cold Fusion is strong, enabling the developer to gather information about CGI variable contents and information related to queries (time, records, and SQL statements). In addition, it is possible to isolate information from specific IP addresses that query the database. All of this information can either be written to a log file, or sent as email to a specified address.

To support rapid application development, Allaire provides Web Application Wizards—progressive dialog boxes that enable you to build data in-

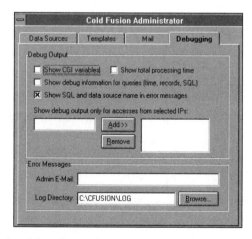

Figure 12.3 Cold Fusion debugging options.

put screens or drill-down query screens for finding and displaying information in a database. Figure 12.4 shows the starting point for building a query application using the Data Drill-Down Wizard.

The entire application is built by using a sequence of nine dialog boxes, which provide the information that Cold Fusion needs to build the HTML input form the user sees on the screen. This information includes:

- Identifying the SQL/ODBC data sources

- Selecting the database tables to be used

- Specifying the fields to be used for table joins

- Selecting fields to search against, as well as the condition a match is based on (such as less than or equal to)

- Customizing the fields for use on the input form, such as a text box or radio button, and selecting the validation rules for input (for example, if it must be an integer)

- Picking the fields to be displayed on the results screen

- Specifying the caption and column widths for fields displayed as results

- Choosing the fields displayed for a detailed drill-down from the results screen

- Selecting a unique identifier on the detail screen to serve as an anchor for drill-down

Figure 12.4   The Data Drill-Down Wizard for building a query application.

By following this simple sequence of events, a developer can use Cold Fusion to generate both an HTML input form and a results screen that can either integrate with a database, or execute multiple SQL statements against several databases.

As we indicated earlier, Cold Fusion is by no means the only application development product available, but in terms of cost, flexibility, and ease of use, it has certainly established a benchmark that can be used to compare similar products in its class.

At the high end of the tools available for Web application development are products like Bluestone's Sapphire/Web, which was used to construct the hypertext-based applications for Eli Lilly and Company and the Kellogg Peat Marwick Group (KPMG), which were discussed in Chapter 4. Although Sapphire/Web is considered to be a professional developer's tool, its interface and program logic are such that it is highly useable for a more casual programmer, who has moderate skills in CGI-database interface programming. This product is a visual programming tool, which treats all the components in a given Web application (stored procedures, database SQL commands, files, and so on) as objects that can be linked by the programmer to build an application. Any required CGI is generated by Sapphire/Web as C++ executables, which offer the advantage of portability and fast execution speed. It also means that existing C/C++ code, files, and libraries can be fully integrated into applications developed using the product.

Sapphire/Web supports a broad range of platforms (SGI, Sun, HP, IBM, DECAlpha, Intel), browsers (HTML 2.0 or later), servers (any HTTP, S-HTTP, or SSL), authoring tools (any capable of handling HTML 2.0 or greater), databases (Oracle, Sybase, Informix, Microsoft SQL Server, ODBC), and object types (Database Stored Procedures, Dynamic SQL, Files, Executables, Functions, OLE).

In addition to providing a robust visual programming environment that automates all the programming tasks, the product also includes editors to allow the developer to manually edit different code, such as the HTML pages and functions. (Editors are built into the product, but full support is provided for most of the third-party editors you might want to configure to work with Sapphire/Web.)

As an added bonus, Sapphire/Web provides an application-development management function for use in developing larger applications that consist of hundreds of screens and images. Each application is treated as a separate project, with all components tied to the project name, making them easy to track and maintain. This visual tool for application management is illustrated in Figure 12.5, which shows the map for a project called "bookstor.swb". If an element shown on the map can be directly edited, by double clicking with the mouse when the cursor is on the element's name will invoke the appropriate editor.

The steps required to create a Web application that integrates databases and hypertext pages are fairly simple, and are as follows:

1. Create your HTML forms (used for data input) and HTML templates (used to control the appearance of the data returned to the user from the query operation). These can be created with either the built-in editor or other HTML authoring tools like Microsoft Word, Front Page, or HoTMetaL, all of which can be configured to work with Sapphire/Web.

2. Use the object browser to find the application objects from Sapphire/Web. These can be:

   • Dynamic SQL

   • Functions

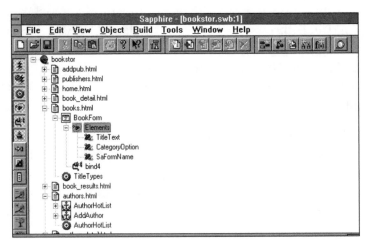

Figure 12.5 The map of a bookstore project, showing pages, links, and elements.

- Executables

- File (for read and write)

3. Select the object you want to use, and Sapphire/Web will bring up an "Object Bind Editor" with appropriate arguments, results, and special editors that can be used.

4. Drag-and-drop from your HTML documents and components onto the Object Bind Editor. This "binds" HTML elements—such as a text input field or an option menu—to search arguments, and binds search results to other HTML elements, such as an ordered list or table. Sapphire/Web automatically populates the returned data into your HTML templates.

5. Add conditional processing code, or modify the default methods of populating data.

6. Generate code in pure C or C++. This generates a CGI program for immediate use. The CGI program can be then be loaded and tested in the HTTP server CGI directory that was specified when Sapphire/Web was installed.

The Data Object Browser, shown in Figure 12.6, allows the user to browse data sources, in this case an SQL database for a bookstore application. By

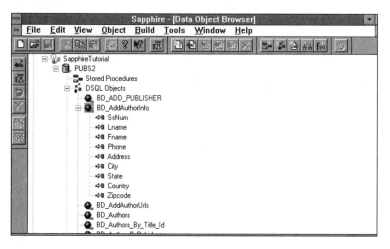

Figure 12.6 Using the Data Object Browser to view data sources.

selecting an object, for example, the BD_AddAuthorInfo record in Figure 12.6, the Data Object Editor can be invoked to directly edit the object, as shown in Figure 12.7.

With tools like Sapphire/Web, it is possible to quickly build and deploy sophisticated Web-based applications throughout your organization. In addition, these Web pages, and the information they contain, are dynamically updated because of the way this product handles HTML files. Sapphire/Web uses a concept the vendor calls "HTML templates." These are normal HTML files that are read and updated by the CGI at runtime (in other words, when they are requested). When a page is altered, any changes are reflected immediately, and are displayed the next time the page is accessed, providing employees with direct access to the most current information.

Table 12.1 provides a listing of the many interface and application building tools available today, and were selected because they are non-proprietary. For example, dbWeb, from Microsoft, was not included, because it would only work with the Internet Information Explorer.

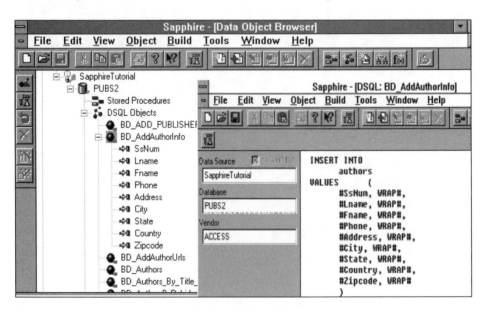

Figure 12.7　Using the Data Object Editor to edit an object.

Sharing Information: Web Server and Workgroup Software

The Web server forms the core of your intranet; consequently, the Web server software is a critical component of the system. The basic function of this software is to process and respond to all incoming requests for files, whether they are hypertext pages or other file types specified in the pages, like inline graphics. (Like other Internet-related products, the selection of available server software has increased dramatically in less than 2 years, from 3 or 4 in 1994, to 28 at the time this was written. This tally includes only the server software that runs in a Windows environment, so there are even more available.) Given this large group of products to select from, it should come as no surprise that levels of functionality and cost vary greatly. Disregarding cost, server software can be reviewed on the basis of features and specific functions, which we've grouped into the following categories:

- *Platforms*—The processor platforms the software will run on

- *Launching*—Refers to how server software can be configured to operate on the server hardware—for example, support for multiple Web sites

- *Logging*—The method and scope of activity logs kept by the Web server system as a whole

- *Protocol Support*—The variety of protocols the server can support in addition to the HTTP 1.0 specification

Table 12.1   Products to Automate Hypertext Application Building

Name	Source	Internet Location	Commercial, Freeware or Shareware	Evaluation Copy Available?
Butler, Tango	EveryWare Development	http://www.every-ware.com	Commercial	No
Cold Fusion	Allaire Corp.	http://www.allaire.com	Commercial	Yes
iBasic	iBasic.com Inc.	http://www.ibasic.com	Commercial	Yes
JAM WEB	JYACC	http://www.jyacc.com	Commercial	Yes
Sapphire /Web	Bluestone Inc.	http://www.blue-stone.com	Commercial	Yes

- *Includes*—Information can be included in HTML documents from either the client or server side

- *Security*—Covers authentication, encryption, and access control to the server and the information residing on it

- *Other*—Nice-to-have features that generally make life easier for a Web server administrator

For more technically inclined readers, we've provided Tables 12.2 through 12.7, which provide a listing of specific items in each of the preceding categories, and can be used as a checklist for evaluating server software. To simplify matters, we'll assume that you're using a CPU as your platform.

We're now going to take a closer look at one server product that will serve to illustrate the features you would expect to find in an easy-to-use, non-proprietary server software. The program is WebSite, from O'Reilly. It's a well-rounded product that is easy to work with, and provides the functionality needed for an internal Web site server. For non-Unix types, such as myself, the WebSite interface is very intuitive; I was able to get the server (WebSite version 1.0) up and running as a Windows NT service in about 20 minutes. It took an additional 10 minutes to try on the T-shirt that comes with the software and to install a complete Web site (using files on hand from a site we had previously created for a client).

Table 12.2 Launching

Item	Description
Different directory roots	If the OS permits a single CPU to have more than one IP address, the Web server can use different IP addresses to indicate different Web sites on the same computer. Each address would get a different directory tree to serve from.
Operation under Windows NT	The server can run as an NT application, service, or both.

Table 12.3   Logging

Item	Description
Log file recycling	New log files can be started according to a set schedule, and old ones archived.
Customization of normal (hit) log entries	The format of these log entries can be changed, and new fields added.
Support for multiple logs	The server can write to multiple log files using different formats for each file.
Support for non-hit log entries	Events outside of normal logging (server load or elapsed time, for example) can be recorded in log files.
CGI log entry	CGI scripts can be used to create log entries.
Performance measurement logs	The server collects performance measurements such as load, hits per minute, requests refused due to load, and number of requests aborted.
User tracking	The server automatically tracks user movement around the pages on the Web site.

Table 12.4   Protocol Support

Item	Description
HTTP 1.0 header handling	The aspects of the HTTP 1.0 specification that relate to how some header information is handled (If-Modified-Since, Accept, and User-Agent). It is assumed that the server information can accommodate these items without using CGI scripts.
HTTP 1.1 PUT	Supports the HTTP 1.1 PUT command that allows remote users to transfer files to the Web server.
HTTP 1.1 persistent connections	Connection with an HTTP 1.1 client can be kept open for more than a single request.
HTTP 1.1 full URI (Universal Resource Indicator)	The server can understand requests using absolute paths or the full URI, as specified in HTTP 1.1.
Server name response	Each server should respond with its name in the "Server:" response header without any spaces in the name.

(Continued)

Table 12.4   Protocol Support (Continued)

Item	Description
Non-supported methods response	The server will automatically start a program or script in response to a non-supported method sent by a client.
Server state variables	The administrator can access server state variables from CGI or other scripts.
Image mapping	There is built-in image map handling, which eliminates the need for CGI scripting.
SNMP agent	The software includes an SNMP agent for handling remote services.
Scripting language	There is a built-in scripting language that the administrator can use for customizing the site.
Windows CGI	The software supports the Windows implementation of the CGI protocol.

Table 12.5   Includes

Item	Description
HTML comments	Comments in the HTML document can be expanded by the server before the page is sent out.
Request headers	The values of request headers can trigger server-side includes, for example, "if-User-Agent-is Netscape".
Forced includes	The server can force includes at the beginning or end of a document. This can be applied to all documents, a certain document type, or documents in a particular directory.
HTTP headers in response	The server can automatically include any administrator-defined headers in all documents.

Table 12.6   Security

Item	Description
Password	Can require a password from the user.
SSL v.2	Supports SSL version 2 protocol.
SSL v.3	Supports SSL version 3 protocol.
S-HTTP	Supports S-HTTP.
PCT	Supports the PCT protocol.
Domain name restriction	Can deny access to some or all documents based on the domain name of the user making the request.
IP address restriction	Can deny access to some or all documents based on the requester's IP address.
Configurable user groups	The administrator can create multiple user groups based on domain name, IP address, or authenticated user name.
Changes to access control list	The user access control list can be changed without having to restart the server.
Access restrictions on portion of document	Portions of a document can be hidden based on the user access control list.
URL-based access rules	Access can be controlled based on the URL specified, rather than a specific file.
File-based security model	Basic security rules are applied to all files if no other rules have been explicitly invoked.
Hierarchical permissions	In the absence of permissions, directory permissions are based on those in place higher in the directory structure.

Table 12.7 Other Features

Item	Description
GUI for setup	The server is configured using a GUI.
GUI for maintenance .graphically.	Server running information is displayed.
Remote maintenance	The server configuration can be changed from a computer other than the server.
Real-time performance measurement	The software provides real-time information about server activity, such as requests refused or request turnaround time.
Action according to output media type	Specified action is taken, or programs are run automatically, if the document being sent out is a specified media type.
Serves other TCP protocols	This can serve other protocols, such as FTP and Gopher.
Automatic directory tree	If a URL requested is for a directory rather than a specific file, the server can provide a listing of all the readable files in that directory.
User directories	Without using aliases, the server can remap directories from outside its normal directory hierarchy to within its hierarchy.
Search engine	The server has a built-in search engine.
Direct DBMS links	The server supports direct links to a DBMS without requiring a CGI script.
User interaction tools	Tools are provided for user interaction as part of the server software.
Server-side image support	Supports either the CERN or NCSA formatting of the image map file.
Nonblocking DNS lookups	The server accepts and parses requests in parallel with the DNS look-up.
Technical support	The vendor provides a technical support mailing list.
Proxy server	The software can be used as a server proxy.
Caching	The proxy server can act as a caching server.
Source code	The server software includes the full source code that can be compiled.

Although these tables would seem to make server selection daunting, remember that the server is at the center of your Web site, and the extra time taken to select Web server software will pay off in the long run.

Browsing the vendor's technical support mailing list will help determine the level and quality of technical support you can expect for a given server product.

Access control is set for a URL path rather than a specific document, and is allowed or denied, according to the user or user group. Restrictions to the path are dependent on IP address or domain hostname. Figure 12.8 shows the screen used to set access permissions.

Server activity is logged in three files: access.log, server.log, and error.log, and several tracing options are available. One of the most useful of these options provides the ability to set a flag for CGI tracing, which permits interactive debugging of CGI scripts as they are being run. The other tracing options are shown in Figure 12.9.

Of the features that WebSite provides, the most attractive is the ability to manage all the files contained in a given Web site through the use of several visual tools, the main ones being WebIndex and WebView. WebIndex is used to index the files in a specified URL path, and provides the information needed by WebView. The information gathered by WebIndex can

Figure 12.8   Setting access permissions to a URL path.

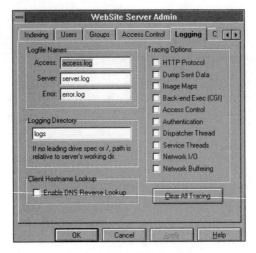

Figure 12.9 WebSite options for logging and activity tracing.

also be used to provide a site search capability for users accessing the site, by creating an online form that incorporates an existing WebSite CGI named websearch.exe.

WebView displays a graphical map of the site, showing all the internal/external links, broken links, and individual file information. Figure 12.10 lays out the Grower Direct site we're using as an example, and Figure 12.11 shows the properties of an individual file (help.htm, highlighted on the screen) chosen at random from the map.

In addition to displaying the general properties of a file, the site administrator can also run HTML diagnostics, set access permissions, and check access activity related to the file. Another particularly useful feature provided by Webview is QuickStats, which gives the administrator a brief summary of site activity, as shown in Figure 12.12.

This product is now at version 1.1, and several functions have been added since the 1.0 release we used for our examples:

- Multiserver capability on a single machine

- Server-side includes

- Support for Visual Basic 4

- Remote administration

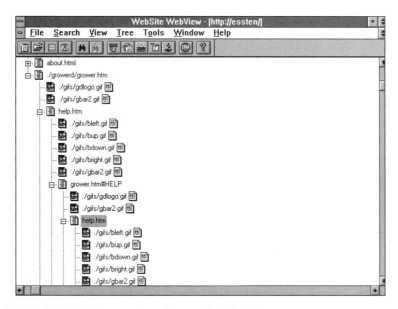

Figure 12.10   The WebView mapping of a specified Web site.

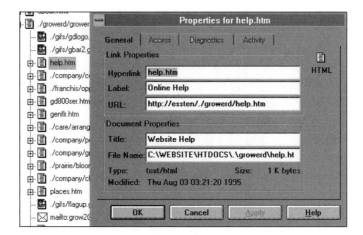

Figure 12.11   File properties of a file selected from the WebView site map.

A new version of the WebSite program, named WebSite Pro, is now available from O'Reilly. This release includes:

- API integration with Cold Fusion, which is bundled with the WebSite software

- WebSite API (WSAPI) and support for ISAPI (Microsoft)

QuickStats

Last 2 Days

Requests	14
New Unique Hosts	1

From 07/01/96 to 07/02/96

HTML Files Served	5
Non-HTML Files Served	9
CGI Documents Served	0
Erroneous Requests Served	3
Total Requests Served	17
Average Requests Per Hour	0.8
Average Requests Per Day	17.0
Unique Hosts Visiting	1

Figure 12.12 Site usage statistics provided by WebView.

- Support for Java and FrontPage

- Support for both SSL (v2) and S-HTTP transaction security

The functionality and ease of use supplied by WebSite provide a good benchmark for selecting Web server software. Any server software that you consider for a Windows environment should meet or exceed WebSite in terms of cost effectiveness, performance, ease of use, and functionality. Given the current crop of products to choose from, it should be possible to find several solid products that can meet your requirements. And, in light of the announcement discussed in the sidebar, even more server programs will appear quickly—products that offer increased functionality and performance gains.

Jigsaw: A New Product Created with New Tools

"Jigsaw lets us demonstrate a lot of the ideas that have been on the drawing board for years...," said W3C director Tim Berners-Lee.

Jigsaw is an HTTP server written entirely with Java. Its design goals were portability, extensibility, and efficiency, and have re-

> sulted in highly portable software, since Jigsaw runs on any CPU that can run Java. New resource objects can be written as extensions to the server rather than using CGI for extensions, which are written as processes. Finally, the software has been designed to operate more efficiently by using caching mechanisms to minimize, and eventually eliminate, the majority of file system accesses.

The current selection of Web server software for the Windows NT platform is provided in Table 12.8.

Table 12.8 Web Server Software for the Windows NT Platform

Name	Source	Internet Location	Commercial, Shareware, or Freeware	Evaluation Copy Available
Alibaba	Computer Software	http://alibaba. austria.eu.net	Commercial	Yes
Commerce Builder	Internet Factory	http://www.ifact.com	Commercial	Yes
Esplanade & Esplanade Secure Edition	FTP Software	http://www.ftp.com	Commercial	Yes
ExpressO HTTP Server	Peak Technologies, Inc.	http://www. capitalcity.com	Commercial	Yes
GNN Server	Global Network Navigator	http://www.tools. gnn.com	Commercial	Yes
IBM Internet Connection Server	IBM	http://www.ics. raleigh.ibm.com	Commercial	Yes
Microsoft Internet Information Server	Microsoft	http://207.68. 137.8:80	Commercial	Yes
Netscape Enterprise Server	Netscape	http://home. netscape.com	Commercial	Yes

(Continued)

Table 12.8   Web Server Software for the Windows NT Platform (Continued)

Name	Source	Internet Location	Commercial, Shareware, or Freeware	Evaluation Copy Available
Netscape FastTrack Server	Netscape	http://home. netscape.com	Commercial	Yes
Open Market & Open Market Secure Webservers	Open Market	http://www. openmarket.com	Commercial	Yes
Oracle Webserver	Oracle	http://www. oracle.com	Commercial	No
Purveyor WebServer	Process Software	http://www. process.com	Commercial	No
Quarterdeck WebServer	Quarterdeck	http://arachnid. qdeck.com	Commercial	No
Spinnaker Web Server	Searchlight Software	http://www. searchlight.com	Commercial	Yes
SPRY Web & SPRY SafetyWeb Servers	SPRY Corporate Software	http://server.spry. com	Commercial	Yes
SuperWeb Server	Frontier Technologies Corporation	http://www. frontiertech.com	Commercial	Yes
VBServer	World Wide Web Development	http://wwwdev.com	Commercial	Yes
O'Reilly and Associates' WebSite	O'Reilly and Associates	http://website. ora.com	Commercial	Yes
Quarterdeck's WebSTAR 95/ NT	Quarterdeck	http://www. quarterdeck.com	Commercial	No
EMWAC Freeware HTTPS	European Microsoft Windows NT Academic Center	http://emwac.ed. ac.uk	Freeware	Yes

(Continued)

Table 12.8 Web Server Software for the Windows NT Platform (Continued)

Name	Source	Internet Location	Commercial, Shareware, or Freeware	Evaluation Copy Available
Fnord Server	Brian Morin	http://www.wpi.edu	Freeware	Yes
FolkWeb	Ilar Concepts	http://www.ilar.com	Freeware	Yes
Jigsaw	W3 Consortium	http://www.w3.org	Freeware	Yes
OmniHTTPd	Omnicron	http://www.fas.harvard.edu	Shareware	Yes

Workgroup or Collaborative Computing: Groupware

Collaborative, or workgroup, computing is another of the computing world's activities that suffers from too many definitions—as well as too many nouns—each supplied by competing product vendors. In fact, the main activities that make up workgroup computing are *messaging, forums and conferencing,* and *workflow automation*; common to each is an element of document sharing and management.

- *Messaging*—This function is provided by email, which gives users the tools to create, respond to, forward, and store electronic communications. Communication can be one-to-one, or one-to-many (distribution lists), and through the use of attachments, can facilitate document-sharing among members of a workgroup. A message storage and archival system may be provided, depending on the email program employed.

- *Forums and Conferencing*—A variant of email, the forums function serves to provide an electronic bulletin board where participants can create and view messages that are normally organized by topic. Most systems provide threading, which is a means of showing the reader the interrelationship between messages and replies. As with email, a variety of storage, retrieval, and search mechanisms for messages are usually available. Conferencing, on the other hand, provides for real-time, interactive communications between participants. For the most part, these "chats" take place using the computer keyboard and monitor to compose and read messages.

- *Workflow Automation*—Workflow software provides the means with which to expedite and track the routing of information or documents among people in a workgroup, through the use of a component called the workflow engine. Active workflow systems monitor the status of the actions in the system (for example, whether or not a certain report has been received, opened, and forwarded on to the next person in the chain), and trigger notices to the users regarding deadlines. Passive systems, on the other hand, don't actively manage the workflow process.

The convergence of these three activities is what we define as workgroup computing, and the products that support and integrate these activities are called *groupware*. An example of this convergence is shown in Figure 12.13.

The product that defined groupware, and the one that is still generally recognized as the industry leader, is Lotus Notes (or simply, Notes). For years, this was the only product that fully integrated the activities associated with workgroup computing; now the appearance of the World Wide Web model in the office environment has changed the playing field. The open, easy-to-use Web architecture provides document sharing and broad distribution, email, and forums or conferencing capability. Given the lower cost of the software required to furnish these workgroup functions (lower in relation to the cost of an equivalent Notes implementation), reduced training needs, and general ease of use, Web applications provide an at-

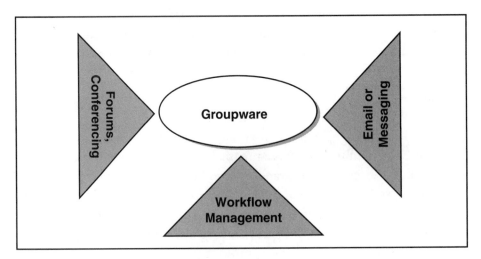

Figure 12.13   The convergence of workgroup activities.

tractive alternative to proprietary groupware. However, it must be kept in mind that Web software is not groupware, but essentially a communications infrastructure that supports workgroup activity. There are two options for achieving groupware functionality on your intranet: either custom-build the system, or buy a Web-enabled groupware product. In either case, you need to seriously consider items such as cost, the existing technical infrastructure, technical resources, time-frame demands, and the nature of the application itself.

BUILDING GROUPWARE APPLICATIONS

Constructing your own custom groupware application from scratch is not a trivial task; it is a programming-intensive activity that should not be entered into lightly. Should you decide to take this approach, we recommend using commercial workgroup components that can be customized and integrated.

There are several products available that can provide the desired messaging, forum, and workflow functionality. In most situations, building from the messaging base, which is the glue that binds all the components together, is the logical strategy. The next step is adding forum/bulletin board capability with products like Allaire Forums and O'Reilly's WebBoard. Web-specific workflow software is less plentiful, but WebFlow Corporation's SamePage and Ultimus' WebFloware are good examples of what is available. Finally, all these elements need to be linked to the document collection itself, which must be indexed in order to support search and retrieval. One of the biggest issues you'll face here is keeping document versions in synch when multiple copies of a single document are distributed throughout the network. Document replication and synchronization is one of the major strengths of Notes, and has contributed to its huge success in the groupware field. Groupware vendors like Lotus have modified their software to interface with Web pages and use the Internet's infrastructure—in other words, Web-enabling the software.

WEB-ENABLED GROUPWARE

Currently, the Web-enabled groupware marketplace only has two products that we consider groupware by our definition: Notes, from Lotus, and LiveLink Intranet, from OpenText. These two products provide integrated tools for developing/maintaining groupware applications, and support typical workgroup activities, such as workflow management and tracking, project collaboration, library management, and information search and retrieval. Table 12.9 lists the various workgroup and groupware products that are currently available.

Table 12.9   Workgroup and Groupware Products

Name	Source	Internet Location	Evaluation Copy
Actionworkflow Metro	Action Technologies, Inc.	http://www.actiontech.com	No
Allaire Forums	Allaire	http://www.allaire.com	Yes
FrontPage	Microsoft	http://www.microsoft.com	No
LiveLink Intranet	Open Text Corp.	http://www.opentext.com	No
Notes, Domino, InterNotes	Lotus Development Corp.	http://www.lotus.com	Yes (Domino, InterNotes)
SamePage, Action Item Manager	WebFlow Corp.	http://webflow.com	No
Vineyard	Data Fellows	http://www.datafellows.com	Yes
Web Crossing	Lundeen and Associates	http://webx.lundeen.com	Yes
WebBoard	O'Reilly and Associates	http://www.ora.com	Yes
WebShare	RADNET	http://www.radnet.com	Yes
Workflow Starter Kit	Ultimus	http://www.ultimus1.com	No
Workgroup Web	Digital Equipment Corp.	http://www.digital.com	No
Workgroup Web Forum	Digital Equipment Corp.	http://www.digital.com	No

Managing, Indexing, and Retrieving Web Site Information

In a very short period of time, you'll discover that your Web site has begun to accumulate a large collection of electronic documents. Consider, for a moment, the collection of electronic information in word processing documents and spreadsheets that exists in your office today; this collection is, by and large, without coherent organization or integration. Since these collections seem to grow exponentially, the only opportunity you'll have to manage your intranet information—with some possibility of success—is by taking the information situation in hand and installing document indexing tools before any documents are even made available on the server; attempting to add controls and manage this information at a later time is next-to-impossible. It can be done, but not easily, quickly, or inexpensively.

In addition to managing information, you want to ensure that your users can find specific material easily and quickly. One of the major premises of an intranet is that it provides improved access to information; therefore, if your users have to work through multiple hypertext indexes and layer upon layer of pages, this premise is negated. It won't take too long for the users to get frustrated, and quit using the system.

The cornerstone of any document-management system is indexing, beginning with the identification keys (key words or phrases) within each document for use in building a master index. Search engine software not only provides the final search capability, but is used in the initial phases of indexing to:

- Identify the material to index
- Select indexing rules and filters
- Index the material
- Build the search screens

Search engines can take one of two approaches to creating an index. Some programs first build a thesaurus linked to the document collection, and then update the thesaurus as new material is added. The second method is to simply build indexes using selected rules and filters; however, when new material is added, the entire collection must be re-indexed.

Search programs may be integrated with, or at least sold with, the server software—the Quarterdeck server, for example, includes the Topic search engine (Verity). Prices vary significantly among the products, ranging from free to over $12,000, depending on the licensing arrangements. The type and number of document formats that are supported by the different programs account for this variation—some support only ASCII text and HTML, while others cover more than 50 different file formats. The diversity of your Web site document collection, then, is the determining factor in selecting a search engine product.

As an example, we've provided a walk-through of the indexing procedure used by Excite for Web Servers (EWS), a search engine provided by Excite, Inc. This particular program uses an index rather than thesaurus approach, and is well-suited for indexing collections that contain only HTML and text files. EWS supports keyword and concept searching, as well as query-by-example searches based on search results.

The complete indexing operation for EWS is done using the browser, and consists of a series of HTML pages that provide forms to fill out as you work through the procedure. The first step is to indicate whether you are working on an *existing* collection of material, or if this is a *new* set of documents being indexed. We chose new, and then provided a name for the collection—ESSTEN (for ESSTEN Communications, Inc.). Next, the method for determining the collection's contents is chosen; you are given the option of indexing using rules, or an explicit list of files. Figure 12.14 shows a portion of the configuration panel used to set the indexing rules.

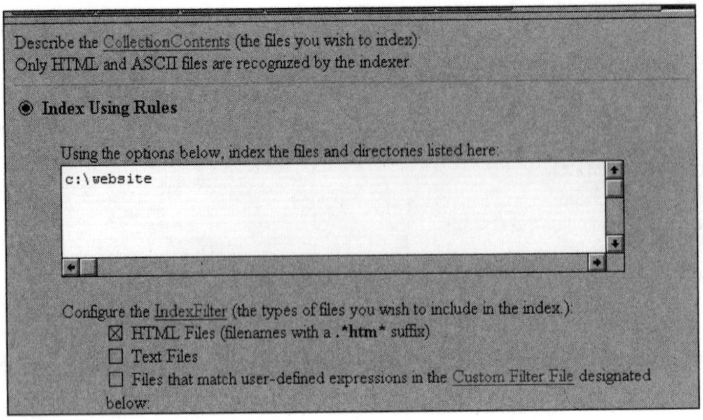

Figure 12.14   Setting indexing rules for the Excite Web Server.

After this configuration information has been saved, the actual indexing is started. One nice feature of EWS is that it provides a status report during the indexing process; it also creates summary and detailed logfiles, as well as an error logfile for all indexing runs. After the indexing is finished, you have the option of letting Excite build a search panel that can be used to search the collection. Using the default screen layouts provided by the software, we used EWS to generate the search panel shown in Figure 12.15.

Since the search panel created by EWS consists of an HTML form with CGI calls to the index, it is fully customizable at any time.

As a test of the search panel and the indexing, we ran a search against the newly-indexed collection, which incorporated all the pages for the Grower Direct site. We used a keyword search specifying the words *defects* and *diseases*. The results, shown in Figure 12.16, are grouped by confidence, and a score assigned to each match (called a *hit*). This scoring, expressed as a percentage by Excite, is called *relevance feedback*, and is simply a tool to help the user refine a search. A very low score, for example, could indicate that the words or phrase submitted for the query were too restrictive; this feedback lets the user conduct a new search using less restrictive keywords. (Then again, it might just mean that the information you're looking for is not in the collection being searched.)

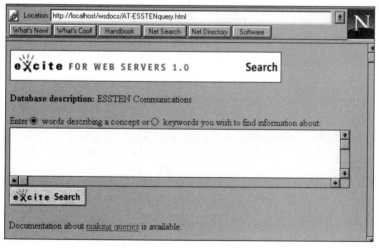

Figure 12.15 Database search panel generated by EWS.

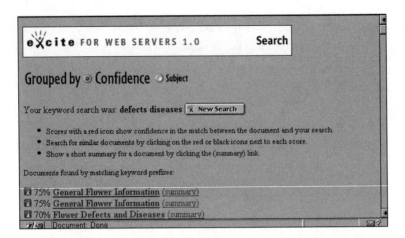

Figure 12.16   The results of a search using the keywords *defects* and *diseases.*

You will notice that to the left of each score is an icon of a figure (displayed in red on the screen). This indicates that the Excite query-by-example feature can be used to broaden your search, since the original search found items similar to the particular match shown on the screen. Clicking on the icon triggers a fresh search, using the match corresponding to the icon as the basis for its search. Table 12.10 shows the search engines that are currently available.

Table 12.10   Search Engine Summary

Name	Source	Internet Location	File Formats Supported	Commercial, Freeware, or Shareware
CyberFTS	Cyberiad Software	http://www.cyberiad.com	ASCII text, HTML, WordPerfect, MS Word, and binary	Commercial
Fulcrum Surfboard	Fulcrum Technologies, Inc.	http://www.fulcrum.com	52 file formats, including ASCII test, HTML, WordPerfect, MS Word	Commercial
InTEXT Retrieval Engine	InTEXT Systems, Inc.	http://www.intext.com	40 file formats including ASCII text, HTML, WordPerfect, MS Word	Commercial

(Continued)

Table 12.10   Search Engine Summary (Continued)

Name	Source	Internet Location	File Formats Supported	Commercial, Freeware, or Shareware
Livelink Search*	Open Text Corp.	http://www.opentext.com	40 file formats including ASCII text, HTML, Adobe PDF, MS Word, MS Excel, SGML, WordPerfect	Commercial
PLWeb	Personal Library Software	http://www.pls.com	ASCII text, HTML, PDF	Commercial
Tecumseh	Tippecanoe Systems, Inc.	http://www.tippecanoe.com	ASCII text, HTML	Commercial
Topic Internet Server	Verity Inc.	http://www.verity.com	50 file formats including ASCII text, HTML, Adobe PDF, MS Word, MS Excel, WordPerfect	Commercial
WebCatalog	Pacific Coast Software	http://www.pacific-coast.com	tab delimited ASCII text	Commercial
ZyIndex for Internet	ZyLAB International, Inc.	http://www.zylab.com	20 file formats including ASCII text, HTML, MS Word, WordPerfect	Commercial
Excite for Web Servers	Excite , Inc.	http://www.excite.com	ASCII text, HTML	Freeware**
WAIS Server and WAIS toolkit.	EMWAC (European Microsoft Windows NT Academic Centre)	http://emwac.ed.ac.uk	ASCII text, HTML	Freeware

Livelink includes Netscape Commerce Server and the Open Text T5 search engine.

**Although freeware, any product support is only available through a licensing arrangement.*

Bundled Solutions for Intranet Development

13

Bundled Solutions for Intranet Development

An alternative to piece-by-piece acquisition of the products needed for intranet construction is the bundled solution, which combines aspects of the mix-and-match and end-to-end approaches, giving you the benefits of both. We'll examine the rationale for using a bundled solution, and then look at several representative product bundles in detail.

What is a Bundled Solution?

There is no industry standard that defines what constitutes a bundled solution for delivering product suites, nor is there a minimum product set that qualifies a product suite as being bundled. However, a bundled solution can be characterized as a *collection of products* that is priced and sold as *one unit* by a *single vendor*; the collection may make use of either a mix-and-match or an end-to-end approach to product selection. In the case of a bundled solution designed to construct an internal Web site, the products required would include: Web server software, a browser, an editor, interface development tools, database software, and possibly workstation and server hardware. Any suite

that includes these components, and is priced as a single product, can be defined as a bundled solution for intranet development.

Why Use Bundled Solutions?

The cross section of products needed to construct an intranet represents a fairly diverse shopping list, and if you have no one on staff with knowledge of this particular area of computing, selecting products can be a time-consuming activity. (Be extremely wary of late-night Web surfers who assure you they know everything about Web software.) There are also other issues, such as installation and configuration, that arise after products are acquired. The bundled solution (see Figure 13.1) is an acquisition alternative that can ease and shorten the selection process, and address some of the follow-up issues.

Product Selection

Those of you who have had any involvement in product selection and acquisition can appreciate the amount of time and resources spent in selecting a single software program. This process, which often involves setting up a project team, includes:

- Developing a list of likely products

- Preparing evaluation criteria based on desired features (similar to the server checklist we provided in Chapter 12)

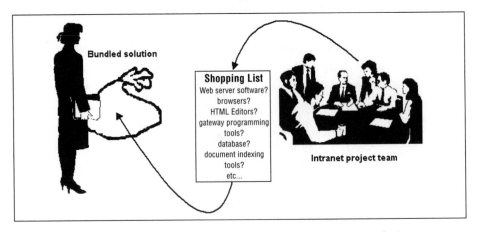

Figure 13.1 The bundled approach to acquiring intranet infrastructure products.

- Conducting product research (interviews and trade press reviews, for example)

- Doing a preliminary assessment of products and developing a short list

- Acquiring evaluation copies of the short-listed products for an in-depth review

- Conducting a final assessment

- Preparing a recommendation

- Acquiring the product

In the case of Web server software, your project team will start out with a list of more than twenty products. Based on a preliminary assessment of how closely each product's documented characteristics match your evaluation criteria, the list can be shortened to the eight or ten that best meet your needs. After you develop a short list, it will be necessary to bring in evaluation copies of each product for testing on-site. (It should be noted that this isn't possible with all products, since not every vendor is prepared to provide evaluation software.) The on-site testing activity will require that each product be installed, configured, and tested in the same hardware environment. This, of course, has its own cost and resource implications, and can only be done if there are staff members available who have the requisite skills. If there aren't, training, with its own cost and time requirements, must be added to the steps in the selection process. Only after testing has been completed, benchmarks assessed, and evaluation criteria scored, can a recommendation be made.

This process, then, will be time-consuming and costly, and must be taken into account when developing your intranet project schedule. And remember—the evaluation activity we've outlined covers only *one* product; when you're looking to acquire the minimum of four products needed to build your Web site, the cost and complexity of evaluation activities increase dramatically.

Product Installation and Configuration

Selecting and acquiring the software is only the first phase of development; the next step is getting the various products installed and working in harmony with each other. The knowledge and skill of your development staff is critical at this point, since each piece of software must be installed and configured, not only to each of the other components, but to the system as a whole.

 When you're figuring out the time needed to configure software, estimate the time you think it will take, then multiply by two, as demonstrated in Figure 13.2.

Unfortunately, it is rarely possible to test the various software packages in conjunction with one another during on-site product evaluations. The issue of compatibility can be addressed only after the products are purchased and installed. In the interim, you have to take vendor compatibility claims on faith, and assume there will be no problem. Since this is rarely the case, the cost in manpower and time spent getting products to coexist is often significantly higher than the total cost of product acquisition.

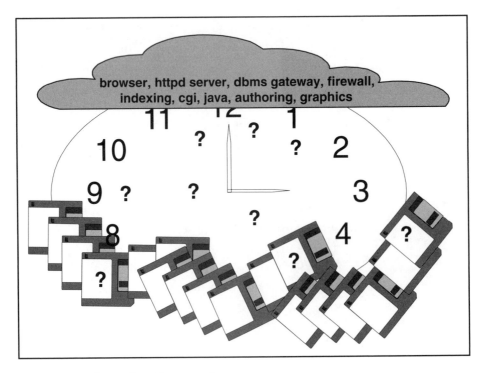

Figure 13.2 The configuration conundrum.

This is the time when the finger-pointing we talked about in Chapter 9 starts, with each product vendor insisting that the other guy's product is at fault. This unwelcome and unproductive feature of the computer-products industry can be the most frustrating and time-consuming aspect of the entire installation process, and is the reason why many companies have adopted the single-vendor philosophy.

The Bundled Solution: Benefits

The greatest single benefit of a bundled solution is the accumulated time saved during product selection, installation, and configuration. The selection phase is considerably simplified because you're assessing single products (entire suites) that have been designed to meet all your needs. However, your greatest savings will be realized during product installation and configuration, since the products bundled together by the vendor have been tested to ensure their compatibility with each other. This will dramatically reduce the time spent reinstalling and reconfiguring software programs in an attempt to reach some level of coexistence.

Training is another area where bundled solutions provide an advantage. Vendors often offer complete training packages, which provide a broad approach to addressing the skills required across the entire product collection. These packages generally provide a more balanced and integrated system of instruction than piecemeal training does, and are usually more cost-effective. The availability of training, its scope, and its cost vary from vendor to vendor, so training should be one of the criteria used when evaluating bundled solutions.

The final major benefit is the single point of contact, with its attendant elimination of vendor finger-pointing. With the bundled solution, a single vendor is responsible for ensuring that the various products in the suite, whether end-to-end or mix-and-match, function properly and perform well together.

Examples of Bundled Solutions

Now we'll examine some of the bundled solutions that are currently available for the Internet/intranet consumer. These examples have been selected from the major product vendors in this market; the three most notable are available from Silicon Graphics Inc. (SGI), Sun Microsystems, and Netscape Communications Corporation. Several firms, such as Oracle and Microsoft, offer "Internet/intranet solutions" (discussed later, in the section titled *Intranet Solutions*), but typically, these are simply collections of their own Web products, marketed under this catch-phrase. They are product suites, but not bundled solutions.

SGI: WebFORCE Workgroup

Silicon Graphics, which produces an extensive line of Web-related products marketed as WebFORCE, was the first company to offer a bundled solution for building intranets. Their WebFORCE Workgroup is a robust, integrated hardware and software solution that combines selected WebFORCE products with software from Netscape Communications and Adobe. The bundle is intended to be what the company calls "intranet in a box," an end-to-end solution that includes workstations and servers, as well as all the software necessary to build and maintain a Web site. The software includes tools for site creation, site management and monitoring, applications and database integration, publishing, and document creation.

HARDWARE

At the workgroup level, SGI provides Indy workstations (available in low, middle, and high-end configurations), and a line of high-performance dedicated servers that have been preconfigured to deliver high-traffic, media-rich, and database-intensive Web applications across the enterprise.

SITE CREATION, MANAGEMENT, AND MONITORING

WebFORCE Workgroup provides two SGI tools to deal with creating, managing, and monitoring a Web site: Intranet Junction and Cosmo Site. Intranet Junction is used to automatically generate customized Web sites using a point-and-click interface to handle the routine activities associated with setting up a site. Cosmo Site is a graphical tool for managing site content and real-time monitoring of site activity, and includes tools for statistical reporting and log file analysis.

Applications/Database Integration and Publishing

WebFORCE products are bundled with Netscape SuiteSpot, an integrated set of products in itself, to provide the tools for document publishing, applications integration, database integration to Web pages, and Web server software.

Document Creation

SGI has provided several tools for content creation, not only for HTML documents, but for VRML documents, as well. Currently, the Workshop bundle includes:

- *WebMagic Pro*—A WYSIWYG editor for HTML documents

- *WebSpace Author*—A WYSIWYG editor for VRML documents

- *WebMagic Digital Media Tools*—A selection of tools for capturing, editing, and playing back audio, video, and images

- *Cosmo Code*—A visual Java development environment

- *Adobe Photoshop*—A package for working with scanned images and photographs

- *Adobe Illustrator*—A graphics-creation package

Sun Microsystems: Netra Internet Server

Sun's Netra Internet Server series provides another end-to-end bundled solution. Netra, which consists of Sun's hardware, several of its own software packages, and software from Netscape Communications, includes tools for: site development and management, security, and Web application development programs.

Hardware

The Netra servers are based on the SPARC hardware configuration, using Sun's Solaris operating system.

Site Development and Management

Site development and management is provided by custom Netra administration tools, as well as by Netscape's LiveWire Site Management software. The delivery mechanism for Web site content is Netscape's Enterprise Server.

SECURITY

Netra's Web site security supplies three applications: standard OS security mechanisms, firewall software (Solstice FireWall-First!), and virus-scanning software (InterScan VirusWall).

WEB APPLICATION DEVELOPMENT

Netscape's Navigator Gold WYSIWYG editor/browser enables development activities, and the Java Developer's Kit helps build applets and interfaces.

Netscape Communications: SuiteSpot

Netscape's SuiteSpot has five Web server products to choose from, plus a collection of programs for site management, document creation, applications development, interface programming, and a relational database. No hardware is included in the bundle.

SERVER PROGRAMS

The Netscape server line consists of the following programs:

- *Enterprise Server*—A high-performance Web server that has a built-in security mechanism for data transmission between the server and client (SSL)

- *Catalog Server*—A document and file management system

- *Proxy Server*—A server that can be used to improve performance through document caching, and to filter access to Web site documents

- *Mail Server*—A client/server messaging system for internal and Internet email

- *News Server*—A secure server for handling public or private discussion groups—internally, or across the Internet

THE APPLICATIONS ENVIRONMENT: DEVELOPMENT AND MAINTENANCE

LiveWire Pro is a collection of software programs used for a variety of activities associated with Web sites: creating site content, developing applications and interfaces, and managing the entire site. The following products make up the LiveWire Pro suite:

- *Netscape Navigator Gold*—Navigator Gold is an enhanced version of the Navigator 2.x browser, and is used to create and edit HTML documents, plug-ins, Java applets, and JavaScripts in a WYSIWYG environment.

- *LiveWire Site Manager*—This tool provides graphical representations of a Web site, and allows the site administrator to restructure the site using drag-and-drop technology. In addition, Site Manager can be used for link checking, link restructuring, importing entire document collections (complete sites), editing and updating, and deploying a site from the central server to distributed servers on the network.

- *LiveWire JavaScript Compiler*—This compiler is used for producing byte code from Netscape JavaScript source code.

- *LiveWire Database Connectivity Library*—The library provided supports SQL and ODBC database connectivity, includes transaction processing features, such as commit and rollback, and can execute stored procedures.

- *Informix OnLine Workgroup*—This is a relational database supplied by Informix, that is upwardly-compatible with the Informix OnLine Dynamic Server SQL database.

- *Crystal Reports (Professional Version)*—Crystal Reports, from Crystal Software, is a visual-forms builder and data-analysis tool that supports cross-tabulation, as well as table and graph drill-down. It can be used to add reporting capability to Web page/database applications.

Intranet Solutions

As mentioned earlier, there are several vendors providing products grouped under the banner of Internet/intranet solutions, and while they aren't bundled solutions, it's useful to know which companies are offering these groups of products (see Table 13.1). Also, given the fast-paced dynamics of the computer industry, they could be offered as bundled solutions next week.

As you may have noticed, there aren't many commercially bundled solutions available at the present time. However, because they provide an efficient, cost-effective approach to Web site creation, local retailers of computer products often put together and market bundles, and many consulting firms provide standard bundles of their own design to clients. Alternately, you can use the Wesley Website-Building Bundle:

- *Authoring Tools*—FrontPage, HotDog or SwagMan

- *Interface Building/Applications Development*—Cold Fusion Professional

- *Graphics Manipulation, Touch-up*—Paintshop Pro

Table 13.1   Internet/intranet Product Groups Provided by Various Vendors

Company	Location on Internet	Description	Evaluation Copy
IBM, Lotus	http://www.ibm.com http://www.lotus.com	Server (Domino), connectivity (InterConnect), groupware (Notes 4.5)	Yes, for some products
Microsoft	http://www.micro-soft.com/workshop	Browser (Internet Explorer), server (Internet Information Server), document creation (FrontPage, Internet Assistant, ActiveX Control Pad), database integration (dbWeb), development tools (Jakarta, VBScript), conferencing (NetMeeting)	Yes, for most products
Oracle	http://www.oracle.com	Browser (Power-Browser), server (WebServer), database integration (PowerBrowser)*	Yes

* The Oracle products provide full integration with Oracle database and groupware products.

- *Java Development*—Java Workshop

- *Document Indexing and Retrieval*—Excite for Web Servers

- *Server Software*—WebSite Pro

These products are all reasonably priced, proven easy-to-use, non-proprietary, and have proven effective in Web site development. It works for us.

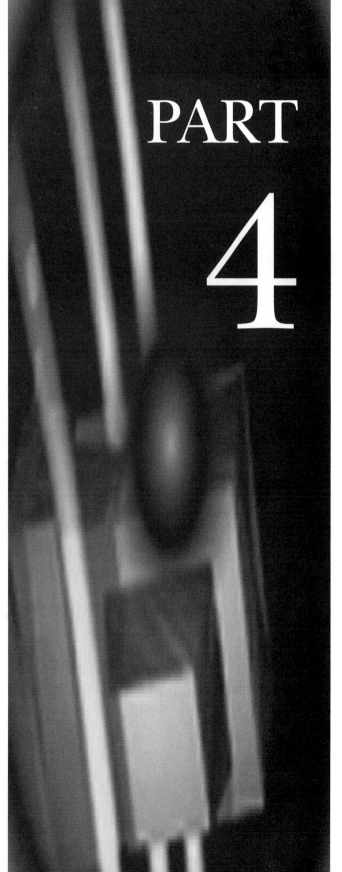

PART

4

An
Intranet
Blueprint

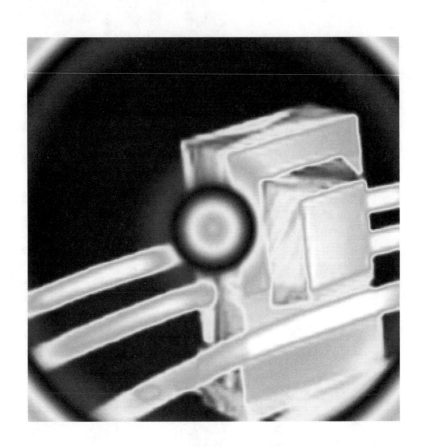

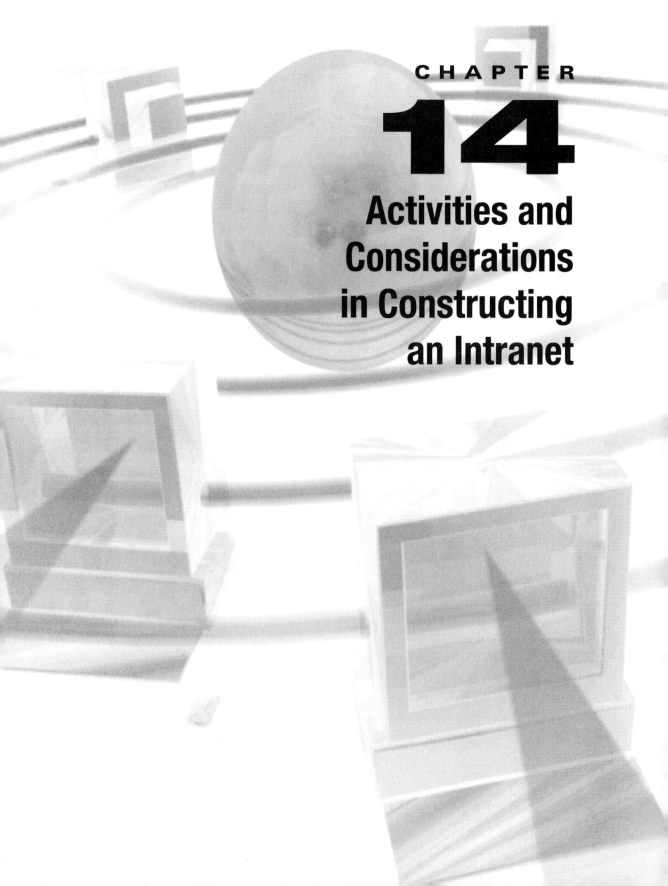

14

Activities and Considerations in Constructing an Intranet

Activities and Considerations in Constructing an Intranet

Despite the relative ease and speed at which an intranet application can be developed, disasters can occur—unexpectedly and quickly. A well-planned project will have a far greater chance of avoiding outright disaster and achieving a reasonable level of success than one that's been short-changed in the planning process. The guidelines we've provided can be used as a checklist to help you through the planning, building, and implementation phases of an intranet project. Remember, however, that no two organizations are the same; you may have to revise these guidelines somewhat to suit your own organization's unique needs.

Since an intranet simply provides the infrastructure for delivering Internet services, a specific deliverable is needed for your first project. Typically, an online publication is used for proof-of-concept, before moving on to develop broader and more sophisticated intranet applications.

Prior to beginning the actual development of an application, there are four fundamental questions that, when answered, generate the specific detail needed to construct an intranet application (see Figure 14.1).

Figure 14.1   Your questions to assist in intranet planning.

For your first intranet project, select an application or publication that is fairly simple, can be developed quickly, and provides the best (that is to say, quickest and maximum) payback for your effort.

What Are We Building, and Why?

This question is used to define the application by establishing its scope, specifying deliverables, and identifying the project's immediate goals (see Figure 14.2). Long-term, broader goals are developed later, and are predicated on the results of the project.

Objectives and Goals

You must first determine the overall objective of your intranet, as well as its underlying goals. An objective for your project can be fairly general, such as technology investigation (computer speak for testing the waters), which is a perfectly valid reason for an intranet pilot project. Since an intranet itself is only a delivery vehicle, you will need a test application or publication to get a true measure of this technology. In many cases, the objective is quite specific, since the project sponsors will already have identified something they want to put online, such as a company phone directory or procedures manual.

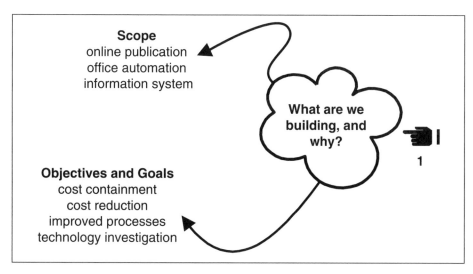

Figure 14.2   What are we building, and why?

Goals support the objective, define quantifiable deliverables, and generally supply the answer to the "why" part of the question. An example of a fairly common goal is cost reduction, which is too general, and needs to be broken down further into specific costs and dollar values.

Scope

The next step is defining the scope of the project: what is included, what is not included, and what can be expected as the final product? Scope is also important for laying the foundation for future application deployment in the organization.

Contrary to what many articles in the trade press say, intranets will *not* immediately solve everyone's communications and information distribution problems, nor should they be viewed as a replacement for every system currently in place.

It's during scope definition that the initial decisions are made regarding the Internet services you're going to include on your intranet. Remember that an intranet is not just a Web server—it can also be used to provide other Internet services (as discussed in Chapter 1). A recap of these services is set out in Table 14.1.

Table 14.1   Internet Services

Service	Description
Chat	Real-time, text-based interpersonal communications
Conferencing	Real-time, audio-video interpersonal communications
FTP	File transfer between hosts and clients
Gopher	Text-based and menu-driven information distribution using client/server
List Services	Automated mailing lists and batch discussion groups
Mail	Email batch communications
News	Batch discussion group communications
Phone	Real-time, audio interpersonal communications
Telnet	Remote terminal access
World Wide Web	Multi-media, hypertext-based information distribution, using client/server

In addition to Internet services, there may be other services you would like to provide for your users, or that are needed to supply functionality unavailable in the Internet services collection. Some examples of these services are workflow management, discussion groups/bulletin boards, or electronic whiteboards. These should be identified now, even if they're not going to be implemented as part of this project, but in the future. The reason for doing this is to provide as much information as possible to help in capacity planning for the intranet and the network infrastructure supporting it.

Don't take any shortcuts at the expense of activities related to setting the scope of the project.

Scope is one of the most important elements of project planning. A poorly defined, unclear scope is the most contentious issue there is between application users and developers. The litanies of, "the users changed the specification," and, "the systems group didn't build what we wanted," are constantly heard in corporate boardrooms all over North America. Most projects start with the best intentions from all involved parties, but during the course of the system's design, construction, and implementation, little items fall through the cracks. These items later get magnified, and linger on as major irritants—not only for the project's participants, but for those involved in future projects.

Who Is This Going to Affect?

It's very important to know who the project will affect, since it will have an impact not only on the area sponsoring the project, but on the systems group and other areas as well (see Figure 14.3). In today's office environment, most workgroups don't exist in isolation; therefore, the impact of an application such as this usually has further-reaching consequences than you might think. And, even if your intranet application will be fairly localized, this is a good time to start involving other groups within the organization, even if only by providing them with general information about the project. The three important reasons for doing this are associated with information management, intranet benefits, and issues management.

Information management concerns how general information publishing and intranet application development within your company are to be managed: Will they be centralized, completely distributed, or use a model that falls somewhere in the middle? This is an important decision with long-term consequences for the future deployment of intranets in your organization (remember the islands of information!). Chapter 15 covers the information-management topic in more detail.

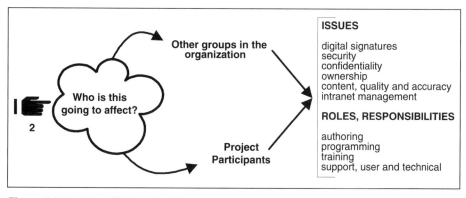

Figure 14.3 Who will this affect?

Another reason for carefully defining who will be affected relates to three major benefits to be gained from an intranet—the ability to pool all the organization's data, eliminate redundant information, and make better use of corporate data resources. Aside from being aware of what information input may be required from them, having an awareness of your project will allow other branches, divisions, or workgroups to identify similar opportunities for their own areas, and perhaps enable them to build on the intranet foundation you've provided.

Finally, this activity helps identify a variety of issues, such as security, roles, responsibilities, data ownership, and intranet management.

Issues, Roles, and Responsibilities

- *Digital Authorizations*—In the case of applications where user authorizations are involved, you'll need to establish what form of electronic authorizations will be necessary. In some cases, a User ID may be adequate, while in others, it may be necessary to install software to generate digital signatures that can be authenticated.

- *Confidentiality and Security*—Depending on application/document content, confidentiality and security may be a concern. Take, for example, a human-resources application in which staff can access and update their own personnel files (address or phone number change and tax information, for example). It is essential to ensure that no one other than the employee and authorized human resources staff have access to an individual's personal records. The security issue is elevated significantly if dialup access to the intranet is provided, or if the system is linked to the Internet. In the latter case, even if the Internet is only used as a transmission medium (see Chapter 16), you must determine whether or not encryption technology should be implemented to protect the contents of company communications and documents transferred across this network.

- *Data Ownership*—Ownership of data has always been a major issue in many organizations, since different groups generate, use, and are responsible for maintaining it. As intranets are increasingly used to draw data from various sources throughout a company, the issue of ownership and care (data accuracy, integrity, and security) takes on even more significance. Consequently, this particular issue must be addressed early in the implementation of an internal information system.

- *Authoring and Programming*—It's necessary to identify the staff who will be responsible for authoring the hypertext pages, as well as who is going to handle any interface programming. In some cases, both can be handled by staff from the group sponsoring the application and building the hypertext pages, without assistance from the systems group.

- *The Editorial Function*—With applications involving more than one area, someone must be made responsible for the editorial function. That person must ensure that content is acceptable, and that the publication conforms to any internal policies that may be in place.

- *Intranet Support*—The intranet's users will need training and ongoing support for using the system, as well as technical support. If both the application owners and systems staff are involved, clear delineation of responsibility is essential—users need to know who to talk to about the different kinds of problems they encounter.

- *Intranet Management*—Unlike traditional information systems, where the bulk of system-management activities reside with the systems group, an intranet opens up the possibility of transferring this management role to the application's owners, leaving the systems group with overall responsibility for the network, but not Web site management. (This is not unlike LAN administrators, who for the most part are knowledgeable computer users in a particular area, rather than systems staff.) The Web site manager (the *Webmaster*) ensures that the system is functioning properly and all hypertext links are intact, and manages the updating of documents as well as the addition of any new material.

These activities serve to refine the composition of the project team, after which it's possible to assess the available skills, and determine training requirements, for the development team itself.

Identifying and resolving the issue of roles and responsibilities lays the groundwork for future intranet applications in the organization, so consider the time used for this activity well spent.

What Do We Have, and What Do We Need?

The purpose of the third question is to document all your staff and technical resources, since they provide the foundation on which to build the system. Once the existing resources have been identified, it's possible to determine what the additional requirements will be, in terms of staff training, consulting services, hardware, and software (See Figure 14.4).

Technical Resources

A technical infrastructure analysis, undertaken by the systems group, determines the existing environment's suitability for supporting your intranet application. The systems group can identify any additionally needed hardware and software (at a minimum, Web server software will be required), and should specifically consider the network, server hardware, development tools, and the testing environment.

THE NETWORK

The corporate network must support the TCP/IP protocol—a factor that isn't a problem with the major network operating systems, since those that command the bulk of the market share, such as Novell and Windows NT, provide full TCP/IP support. However, if you aren't already using TCP/IP, network reconfiguration will be required, and can take a significant amount of time to implement and test.

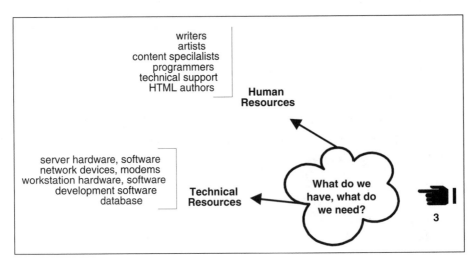

Figure 14.4　What do we have, what do we need?

Additionally, if remote access is provided to the intranet, it's necessary to determine how this will be handled. If an existing modem pool can be used, then capacity analysis must be done to ensure that it can handle the increased load. On the other hand, if a modem pool needs to be created, hardware and line specifications must be drawn up for the necessary equipment.

SERVER HARDWARE

You need to determine whether or not an existing production server can be used to host the Web server software. If an existing server is used, you must do capacity analysis (of memory and hard drive space), in order to ensure that the computer can handle the new application, as well as the current production load. If a new computer is required, then specifications for a suitable machine must be prepared.

DEVELOPMENT TOOLS AND THE TESTING ENVIRONMENT

Based on what's known of the application at this point in the planning phase, it's possible to determine the development environment that will be needed. Since development is typically done outside the production environment, it will likely be necessary to set up a Web server for development purposes, although existing workstations can be used to develop the Web pages and interfaces. In addition to the Web server program, the following software may be required for intranet development and deployment.

- *Authoring Tools*—This category covers all the software needed to create the hypertext pages, and includes HTML editors, graphics programs for creating or manipulating images contained on pages, and multimedia software for creating the multimedia content. If a large volume of existing documents will be converted to hypertext, you may want to use conversion or filter programs to automate this process, thus reducing conversion times and the amount of manpower required.

- *Browsers and Viewers*—You will, of course, need a browser program for the employees developing and using the system. Additional viewers may be needed during development, to view data files that don't contain text or hypertext information—for instance, PDF or graphics files.

- *Programming Languages*—In addition to general-purpose languages such as C or C++, your programmers may require utility languages, such as Perl or REXX, to produce CGI scripts or to develop Web site-maintenance routines. Depending on your application, additional programming languages and tools may have to include ActiveX, Java, VBScript, or JavaScript.

- *Interfaces and Interface Development Tools*—If your Web pages are interfacing with databases, then specific DBMS gateway programs, or tools like Cold Fusion and Sapphire/Web, can be acquired to automate as much of the interface development as possible.

- *Internet Services*—Additional Internet services, such as email and chat, require their own software programs. Some, like Telnet and FTP, are already included with the Windows NT OS, so third-party software isn't required.

- *Other Services*—This category includes functions such as electronic whiteboards, workflow management, and group discussion/bulletin boards. Since many of these aren't provided by the current set of Internet services, you'll need to purchase the software.

- *Database*—Unless databases for storing information collected from the Web pages already exist in the organization, and can be used, you will need to acquire this software as well.

- *Search Engines*—An intranet application composed of a large volume of documents should provide users with the tools to search this collection and retrieve the specific documents or pages they need. There are two alternatives for providing this function: programming search utilities in-house, or purchasing third-party software.

- *Site Maintenance*—Third-party software may also be required if your Web server software doesn't provide the tools for basic site-maintenance activities, such as site mapping and hypertext link checking.

- *Other*—If users will have remote access to the intranet, then you need to provide software that has dialing capability and supports TCP/IP communications over the telephone system.

Staff Resources

The project's human resources need to be assessed in a manner similar to that used in the technical assessment. You should have a team comprised of staff from the sponsoring group, other areas affected by the application, and people from the systems group. The types of skills you'll need to have, or develop, within this group can be categorized according to the following general activities.

- *Content Selection and Preparation*—A solid understanding of the content, how it should be structured, and good general writing skills

- *Page Authoring*—A basic understanding of HTML, or word processing experience, on which to build these new skills

- *CGI Script Preparation*—Experience with HTML and Perl, or solid experience with another programming language

- *Hardware and Software Selection and Installation*—Good general microcomputer technical skills

- *Network-related Activities*—Solid LAN experience, and a basic knowledge of TCP/IP and HTTP, at a minimum

Once you've inventoried your in-house expertise, it's possible to determine what training the project team members will need. Before going outside the organization to arrange training, check to see if any staff other than those involved in the project have some of the skill sets needed (another reason to keep other areas informed about the project). You may find that some of the skills, especially in the areas of browser installation and rudimentary HTML authoring, are available internally. Using in-house experts can reduce, if not entirely eliminate, some training costs.

The greatest need for training will most likely be in the network area. However, this will largely depend on the experience of the technical staff and the amount of exposure they've had to a diversity of networking situations.

What Do We Have to Do?

Our fourth, and final, question serves to map out the project's tasks, and helps to further clarify roles and responsibilities. In addition to getting the details nailed down, this activity offers another opportunity to identify any issues that may have been missed earlier in the planning process (see Figure 14.5).

Environmental Activities

Environmental activities cover everything that must be done in order to set up the computer environment needed for developing, testing, and delivering an intranet application or publication. This includes product selection, hardware and software installation, and testing the complete environment.

PRODUCT SELECTION

Once the functional requirements are established, you must assess the various product alternatives and, based on research or in-house testing, select specific software programs. The amount of time and rigor each company chooses to apply to software testing is really a matter of preference. Given that most software you might use has been reviewed extensively in the trade press, and since most of it is available for evaluation, we recommend spending enough time on this activity to feel reasonably comfortable with your choices. Remember, your first intranet application is a pilot project, so it isn't necessary to establish corporate standards at this point.

Likewise, you must also undertake reviews for any hardware acquisitions you make. In the case of hardware, most of the effort will probably be spent developing specifications for the machine's configuration, since product standards probably already exist in the organization.

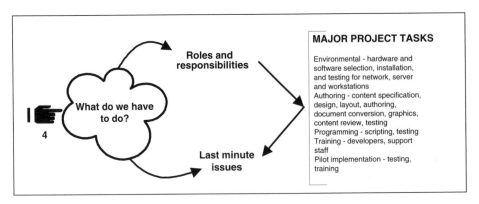

Figure 14.5   What do we have to do?

Hardware and Software Installation

It goes without saying that any new hardware and software will need to be installed, configured, and tested. However, there is a danger in taking things for granted and putting off this work until the last moment. This often happens when dealing with computers, because we assume that pre-installed and preconfigured computers must simply be unpacked and plugged in. A case in point is a server installation we were involved with not too long ago. The machine was purchased with Windows NT Server pre-installed, so we delayed unpacking until we absolutely needed the computer. When the technical staff set up the machine, they discovered that Windows NT was indeed installed, but the software was NT Workstation, not NT Server. No problem; we rushed through a purchase order and had the correct software sent over by courier. The next surprise came when the technical staff member tried to install the software from the CD; he discovered that the six-speed CD-ROM drive that was supposed to be part of the configuration we had purchased hadn't been shipped with the computer, let alone installed.

Testing the Environment

Finally, the entire development environment, including all the workstations, as well as the server, must be tested to ensure that all the pieces do, in fact, coexist with each other. Since rigorous testing of the entire system can't occur until some development has been done, or portions of the application are available, an alternative is to create a small hypertext application for testing purposes. This is particularly useful for testing products like Sapphire/Web, which is used to automate interface development, or if there are DBMS gateways in use. Once again, dealing with testing as soon as possible avoids a last-minute scramble to get things working properly.

Authoring

Authoring encompasses all the activities required to prepare the HTML source files that make up the hypertext pages, but excludes any external programs used to send, receive, or manipulate data. The following tasks are part of authoring activity.

Publication/Application Structure

The relationship and flow (movement) between the various hypertext pages that make up the application or publication must be planned prior to creating the pages. The three primary structures that can be used (as we discussed in Chapter 7) are hierarchical, linear, and blended. The easiest way to plan your structure is to prepare a graphical representation of the relationships between pages. These maps, or diagrams, are an essential element of designing the application, and are not that dissimilar to the flow charting computer programmers use to plan their programs.

Content Specification

Staff members from the area sponsoring the project will have to identify the information to be included in the hypertext pages, and must be responsible for ensuring that the correct content is provided and presented in a suitable format. Depending on the application, providing content may involve staff from more than one area within the organization, so it's necessary to clearly establish who will make the final decisions regarding content (the editorial role).

Page Layout

As you've learned from previous chapters, the electronic medium is different from the paper medium. Although electronic information has many strengths, it's not without its weaknesses. The major limitation is the amount of information that can be comfortably displayed on the screen without scrolling (usually 18 lines of text). The information, whether text or graphics, must be organized in such a fashion that it's comfortable to read and easy to follow as the reader scrolls through the pages. The most likely candidates for handling layout are graphics people, if there are any in-house, or staff who have worked on newsletters or similar publications where layout is more complex than in standard office memos or reports.

Document Conversion

If your application is going to take advantage of existing documents, the documents will have to be displayed in their native format, converted to hypertext, or changed to a document format the browser can display. Since there are plug-ins available for the major word processors, conversion may not be necessary. If you're not using a plug-in, you have to determine which of two kinds of conversion you want to undertake: from the document's native format (Word, for example) to hypertext; or from the native format to a portable format that can be displayed in the browser, such as PDF.

There are numerous tools available to automate document-to-HTML conversion, but the results are not 100-percent perfect. Any staff member can probably use the conversion software, but someone with HTML skills will have to clean up the converted documents. Document-to-PDF conversions are nearly foolproof, since the structure and layout of the original aren't altered—only the method in which the data is stored changes.

 In the case of large document collections where the retention of existing format and layout is important, consider converting the documents to Adobe's PDF. The resulting PDF files can be displayed by the browser using Adobe's PDF reader plug-in. This is what B.C. Hydro elected to do with 1,800 procedures it wanted to provide to users on their intranet (see Chapter 4).

GRAPHICS

Simple graphics can be used effectively to brighten pages and make a document more pleasant to read, and images can also be used as hypertext links, to aid readers in navigating through the pages. Several collections of icons and clip art are freely available to page authors on the World Wide Web. To use these images, the level of graphics skills required is not extensive. If, however, you want to create or manipulate more complex graphics, you'll need someone in your organization who is familiar with computer graphics software.

Including and displaying graphics images on a page is an area where page layout requires particularly careful consideration. Far too many page authors insert images too large to be displayed on a single screen without scrolling.

 If an image cannot, for whatever reason, be reduced, consider using a thumbnail of the picture, so the user has some idea of what is coming.

PAGE AUTHORING

All the hypertext page source files that contain HTML tags will have to be created using a conventional text editor, word processing software, or an HTML editor/authoring tool. There are two approaches for doing this. The first involves having content specialists create the content in a word processor, and then having someone familiar with HTML add the tags; the second is to create the content and add the tags at the same time. In terms of skills, anyone with rudimentary typing and word processing experience can learn the basic HTML formatting tags in one day. However, more complex structures, such as tables and forms, take a bit longer to learn. Generally speaking, preparing HTML documents isn't complicated, but it can be time-consuming and tedious—a good reason to consider investing in one of the more robust authoring tools, such as FrontPage.

CONTENT REVIEW

After pages are created, the content specialists should review them, to ensure that the content is accurate, the layout works well for the material, page flow is suitable, and writing style is appropriate for the readers.

PUBLICATION/APPLICATION TESTING

Completed sections of the application or publication can be made available on the test environment, to ensure that all the links and CGI scripts are operating correctly. Doing this also provides further opportunities for technical tests, content review, and structure review, before the application goes into production testing.

Programming

CGI scripting will be required for any applications that require user input (via forms), or that retrieve data from a source such as a database. In most cases, this programming is handled by someone from the systems area, but user programmers are becoming more and more evident in many organizations. If you have non-systems staff on your team who have acquired some programming experience on their own, they may be perfectly capable of handling basic CGI scripting. However, the final testing of these scripts should be the responsibility of the systems group, since they're the ones responsible for ensuring that the technical environment works correctly. They must also make sure your application doesn't bring down everyone on the network when the server is running multiple applications.

Training

Initially, training may be needed for the development team members and the technical staff involved with the project. As we indicated earlier, the amount and level of training needed will depend on the skill sets the project team already possesses. Given the requisite in-house skills, it may not even be necessary to obtain any outside training resources.

Related to training is the necessity of providing general information about intranets (for instance, hypertext and the World Wide Web) for interested groups in the organization. It's important that the project's supporters, opponents, and interested spectators understand what you're trying to do, as well as what an intranet can do. Therefore, general information sessions should be provided at the beginning of the project. Prior to the pilot implementation, training requirements for the pilot group will also have to be determined, and training developed for this group.

Pilot Implementation

Once the development phase is finished, and as much testing as you feel is necessary has been done by the development team, the application can be implemented on the intranet for use by the pilot user group. This group provides that final level of stress testing needed to shake the bugs out of the system, and gives the systems group a chance to get a more accurate picture of the load on the server and the network in general.

The pilot group is also used to test the training material that was developed. Based on these results, this material can be revised for system users before the application is fully deployed throughout the organization.

Application/Publication Development and Implementation

We've examined the major tasks that need to be completed through the development cycle, many of which are fairly routine to computer professionals. The difference between an intranet project and more traditional development projects is that users take a more active role. At a minimum, they author pages, and in many cases have set up their own Web server and done the CGI scripting needed for their applications.

Intranets, then, are dramatically changing the dynamics of the user group/systems group relationship. If your intranet project is one in which there will be a strong user role during the development phase, then there are some valuable things to be learned from the experiences of the systems people.

Tips for Planning Your Intranet

Plan, plan, and plan again. The time spent in planning before development is repaid tenfold, by eliminating surprises that can throw a monkey wrench into the project.

Manage the development process. In a collaborative project, it's very easy to lose track of which is the most current version of the material; this can lead to new material getting lost or being overwritten.

Manage the change process. As you move along through the development process, changes will be identified—some of them important and capable of adding value to your application, others not so important. These changes have to be reviewed, and then implemented based on their merits. At some point, you'll simply have to put a hold on further changes, if you want to finish the project.

Test, test, and test again. No matter how much testing you do, there will always be a bug that doesn't show up during testing. However, it's usually possible to eliminate the fatal bugs at this stage.

Don't hesitate to ask the systems staff for advice. They really aren't the enemy, and are usually happy to provide the kind of help that will reduce their workload in the long run.

In this chapter, we've looked at the various steps in developing an intranet, with the bulk of the emphasis on planning, since this activity lays the foundation for the entire project, and is what ultimately determines the project's success. In conversations with Steve Whan, at B.C. Hydro, and Gary Fendler, at Aetna Health Plans, the message was the same: Take time to do some detailed planning.

In the following chapter, we'll look at several aspects of Web site management, including models for information distribution, and tools for hypertext link maintenance.

PART

5

When
Construction
Is Completed

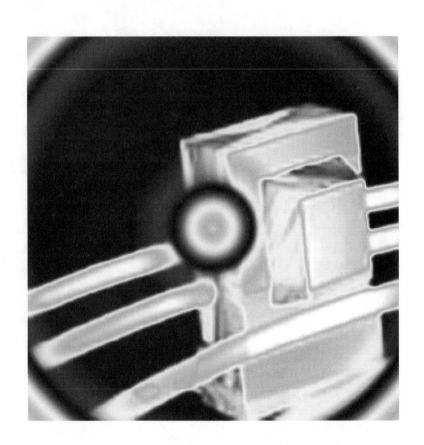

Managing the Web Site: A Necessity, Not an Option

Managing the Web Site: A Necessity, Not an Option

You will discover, as many others have, that it takes just as much work to maintain an intranet Web site and its contents as it does to create one. Site maintenance activities are divided into two general categories: the technical environment and the site's content. In addition to maintaining the site, ongoing capacity planning is necessary to ensure that system capacity and overall performance levels are acceptable.

Maintaining the Environment

The network and server environment is usually maintained by the systems group, although server-related activities may be handled by the local Webmaster, depending on how the individual organization chooses to separate these roles and responsibilities.

Server maintenance focuses on the file collection that resides on the server hard drives, and is carried out to ensure optimal, as well as correct, performance. Over time, as files are created and deleted on a hard drive, the storage area becomes fragmented, and files can no longer be stored in contiguous areas. The end result of this fragmentation is a decrease in data throughput, since it takes longer to locate a specific file and to assemble all of its parts when files are being read from the drive. You need to run software utilities that deal with this problem on a regular basis, to keep the drive unfragmented and ensure that drive performance levels are maintained.

The other file-related activity concerns link maintenance, an essential activity that maintains the integrity of your hypertext system. The hypertext links embedded in a page reference specific files that are retrieved when the link is activated. If the files being referenced have been renamed, moved, or deleted, the link has nothing to retrieve. This isn't the result of carelessness on the part of users or authors, but happens as a matter of course as new material is added to, changed, or deleted from the system. The entire Web site must be checked for these broken links on a regular basis. Most of the newer Web server programs, such as WebSite and Netscape Server, include the capability to scan specified directories and produce a graphical display of the HTML files they contain. This display shows all the links and indicates which ones are broken. There is also software available that's designed specifically for managing Web sites. One such program is COAST WebMaster, which we used to create the Grower Direct Web site map shown in Figure 15.1.

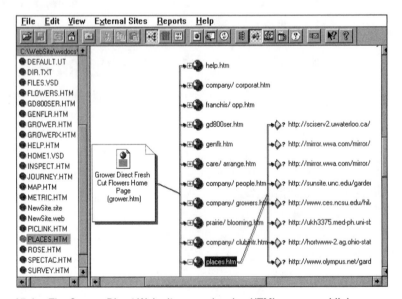

Figure 15.1   The Grower Direct Web site map showing HTML pages and links.

In Figure 15.1, all the links coming from the home page are shown as black arrows, and one of the referenced pages, places.htm, was selected in order to display its external links, shown as large arrowheads followed by a question mark. Products like WebMaster provide a sophisticated collection of tools for link management, including: the ability to display links to other file types, such as graphics files and Java scripts; display broken or duplicated links; launch other external programs (HTML editor, browser, and virus scanning software) from within the program; and report the number of accesses for each hypertext page.

Maintaining the Content

Maintaining and revising the existing content—whether it's publications or office applications—are activities that quickly become more complex and time-consuming because of the increasing volume of information on your intranet, as well as the fact that the publications and applications themselves become more complex as your intranet experience increases. As we've seen with desktop computing, information grows exponentially, and it doesn't take too long for things to get out of control. The issue of publication/application management is one that should be addressed in the planning phase of your first intranet application.

At the same time, you also need to determine how the information on the system will be made available to the users, as well as the procedures the information providers will have to follow in publishing the information. There are two fundamental points of view regarding publishing and distributing information, and each one represents a significantly different philosophical and functional approach (see Figure 15.2). Information-management structures can be based on either the centralized or distributed model; expressed in their purest forms, neither provides a satisfactory way to deal with the issue. The centralized structure, based on a centrally controlled single server, represents information dictatorship; multiple independent servers distributed throughout the organization, on the other hand, are anarchic and chaotic. Some organizations, such as Eli Lilly, espouse strong central control; others, like Electronic Arts, promote user empowerment. Most organizations, however, are still grappling with this issue.

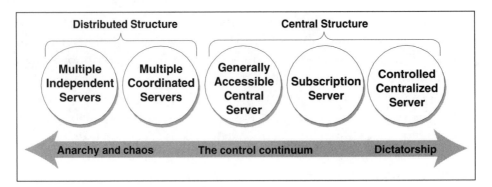

Figure 15.2   The control continuum.

It is the variants of these two models that can provide a workable solution for your particular organization. One of the best works we've seen on this subject is a paper titled, "Collecting and Serving Information Within a Large Organization," by Susana Fernandez Vega and Jean-Yves Le Meur, staff members at CERN. The information on publishing models that follows is summarized from their much broader treatment of this subject.

The paper first addresses two general issues related to electronic publishing: information sources and information scope. Before making a decision as to which publishing structure will best suit your needs, it will be necessary to have a detailed understanding of both the sources and scope of information within your organization.

Information Sources—Because different groups will be using your intranet to publish documents, information will come from a variety of sources within the organization. Consequently, you'll need to consider how much importance to place on each of the following items:

- Maintaining a uniform document style

- Using URLs consistently

- Maintaining consistent and valid HTML syntax

- Data conversion to HTML or PDF

- Publishing the information

Information Scope—Given the diversity of a large organization, there will be a corresponding diversity in the types of information published (for example, personal information, technical reports, or marketing data). As a result, you'll need to establish guidelines regarding the following key items:

- Ease of navigation through the organization's information collection

- Access restrictions needed for sensitive information

- How the information will be represented (rendered)

Based on how an organization chooses to deal with these two issues, Fernandez Vega and Le Meur present five models as alternatives for electronic publishing: "Controlled Centralized Server," "Subscription Server," "Generally Accessible Central Server," "Multiple Independent Servers," and "Multiple Coordinated Servers." The models are grouped into two categories related to the degree of control exercised over publishing activities: *centralized structure* and *distributed structure.*

Centralized Structure

- *Controlled Centralized Server*—In this model, all the organization's Web documents are stored on one server, and a central service group is responsible for collecting, editing, and structuring all the information that's published on this server.

- *Subscription Server*—All Web documents are stored on a single server, but information providers retain direct control over document content and structure. However, they don't have direct access to the server—they must submit documents using the programs provided by the Subscription Server, which, in effect, acts as an electronic publishing agent.

- *Generally Accessible Central Server (GACS)*—In the GACS model, all documents are still distributed from a single server; however, all the information providers have direct access to their own data. They can remove and edit existing documents, or add new ones.

Distributed Structure

- *Multiple Coordinated Servers (MCS)*—In an MCS implementation, each area can set up its own server, but must work through a central coordinating group that approves the setup, and provides assistance to the content providers. This group's role, then, is to coordinate the distribution of information among the various servers distributed through the organization.

- *Multiple Independent Servers (MIS)*—Within the framework of this model, there is no centralized service; all the information is spread out through the organization on servers located in various areas. There is no coordination, and any information provider can set up his own server.

Fernandez Vega and Le Meur's document presents detailed information on the advantages and disadvantages provided by each of the five models, as viewed from administrative, publishing, and user perspectives. We've provided a summary of their comments on the Generally Accessible Central Server and the Multiple Coordinated Server, which are the most suitable for a business intranet environment.

The Generally Accessible Central Server

With this model, content providers have full access to the central server, and complete jurisdiction over the information they publish. Some organizations choose to develop a process for identifying approved content providers, in order to provide some measure of control in this structure, while at the same time distributing the burden of information publishing across the organization (see Figure 15.3).

To facilitate publishing, it's necessary to identify the process and supply the means for providers to access the central server. Some of these access methods are:

- Direct login to the server, enabling providers to edit and test pages directly on the machine (this is not recommended, since it poses the highest risk to server integrity)

- Using an auxiliary machine that replicates the server configuration, allowing providers to work on the auxiliary machine and then transfer the tested files and scripts to the server

- Letting providers work on their own machines—which may limit testing, particularly in the case of CGI programs

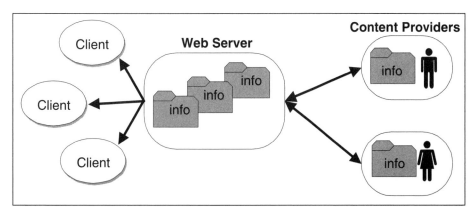

Figure 15.3   The Generally Accessible Central Server model.

ADVANTAGES OF THE GACS MODEL

The greatest advantage of GACS is that duplication of the work required to install and maintain the software on a server is significantly reduced. For areas within an organization lacking in technical skills, this model includes a central service group that can provide needed expertise. Another advantage is ease of navigation through the information, since there is a central structure to provide order to the material. Finally, the GACS approach makes it easier for individuals to be content providers. The only basic skill they need is the ability to create and edit HTML documents; the details of Web server operation are not required.

DRAWBACKS OF THE GACS MODEL

Among the drawbacks of this model is the need to create and manage accounts—as well as to maintain all the software—for a variety of information providers. It can sometimes be difficult to maintain consistent formatting, information style, link consistency, and correct HTML syntax throughout documents.

Multiple Coordinated Servers

With multiple coordinated servers, shown in Figure 15.4, providers have a measure of independence, but the central service that's responsible for coordinating information distribution has to approve each server setup. Depending on the degree of coordination and control desired, the organization can also develop publishing and style guidelines to ensure that

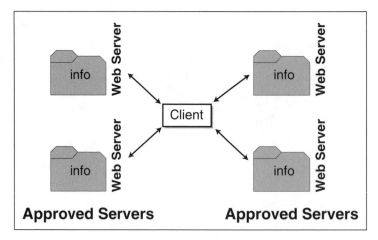

Figure 15.4   The Multiple Coordinated Servers model.

redundant information is eliminated, and that consistency is maintained throughout the company's Web sites.

ADVANTAGES OF THE MCS MODEL

Generally, each area is responsible for the information it delivers, and there isn't a strong reliance on a central service. Within established limits, the information providers have a great deal of control over hardware, software, information format, and content. One of the major advantages of having separate servers is that individual machines are isolated from central hardware failures. While the central service group responsible for coordinating server activity does provide help and instructions on request, its work load, by and large, is reduced by having operational responsibility transferred to individual Webmasters.

From a user perspective, there are also several advantages to this model, among them: multiple access points to company information, the ability to bypass an overloaded or broken central server, and speed of document access.

DRAWBACKS OF THE MCS MODEL

The biggest drawbacks to this model are the increased workload and skill requirements it places on the information provider. In addition to creating information content, the provider also has to take on the tasks of a Webmaster, which include managing the server software (selection, installation, administration, and upgrading) and managing software needed for other facilities, such as CGI scripts, access statistics, or local search engines.

There are some drawbacks from the user perspective as well—most notably, URLs that aren't consistent or homogenous make navigation more difficult. Depending on the degree of central coordination, a lack of uniform document style, and the lack of a global search engine for all the servers, may also be problematic.

Generally, however, the MCS model offers the best solution for supporting user empowerment, while at the same time providing a measure of control over Web site deployment throughout the company.

If you're interested in discussing these models with the authors, you can contact either Susana Fernandez Vega at **susana.fernandez.vega@cern.ch** or Jean-Yves at **Jean-Yves.Le.Meur@cern.ch.** The full text of "Collecting and Serving Information Within a Large Organization" is available in PDF format and can be downloaded from **http://preprints.cern.ch/archive/ electronic/cern/as-96-001.pdf**.

Capacity Planning

As the amount of information contained on the server grows, and general network traffic increases, the capacity of the both the network and server will decrease. The key areas where capacity needs to be monitored on an ongoing basis are: network traffic, server processing, and server hard drive capacity.

Network Traffic

Network traffic will increase as intranet applications are deployed throughout your organization—not necessarily as a result of the increased number of users, but as a consequence of the types of data transferred among the various nodes. As a general rule of thumb, you can estimate that a hypertext page, containing text and a couple of small GIF files, consumes approximately five times as much bandwidth as an ASCII text email message (2 or 3 K, on average).

Since bandwidth on a LAN is finite, the answer lies in spreading the traffic more evenly over the network. At first glance, it would seem that adding more servers provides a simple solution, but this isn't the case. Network load distribution is not a straightforward activity because Ethernet and token ring networks function so differently from one another.

ETHERNET LANs

Since Ethernet is a self-balancing, broadcast network, the addition of servers merely adds to the problem by increasing the broadcast level. The solution, then, is to segment the LAN, using either routers or smart switches to route traffic between the segments.

TOKEN RING LANs

Token ring networks can be optimized either by adding servers, or by adding rings to the network. The server alternative works, providing that these computers are strategically placed on the ring. The use of additional rings is also a viable alternative, but in either case, serious attention must be paid to network redesign, to ensure that an optimal configuration is achieved.

Server Processing

At some point, the Web server hardware will not be able to handle the volume of information requests received, and its ability to serve documents will degrade. The two most common solutions are to split the Web site information across several servers, which has both support and network consequences, or to install a *caching server*. A caching server (also called a *proxy server*) enables the site administrator to store, or cache, frequently accessed documents on another computer, thereby reducing the traffic to the primary server.

Server Hard Drive Capacity

Routine file maintenance should be done to ensure that obsolete or redundant files are purged from the server's hard drives. This maintenance activity will address the capacity issue to some degree, but after a certain point, you'll simply have to increase drive capacity—either by adding more drives, or by replacing existing drives with ones that have more capacity.

Through the course of this book, you've learned what constitutes an intranet, seen some of its uses, and found out what's required to construct, implement, and maintain one of these internal networks. In the next chapter we'll look at connecting to the biggest network, the Internet. Last but not least, in the final chapter, we'll look at some of the general trends related to this topic, and highlight some specific technologies that will be grabbing the spotlight in the near future.

16

Looking Outward: Connecting to the Internet

16

Looking Outward: Connecting to the Internet

"**A**re we connected to the Internet?" is the most common question you will hear before, during, and after the construction of an intranet. If you're not connected, this question will immediately be followed by, "Why not?" But the important question, of course, is, "Why *should* we be connected?" In this chapter, we'll look at the reasons so many organizations are building firewalls and venturing out onto the Internet, what issues are involved, and how to establish a secure connection to the larger network outside the organization.

Reasons For the Intranet-to-Internet Link

There are many good reasons for a company to connect its business to the Internet. The most common are:

- Marketing

- Communications

- Cost reduction

- Customer support and service

- Electronic commerce

- Product/service delivery

- Research

Marketing

Marketing has been the single most compelling reason for corporate Internet connections; it is also the most poorly understood, and probably the most disappointing. In the past two years, literally thousands of companies have scrambled to the World Wide Web in pursuit of market share, hoping to reach and tap into a vast, global consumer group. (The size estimates for this group deviate wildly, ranging from a low of 4 million to a high of 60 million.) The corporate theme for 1995 was "establish an Internet presence."

Since then, some companies have done well, but many Web sites have been abandoned (they're called *ghost sites* in the lingua franca of cyberspace); mostly, however, valuable lessons have been learned. The first lesson has been that commerce on the Internet is still in the process of defining itself, and is by no means stable and predictable. The Internet entrepreneurs have also discovered that the well-oiled and refined marketing techniques of Madison Avenue don't work on the Internet. Web surfers are, by and large, a collection of curious information seekers, disinterested in, and even repulsed by, flashy, 30-second advertising spots. Marketers have also discovered that, instead of one mass market consisting of 30 or 40 million people, the Internet is really composed of thousands of smaller niche markets.

Nevertheless, in spite of the disillusionment numerous businesses experienced during the initial period of the electronic gold rush, the Internet shouldn't be discounted as a marketing tool; it can provide a cost-effective means for marketing your company's products and services. The key is to learn from the experiences of others who have already been there.

Marketing on the Internet: Some Tips

1. Set realistic expectations. Skip Kerr, owner of retail flower franchise Grower Direct Fresh Cut Flowers, set up a Web site on the Internet in the fall of 1995. He had done some research, set a limit on what he was prepared to invest in a Web site, and approached it with an attitude of testing the waters. He didn't expect significant sales increases, but believed that the Internet provided a preview of the way business would be conducted in the future. His investment, then, was primarily to gain experience; if any of the retail outlets had increased sales, or if a franchise was sold through contact with the Grower Direct Web site, he would consider these added bonuses.

2. Understand the medium. Your audience is constrained by several technical limitations, among them screen size and quality, and the speed of individual users' connections to the Internet. Receiving multimedia presentations over a 28.8 modem is not a pleasant experience, nor one that a user would want to repeat.

3. Understand the online culture. For the most part, Internet users are information seekers; if you provide them with useful information, your site will get return visits. Light and sound shows of dubious quality are no substitute for good content—*content is everything!*

Communications

One of the benefits provided by an intranet is improved, low-cost communication among the staff within your organization; the ability to extend this capacity is probably the greatest advantage of having an Internet connection. Unlike the traditional forms of business communication (mail, courier, telephone, and fax), email—used in conjunction with related tools (such as bulletin boards and conferencing)—provides a communications medium that is less encumbered by geography, political boundaries, and time zones. From a user perspective, email provides an opportunity to manage communication more effectively, while at the same time increasing the scope and volume of messages. With the telephone, for example, an employee can normally deal with only one person at a time, and must always be aware of time zones when placing calls. Computer-based electronic communication facilitates ongoing, multiple dialogues that can take place at the convenience of both parties. The communication tools made available by the Internet can also provide improved commerce with business partners, suppliers, distributors, and customers, and is of particular value to broadly distributed companies, since email and other services facilitate effective messaging, regardless of where staff is physically located.

Cost Reductions

Email alone can yield cost reductions, especially if your organization is broadly distributed and relies heavily on long-distance telephone and fax services. The estimated cost of email is six cents per message, and additional savings are garnered by reducing, if not totally eliminating, telephone tag, a common but unproductive office activity.

Another major opportunity for cost savings is in the area of general information distribution—in Chapter 4, we saw how Federal Express anticipated savings of about $120,000 by making just one manual available online. Any cost benefits related to internal publishing apply equally to documents that are published for external use. Not only are production and distribution costs reduced, but there is the added benefit of improved service to your business partners and customers by providing information on demand at their convenience.

Finally, the Internet can be used by companies who want to connect their distributed local networks and create a corporate wide-area network without incurring the costs associated with building, and maintaining, a private WAN. In this scenario, each LAN has an Internet connection, and the larger network infrastructure is used to carry data traffic between sites. This solution is cost effective, but has security implications (see *Network Security: Firewalls*).

Customer Support and Service

Businesses recognize that retaining customers, and the repeat business they generate, is as important as finding new ones. In *The Virtual Corporation*, authors William H. Davidow and Michael S. Malone noted that, "retaining 2 percent more customers has the same effect on the bottom line as cutting costs by 10 percent," and, "for regional banks a twenty-year customer is worth 85 percent more profits than a ten-year one."

And, in a speech he made at the 1990 American Banker Conference, keynote speaker Robert Williams said, "People are no longer buying just products or services...they are buying *relationships.*"

Relationships are built on customer support and service, the foundation of which is communications; customers expect to receive help or information at the time they ask for it—not the frustration of being told that the information they need isn't readily available, or that the person who can answer their question isn't in the office. Customer support and service activities can be enhanced by providing online information repositories (brochures, catalogs, price lists) and lists of Frequently Asked Questions (FAQs) that deal with the typical problems customers may encounter. These FAQs can take the form of, "How do I...?", followed by the solution: "You can fix this by..." Making information available online speeds up information retrieval for your customers, reduces frustration by giving them answers to their questions in a timely manner, and builds the kind of relationship that retains their business.

Electronic Commerce

Electronic commerce on the Internet has not been as successful as anticipated, primarily because of the issue of secure transactions and the current public attitude toward online shopping in general.

Because the Internet is a packet-switched network, packets of data sent from one point to another travel by way of many other computer systems (called hops), giving anyone with the appropriate skills ample opportunity to intercept, copy, and use the information. However, this lack of security in transactions between vendor and purchaser is rapidly becoming a non-issue because of encryption technology now built into Web server software programs (S-HTTP and SSL are the two major secure server protocols). Information can still be intercepted as it travels over the Internet, but the encrypted contents are not easily readable without considerable computing resources—resources that typically aren't available to most thieves on the network. Alarmist articles continue to appear in various magazines, questioning the suitability of the Internet for conducting online commerce, but these fears should be put to rest in light of the following:

- Several major North American banks are rapidly moving towards providing full-service banking for their customers, using the Internet.

- VISA International and Mastercard are working together on a standard called SET (Secure Electronic Transactions), which will ensure secure credit card transactions over the Internet.

SET

A collaborative effort by VISA International and Mastercard (with a total of approximately 700 million customers worldwide), SET will enable secure credit card transactions over the Internet. This new standard combines secret-key, public-key, and digital signatures to secure and validate transactions.

SET is intended to meet the following business requirements:

- Provide confidentiality of ordering and payment information

- Ensure data integrity for all transmitted information

- Provide cardholder authentication

- Provide merchant authentication

- Facilitate software and network interoperability

The second, and perhaps more significant, stumbling block to online commerce is general public attitude. Shopping is still very much a social activity, and provides a chance not only to get out, but possibly to meet friends or family, as well. A major attitudinal change will have to occur before online shopping really takes off. An associated aspect is the types of products and services sold online. Some, such as book and music clubs, lend themselves well to electronic commerce. As direct sales institutions, these have been a part of our culture for decades. Club members select products from a brochure, mail a form, and in eight or ten weeks, ordered products appear along with an invoice. The online incarnation makes this process even easier—members just fill in and submit an electronic form to order the clubs' products. An online ordering system can provide an effective means of facilitating product sales and provide a useful service to your customers.

Product/Service Delivery

Product and service delivery using the electronic medium is limited by what can actually be delivered online, and is being used primarily by companies selling information or computer software (some pioneering work, however, is also taking place with the distribution of digitized music). Information, of course, exists in electronic format, and can either be a product or a service. The real boom in product delivery is happening in the computer software industry, where most of the major vendors have made it possible to download programs from their Web sites. The benefit to the vendor is the elimination of most of the distribution costs (copying programs to media, packaging, and shipping); benefits to the consumer are immediate availability, and the elimination of unnecessary packaging.

Research

The Internet is a vehicle for accessing an incredibly large collection of information provided by individuals, institutions, and corporations. For some companies, direct and immediate access to diverse information sources is a critical element of business. The biggest drawback of the Internet is the overwhelming amount of information available, all seemingly unrelated and disorganized. Fortunately, information collections such as AltaVista, InfoSeek, Inktomi, and Yahoo have given searchers tools that make finding specific information a great deal easier than it was as recently as two years ago. If serious research is one of your primary reasons for connecting to the Internet, two procedures are of particular importance:

- Establish the credentials of an information source.

- Verify the accuracy of information by cross-checking it against other sources.

Because of the vast wealth of information available on the Internet, there are very few subject areas you can't research. However, it's wise to remember that not everything you might find will be accurate and credible.

Use the Internet's resources and tools as an adjunct to your operational activities, *not* as a replacement.

Making the Connection: The Issues

Before proceeding with connecting your company intranet to the Internet, there are several issues you need to be aware of, and that should be addressed before you make the actual connection. They are, in order of importance: security, capacity, and usage.

Security

Your gateway to the Internet is bi-directional, which means it's also a gateway into your intranet; everything available internally (such as financial applications and corporate databases) is potentially at risk to outside intruders. Even if the intranet itself doesn't provide direct access to sensitive information, this gateway provides an access point to the corporate network. In addition to the security mechanisms provided by various applications and the NOS, there are numerous other hardware and software solutions that can be used to secure your network and reduce the risks associated with having a corporate Internet connection.

An additional security risk comes from your staff's ability to transfer software programs from various locations on the Internet to their own computer. In light of this, virus detection procedures will need to be reassessed in order to determine whether or not they are adequate, and to determine if the existing virus detection and removal tools are adequate for the task.

Capacity

If you choose to allow outsiders access to information on your intranet, and your site generates a large volume of data traffic, both incoming and outgoing, then Web server capacity becomes a major issue. The server has to be able to handle the increased traffic load without degrading the performance of your internal network. Depending on the level of activity, hardware and software upgrades may be necessary to maintain acceptable performance levels.

Usage: Acceptable Use Policy

The Internet, especially the World Wide Web, has created a new problem in the corporate environment—a rapidly growing body of electronic loafers. It is akin to the problem of staff using company time to play computer games, only with some significant differences. The staff computer gamers are using company time and workstation computer resources; Web surfers are using time and workstation resources, plus the cost of the Internet connection and its bandwidth, and this can significantly impact system performance.

A related problem is staff use of the company's Internet User IDs when posting to discussion groups on the Usenet or mailing lists. Everything that's posted reflects on your organization, regardless of any disclaimers that appear in the signature of the message, such as, "This is a personal opinion and does not reflect the views of XYZ Corp." Remember, this is a global network; statements made by staff, and their behavior in cyberspace, can have far-reaching business and legal consequences.

A clearly stated acceptable-use policy must be put in place in your organization before an Internet connection is established. It must spell out, in detail, what behavior is acceptable, and what is considered appropriate or inappropriate use of company time and resources regarding Internet activities.

Making the Connection: The Requirements

The basic requirements for an Internet connection are: an Internet Service Provider (ISP), a data line from your host or gateway computer to the ISP, and devices for connecting your gateway computer to the data line. Figure 16.1 illustrates a minimal configuration, which we'll modify later to accommodate issues such as security and performance.

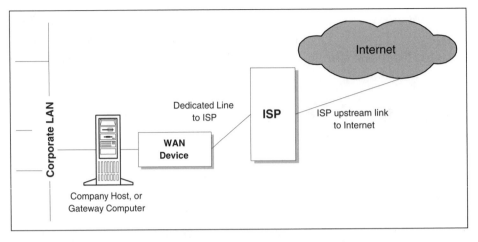

Figure 16.1   Minimal configuration for a corporate Internet connection.

The Internet Service Provider

In addition to providing an access point to the Internet through their computer system, the ISP allocates a *dedicated* IP address to your company. This number identifies your host computer (the gateway) to other hosts on the Internet, and provides the static IP address required if you want to register a *domain name* for your company. The domain name is a unique alphanumeric identifier that identifies your company, and is mapped to a specific IP address. The use of domain names generally makes Internet addressing more flexible and easier for users.

How Domain Names Work

The Domain Name Service (DNS) enables the mapping of alphanumeric information (although text characters are usually used) to an IP address, which consists of dotted-octet numbers. A fictitious IP address would look like this: **127.161.22.12**. By using DNS, we can convert it to an address, or *domain name*, that looks like this: **sparky.research.widgits.com**. In this example, each part of the IP address has corresponding text mapped to it. Table 16.1 shows the mapping of this sample domain name to a fictional IP address, and explains what each part represents.

It should be noted that not all of the four IP address elements need to have text mapped to the numbers; however, at least two must be mapped in order for the domain name to be valid (for example, **essten.com** is a valid domain name).

Individual, organization, and corporate domain names are registered with the Internet Network Information Center (InterNIC), and domain name registration is a service provided by many ISPs. Service provision has become a highly competitive business, with most ISPs offering a broad range of services above and beyond providing Internet connectivity (for example, hosting Web pages, consulting, and so on). These value-added services benefit the consumer, but it does make the selection of a service provider somewhat more confusing. We've put together a list of criteria in Table 16.2, geared towards finding a "no-frills" Internet provider, which will help make the process of selecting an ISP a little easier.

Table 16.1   An Example of Domain Name Mapping to an IP Address

IP Address Element (Octet)	Text	Representation
127	Sparky	The name assigned to the host computer
161	Research	A subnetwork under the host computer
22	Widgits	The company name
12	Com	The type of organization (*com* designates a commercial entity)

Table 16.2   Criteria for Selecting an Internet Service Provider

Criteria	Rationale
Length of time in business	A track record provides some assurance that the company has business experience, and will still be in business next month
Scope of services provided	This provides an indicator of whether or not it has any technical strengths, or if it's primarily a marketing firm

(Continued)

Table 16.2 Criteria for Selecting an Internet Service Provider (Continued)

Criteria	Rationale
Company size	Another indicator of stability, as well as of its ability to provide adequate support for your company
Percentage of staff that is dedicated to support	You want a company that can provide adequate support, which is not usually provided by firms who are top-heavy in marketing personnel
Number of computer professionals employed by the company	You not only need bodies dedicated to support, but bodies with the right skills
Available references	Direct and indirect checks (such as newsgroup discussions) provide a good indicator of the level and quality of service you can expect to receive
The ISP's connection to the Internet	A high-capacity line from your site to the ISP is wasted if its own connection is a low bandwidth link shared by all of its other subscribers
Service guarantees	Does it offer service guarantees, such as the number of hours of uptime during the business week, or the length of time required to fix a problem
Monthly downtime— typical outages, average length of time down per outage	This information provides an indication of the system's stability
Trouble reporting	It will be helpful to know if there is more than one way to report problems, and if you can report problems in your off-hours
Problem response and repair records	The ISP should provide records that demonstrate how quickly they respond to, and resolve problems, as well as whether or not they have escalation procedures if a problem isn't resolved in an appropriate period of time. Your business will be negatively impacted by lengthy periods of downtime

(Continued)

Table 16.2 Criteria for Selecting an Internet Service Provider (Continued)	
Criteria	**Rationale**
Setup costs	You should know the initial cost of setting up a connection
Rate structure	You should also know if are there any additional surcharges for the volume of Internet traffic, or time of day the connection is used
Proximity	There's an advantage to having your ISP in close proximity; remember, there are additional line charges you must pay to the telephone company, and distance is a factor in these rates, too

The Data Line

The data line is the link that connects your computer to the ISP, and that will carry all the traffic between your site and the Internet. There are numerous options available, with availability and pricing for each depending on geographic location. Because of this, we haven't used actual prices for the various options, but have given typical rate structures instead. The current data line options we'll look at, in order of general availability, are: analog dialup, point-to-point (or dedicated leased line), frame relay, and Integrated Services Digital Network (ISDN).

ANALOG DIALUP

An analog dialup connection makes use of a modem over a conventional analog telephone line. The effective throughput is determined by two factors: the quality of the telephone line (that is, its susceptibility to interference) and the speed of the modem. Line quality can be affected by factors such as electrical interference, the age of the telephone lines, and weather conditions. Needless to say, line quality can vary a great deal from region to region, or even from area to area within a city. 28.8 Kbps modems are readily available today at reasonable prices; you shouldn't even consider anything slower for a server connection. Keep in mind that the 28.8 speed rating applies only to ideal conditions; in the event of poor line quality, modems reduce the speed sufficiently to compensate for line conditions.

In the long term, a dialup connection isn't the best choice for Internet access because of its limited transmission speed; in the short term, however, it's an inexpensive way to get your feet wet and carry out testing while waiting for a dedicated line to be installed.

POINT-TO-POINT

Point-to-point refers to a dedicated, leased line connection from your site to the ISP. This is by far the most common type of connection for business, and these lines are available with different speeds and options: 56 Kbps Leased Line, 56 Kbps Frame Relay, T1, Fractional T1, and T3. Installing a point-to-point connection will increase connectivity costs, since additional devices are needed for this type of service.

56 KBPS LEASED LINES

For this type of connection, you lease a line from the telephone company in order to provide a dedicated physical connection from your site to the ISP. You can expect to have *both* the telephone company and the ISP bill you for installation, and a monthly line rate is charged for the service. The installation fee and monthly rate will, of course, vary according to the geographic area you are in, the telephone company providing the service, and most importantly—the *length of the physical connection.*

In addition, you'll require a router and a Channel Service Unit/Data Service Unit (CSU/DSU). The router, as you may recall, is a device that handles the routing of data traffic between networks, and is essential for the connection. The CSU/DSU takes incoming data traffic from the ISP (converted for transmission over the line), and translates this data into an Internet Protocol (IP) packet, which is then routed to its destination on your network. Conversely, outgoing data is converted from IP packets into another format for transmission, and sent to the ISP where the CSU/DSU at that end translates your data back into IP packets and sends it along to the ISP's router. These devices are necessary at both ends of the leased line, and you should be aware of the fact that most ISPs require you to purchase this equipment for their end of the connection as well as for yours. Most are not willing to supply routers and CSU/DSUs for all their customers, since the combined cost ranges from $1500 to $2500 for each installation.

56 KBPS FRAME RELAY

Frame relay is an alternative to regular leased line (56 Kbps), which also provides 56 Kbps of bandwidth. It's a technique used by telephone companies, which allows an ISP's subscribers to share a line from the telephone company to the ISP, rather than having each subscriber pay for a separate line. Each subscriber's frame relay line enters what the telephone company calls a frame relay cloud, where data is routed along a Permanent Virtual Circuit (PVC) into a single high-speed connection (usually a T1 line) to the ISP. The advantage for the ISP is that they only need to maintain one line and set of devices, as opposed to separate lines and devices for each of their subscribers. From the customer's perspective, there are two significant cost advantages to this type of connection. The first benefit is that you only have to provide a router and CSU/DSU for your end of the line; the second, and perhaps most advantageous, gain occurs if you decide to switch your service to a different ISP. Rather than facing an installation fee of approximately $1000 to install a new line, all the telephone company has to do is flip some switches to change your PVC routing—at a cost of $25 or $30. A frame relay connection is shown in Figure 16.2, using a T1 line from the phone company to the ISP. In this particular illustration, the single T1 line has a bandwidth capacity that is the equivalent of 24 56 Kbps lines.

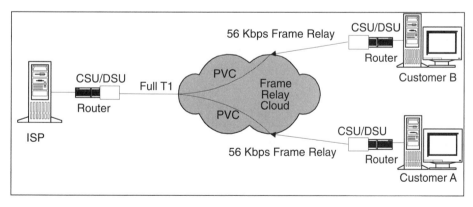

Figure 16.2   Using a frame relay to connect customers to an ISP.

T1

The T1 connection provides data transmission at 1.5 Mbps—about 25 times faster than a 56 Kbps line. The speed is greater, and so is the cost. Installation charges remain much the same, but expect the monthly rate to be approximately five times higher, and the cost of a CSU/DSU (normally $150-$250) to increase to the vicinity of $1000.

Remember, even if you have a T1 connection to the ISP, its sole line upstream may be a T1 that is shared by all its subscribers. If you require full T1, make sure you have an agreement in writing with the ISP, and be prepared to be billed for additional device costs, and perhaps even for the cost of a T1 from the ISP to its access provider.

FRACTIONAL T1

Since a single physical T1 line can be divided, or *fractioned,* into 24 channels, each with a capacity of 64 Kbps, it is possible to lease a fraction of a T1's capacity from the telephone company. They usually lease this capacity in pairs (for example, two, four, or six channels), and set a limit on the number of pairs you can purchase before you have to pay the cost of a full T1 connection.

Installation costs for a fractional T1 line are the same as for full T1, since a physical line must be installed, but monthly rates are lower because you're not using the line's full capacity. If you decide to upgrade your capacity, from, for example, four to six channels, you don't normally have to pay the full installation fee again, but there is usually a small fee for adding channels. Line device requirements are the same as for a T1 connection.

T3

The approximate speed of a T3 line is 45 Mbps, or about 28 times faster than a T1 connection. This type of capacity is really only needed for Wide Area Network backbones like the Internet, and if you need this kind of capacity, it's likely that only your ISP's provider could sell you a T3 connection.

ISDN

The ISDN service is not as broadly deployed as the other types of connections for three reasons. The first is that it requires significant hardware and software upgrades at the telephone companies' sites (it is a digital, rather than analog, transmission service). The second reason is the price of the associated equipment that's needed, and the third is a result of competing and proprietary standards related to this technology. However, ISDN has been gaining ground over the past two years, because telephone companies have upgraded their systems, equipment prices have come down, and the standards issues have begun to be resolved. There are two flavors of ISDN: the Basic Rate Interface (BRI) and the Primary Rate Interface (PRI). BRI consists of three logical channels—D, B1, and B2. The D channel has a bandwidth of 16 Kbps, and is used for control information about the ISDN call. The two B (bearer) channels each provide up to 64 Kbps, and can be assigned to carry either voice or data, or be dynamically combined to provide one data channel with a bandwidth of 128 Kbps.

Cost wise, BRI rates vary a great deal from region to region, and from phone company to phone company. Some provide flat-rate BRI at $90 per month, while others charge from $40 to $90 per month, *plus* a 15 cent per minute surcharge. Equipment for an ISDN connection is still fairly expensive, and you'll need an ISDN router ($450-$750) and a device called a network terminator, or NT-1 ($100-$150 for an external unit) to replace the CSU/DSU.

PRI functions the same as BRI, except that it provides 1 D channel and 23 B channels. Unlike BRI, the D channel can carry 64 Kbps, meaning that the combined capacity of all the channels is the equivalent of T1. The difference between PRI and T1 is that PRI ISDN enables the customer to dynamically allocate each of the channels to carry voice, data, or any other digital transmission. The carrier's rates for this ISDN offering, and the associated equipment, are still a barrier to the widespread deployment of PRI.

Of the options available for connecting to the Internet, your selection should be based on your estimated bandwidth requirements, and will, hopefully, not be restricted by the availability of suppliers and services in your geographical area. Table 16.3 provides a summary of the different types of connections based on:

- *Bandwidth*—The amount of data that can be sent through a line in one second

- *Call Setup Time*—The length of time required to establish a connection if the line is not constantly active

- *Rate Structure*—The way services are billed to consumers

- *General Availability*—The availability of services in most geographical areas

- *Suitability for Incoming Traffic*—The suitability of the connection for incoming traffic, which requires a live connection

Table 16.4 is a sample checklist you can use for preparing cost and service comparisons between the different service providers.

Network Security: Firewalls

The cornerstone of network security mechanisms is something called a *firewall*—an entity made up of hardware and/or software, used to control the flow of information between your organization's network and the outside world. The general perception of firewalls is that having one will make your network impervious to security attacks; unfortunately, this is not necessarily the case. Take a moment to examine the origin of the term firewall. Remember that a building firewall does not prevent, stop, or extinguish a fire; the intent is simply to slow down the rate at which a fire spreads—the

Table 16.3	Types of Connections to an ISP			
Factor	Analog	Dialup	Dedicated or Point-to-Point Frame Relay	ISDN
Bandwidth	14.4 or 28.8 Kbps	56 Kbps to 1.5 Mbps	56 Kbps to 1.5 Mbps	56/64 or 112/128 Kbps
Call Setup Time	30 seconds or longer	None	Negligible	5 seconds or less
Rate Structure	Fixed or per minute	Fixed	Fixed	Fixed or per minute
General Availability	High	High	Medium	Medium
Suitability for Incoming Traffic	Low; only while connection is active	High; connection is always open	High; connection is always open	Medium; only while connection is active

Table 16.4   Service Provider Checklist for a Dedicated Connection

Item	Information
Provider	
Connection Speed	
Line Installation Fee	
Monthly Network Charge	
Monthly Line Charge	
Port Connection Fee	
Local Router Cost	
Remote Router Cost	
Local CSU/DSU Cost	
Remote CSU/DSU cost	
Surcharges	
Other Costs	

firewall is a barrier, but it is not impenetrable. Similarly, in the computer world, a firewall does not totally prevent or stop network intrusions. However, used in conjunction with other security mechanisms and procedures, it does significantly improve the security of your network, by isolating it from direct access by outsiders. *Take note:* Firewalls filter information—they do not encrypt it. This is an important distinction if your organization is using the Internet as an infrastructure for a WAN that links your distributed LANs together. Once data has left one LAN and is being passed over the Internet to its destination, it's vulnerable. However, an approach called Virtual Private Networks (VPN), supported by several firewall manufacturers, enables you to securely extend your intranet's capabilities to include remote sites.

Virtual Private Networks

VPN is an extension of firewall software capability that provides encrypted and authenticated communications between sites using the Internet to carry data traffic. Figure 16.3 illustrates the use of VPN for communications between a remote office and a portion of the head office network.

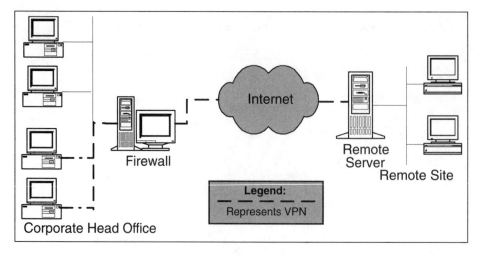

Figure 16.3 Using VPN to secure intra-office communications over the Internet.

Aside from VPNs, there are several types of firewall configurations, each of which employs different techniques for handling incoming and outgoing traffic. Overall, however, firewall design is based on one of two approaches:

- Allow everything to pass through, except specified packets

- Allow nothing to pass through, except specified packets

The jargon of the firewall world can get very confusing: sometimes, one term is used to describe several different configurations and techniques, while at other times, many different terms are used to describe the same thing. Consequently, we'll deal with some of this terminology before proceeding any further.

Host-based Firewall—This refers to any computer running firewall software. If the software is geared to security at the application level, it's also referred to as an application proxy, proxy server, or application gateway. It's not uncommon for host-based firewalls to be called bastion or gateway hosts as well.

Router-based Firewall—This firewall uses routers, called screening routers or packet-filtering routers, to screen packet information.

Dual-homed Gateway—Dual-homing is a TCP/IP term that describes the ability of a device to have more than one IP address. In a dual-homed gateway configuration, the computer has two network interfaces—one for the internal network, the other for the outside network. This gateway combines packet filtering and application proxy features to make it one of the most secure options, allowing no direct access to internal systems.

Firewall Techniques

There are four major techniques employed to handle the data passing through a firewall:

- Intermediate networks

- Packet filters

- Application gateways

- Circuit-level gateways

Rather than rely solely on one technique, systems that require a high level of security often combine all four.

INTERMEDIATE NETWORKS

If Internet access to your intranet is provided by an intermediate, non-TCP/IP network, such as MCI Mail or SprintMail, the risk to your network is significantly reduced. These proprietary networks don't have the vulnerability of TCP/IP and Unix systems. However, there are still risks associated with virus attacks from downloaded files, so virus detection procedures and tools are still essential. This type of firewall is sometimes referred to as a *passive firewall*, and is shown in Figure 16.4.

PACKET FILTERS

Packet filtering is handled by the router, or a computer acting as a router, which examines the contents of each incoming and outgoing packet for its source, destination, and service type. Packet filtering, shown in Figure 16.5, relies on detailed, complicated, predefined rules set out in filter tables. Two forces work against the packet-filtering approach to security: one is the nature of routers themselves—they are devices designed to facilitate, rather than impede, communications. The second is the fact that router technology is, for the most part, proprietary, with each manufacturer using its own syntax and methods to implement filter tables, thereby providing ample opportunity for the inexperienced to program in faulty logic.

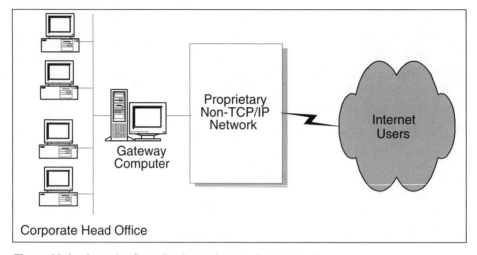

Figure 16.4   A passive firewall using an intermediate network.

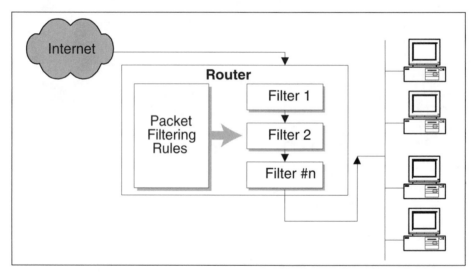

Figure 16.5   Router packet filtering, based on router tables.

There are maintenance issues as well, since every change made to the system, including the router software, requires a reassessment of the programming in place. This activity is not automated, so time-consuming, hands-on programming and testing must be done for each modification.

Packet filtering gateways provide a good measure of security in a Windows NT environment, since this OS is not as prone to hackers as the Unix-based operating systems.

In an NT environment, don't use Dynamic Host Configuration Protocol (DHCP) for dynamic IP address assignments. By not using DHCP you'll have more control over IP address allocation and it'll be easier to maintain router tables.

APPLICATION GATEWAYS

Unlike packet-filtering gateways, application gateways apply rules and safeguards based on specific applications, rather than on packets. The application gateway examines all calls to a specific application. Then, based on authorization (for example, the address of the requester or the correct password), it permits access to the application, through programs called proxies (there are both client and server proxies). All traffic deals with these proxy services, rather than directly with the applications, thereby providing a good level of security.

There are some disadvantages to this approach, one of which is that this type of gateway requires special programs for each specific application. If the appropriate program doesn't exist for one of your applications, the gateway must be custom-developed. (Most of the common Internet applications, such as email, FTP, and Telnet already have application gateway programs.) Application gateways are also more expensive and less flexible than router-based firewalls, and are more complicated to use. However, their superior logging capability and authentication services may justify the inconvenience and increased cost. Figure 16.6 illustrates the use of an application gateway.

CIRCUIT-LEVEL GATEWAYS

Related to the application gateway, circuit-level gateways control access to a system based on port connections between trusted (your network) and nontrusted (the Internet) hosts. The host on the outside of the gateway connects to a TCP port on the gateway machine, and if the gateway computer determines that the calling host is authorized to use the requested service, a connection is established to the port supplying the service. The gateway then serves as an intermediary, passing packets back and forth between the service and the outside host. If authorization fails, the connection is dropped and information about the attempted access is logged.

This type of gateway is also commonly used to place limits on outbound traffic destinations. One of two protocols can be used for this purpose:

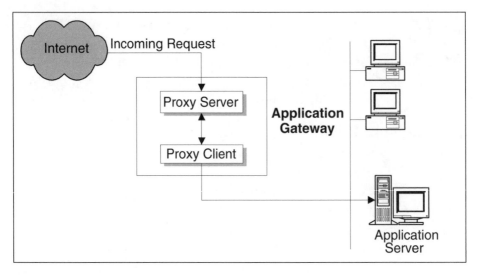

Figure 16.6 Using an application gateway for access control.

socks or proxy. Socks screens on the basis of the IP address, whereas proxy uses the destination's host name.

Like application gateways, circuit-level gateways are very good at hiding internal network names and addresses, and provide good security—but are not easily adapted to new services. The circuit-level gateway concept is illustrated in Figure 16.7.

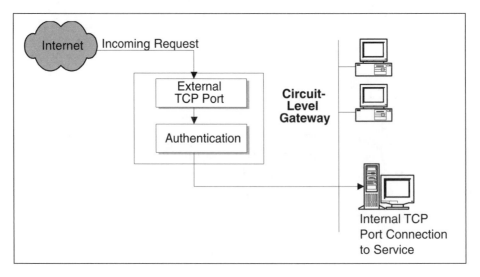

Figure 16.7 Access control using a circuit-level gateway.

Money invested in security will, over the long term, prove a good investment. It's important that security be dealt with thoroughly, in order to minimize the risk to your organization's intranet. Given the complexity of the issue, hiring a qualified security consultant to install your firewall is something we'd recommend.

Connecting your intranet to the Internet is not without its risks, complexities, and costs, but this shouldn't dissuade you from taking advantage of the benefits that can be realized from establishing this connection. The future promises to hold even more opportunities for organizations that link their intranets with the larger, global network.

Themes, Trends, and Technologies

17

Themes, Trends, and Technologies

While making technology predictions is only slightly less risky than weather forecasting, in this final chapter, we will risk identifying some themes and trends that we believe will continue over the next year. In addition, we've also looked at some areas of technology that will most likely play a major future role in the intranet environment.

Themes

The major theme of today's corporate intranet is electronic publishing—a theme that will grow more prevalent as more companies discover the benefits of putting their volumes of paper-based information online. It's clear that hypertext, and the Web delivery system, are without equal as vehicles for delivering different kinds and sizes of documents throughout the organization.

This system is fast, inexpensive, and above all, easy to learn and use. As such, it provides the average worker with a powerful tool that can be used to communicate and collaborate with other staff in the organization—without having to be heavily reliant on the systems group. And viewed from the financial perspective, the publishing aspect of an intranet, more than any of its other applications, provides the quickest and most significant return on investment.

The publishing theme will continue to dominate until other areas of intranet technology, such as Web-based client/server and systems integration applications, become more mature. The intranet concept is, after all, still relatively young, and there are some key issues (performance is one of them) that need to be addressed before other kinds of applications can be deployed at the same speed with which electronic documents are being published. Another major issue is security, particularly if the Internet itself is used as a communications backbone by an organization. And, until corporate management's comfort level with security rises, there will be a reluctance to host mission-critical applications on an intranet.

Trends

The intranet concept will continue to encroach on certain established areas of the computing environment, and as intranet software matures, some of these areas may be eliminated entirely. In the short term, five areas in particular will be affected as Web technology spreads through the office environment: network operating systems, client/server, desktop publishing, imaging, and systems integration.

Network Operating Systems

In March 1996, the Forrester Group, a technology research company, produced a report called "The Full Service Intranet," dealing with networking technology, strategies, and services. In the report, they predict that over the next four years, intranet technology will surpass proprietary NOS technology, such as that supplied by Novell and Microsoft. They assert that intranet technology will provide five core services (directory, email, file, print, and network management) which, when combined with open standards and low cost, will allow this to happen.

We agree with the Forrester analysis—especially their selection of directory services and their comment that, "...directories will be the cornerstone." The major weakness of intranets has been the absence of robust directory services for managing user information, file and systems configurations, and application attributes. We suggest, however, that this will take place far sooner than anticipated by Forrester. In June 1996, Netscape Communications released a strategy paper titled, "The Netscape Intranet

Vision and Product Roadmap," in which the company addressed the "full service intranet" topic. On the subject of directory services, Netscape announced a server software product called *Directory Server 1.0* (scheduled for release in Fall 1996), which will provide universal directory services based on the X.500 naming model.

Client/Server

As we've seen, client/server suffers from being overly complex and expensive to implement throughout an organization. Given the lower cost, relative simplicity, and openness of Web protocols and services, intranet-based client/server will force the current collection of client/server products out of the corporate computing picture. The organization's internal Web will provide the middleware, with browsers as a common user interface. Web-based client/server is scaleable, flexible, non-proprietary, and extensible—features that can't be equaled at comparable cost by any of today's client/server products. There will be some delay (and confusion) in the short term, as a larger selection of easy-to-use and robust development products appear for this segment of the market. Because proprietary architectures, on the whole, provide better performance than open systems, one of the key issues Web client/server has to address is performance. Once the performance issue is laid to rest, and an ample selection of development tools are made available, Web client/server will dominate the office computing environment.

Desktop Publishing

Desktop publishing software products are one of those niche products that we expect to see disappear in the office environment. They have become more reasonably priced in the past few years, but for the most part they're complex and difficult to learn. Some products, like Corel, have been expanded to include every possible desktop function within a single product set (drawing, animation, desktop publishing, imaging, word processing, and so on). The result is an over-priced, complex product suite that consumes more than 150 MB of hard drive space. Corel and similar products continue to remain locked in the paper-based publishing paradigm, and if the vendors of desktop publishing products don't recognize the reality of Web publishing and adjust fairly quickly, market share—and even continued existence—will be at risk.

Imaging

Imaging technology is an area that should benefit from the continued deployment of intranets. This technology has been held back because of cost and proprietary standards, particularly in the area of the user interface/delivery software. The Web's object-based protocols provide an ideal user interface and delivery mechanism for using image technology in the office environment.

Systems Integration

Many office environments have struggled to integrate their various systems over the years, hoping to tie them all together and provide access through a common user interface. Any degree of success has been achieved only through a significant investment in time, energy, and resources, often with an end result that is incomplete and inflexible. The Web's protocols and the browser interface, when coupled with Java or ActiveX, offer an opportunity to provide a common front end to the organization's numerous and diverse applications and data sources. The BC Hydro experience (see Chapter 4) is a good case in point—its users are now able to access local desktop and network applications using the Netscape browser.

Technology Watch

Numerous intranet-related products have appeared in the past several months—products geared toward meeting the needs of virtually every aspect of creating and maintaining intranet applications. Many, of course, will disappear from sight, unable to gain enough market share to survive; a few other especially strong products will continue to exist, although under a different vendor label—the companies that created them having elected to enter into partnership with larger companies, like Microsoft or Netscape. In light of this marketplace volatility, we've focused on product categories, rather than specific products, in looking toward the future. Our selection is based on broad business needs, and includes development tools, conferencing, and intelligent agents.

Development Tools

This category of products will provide the largest area of growth over the next year, as more organizations expand beyond the publishing theme, developing Web applications that integrate existing applications, resuscitate legacy systems, and allow them to use their data stores more effectively. Developing these applications today is still a labor-intensive activity—and in terms of total system cost, the most expensive part of the development process. Under continued pressure to deploy applications more quickly, and at less cost, companies are looking for tools that provide these capabilities. We expect to see more products like Sapphire/Web, which provide a visual, drag-and-drop interface for creating and testing applications. These products will also feature a reduced learning curve, and won't require the high-end technical expertise that has come to typify many of today's development tools.

Conferencing

Conferencing software, which facilitates real-time communication, is conspicuous by its absence in this book, and for good reason; Internet-based conferencing is barely past the proof-of-concept stage. Text-based conferencing software is not a satisfactory business solution because of the legion of two-fingered typists. Therefore, conferencing tools have to be either audio- or video-based, and since audio-based conferencing using a computer doesn't provide much improvement over the existing telephone system, video-based conferencing has to be the solution of choice.

Full video transmission requires a great deal of bandwidth, even when used in internal networks. Extending this video capability to WANs, where the advantages of video conferencing are of the most use, makes bandwidth and network costs a major consideration.

Equipment cost is another roadblock preventing the widespread deployment of this technology: How many organizations can provide full-blown, multimedia workstations for all their employees? Even at an optimistic estimate of $200 per workstation (for software, sound card, microphone, and camera), it's unlikely that a company with several thousand staff members will undertake a large-scale equipment upgrade. However, companies can start testing this technology and assessing its business value by setting up conference rooms installed with multimedia PCs, and feel fairly secure in the knowledge that costs will come down in the not-too-distant future.

Over the long term, we expect further advancements in data compression, and microcomputers shipped with multimedia features as a standard office-computer configuration. When this happens, computer-video conferencing will make significant gains in the office environment.

Intelligent Agents

The individual's electronic workspace in the office environment continues to grow and increase in complexity. As a result, it's becoming more time-consuming and more difficult to manage, use, and cope with the volume of information swamping workers. Tools called *intelligent agents* already exist to automate personal information management, and although rudimentary, are being used on Web sites. For example, one program can be configured to visit specified Web sites, and notify its user of any content changes.

There is ample room for more sophisticated, user-programmable agents in the office environment. These personal software agents could be configured to carry out many routine tasks, such as checking Web pages for content changes, scheduling meetings, forwarding documents, and screening email, based on established rules. This is an area where we expect several new products to appear during the next year. In fact, Netscape Communications has already announced email agents for a product they've code-named *Orion*, which is scheduled for release by 1997.

Industry Watch

The Internet/intranet product industry will be interesting over the next year, and Microsoft, in particular, will be a company to watch. It continues to pursue a strategy designed to dominate any market it's in, and intranet technology is no different. Microsoft is currently giving away Web-related products (for beta-testing purposes) as quickly as the company's developers can produce them, and has announced that these current stand-alone programs will be included free with future releases of their operating systems. This "carpet-bombing technique" (as some pundit so accurately labeled it) may allow the company to capture an even more significant market share than it presently has. The strategy certainly worked for Microsoft's Windows operating system, and for Netscape Communications in the browser market.

If Microsoft is successful, both the developer and user communities will be affected. For developers, it could mean a return to the Windows applications development environment, and for users, a homogenous environment where everything looks like the Windows 95 desktop.

Conclusion

There will continue to be exciting new intranet products appearing, or announced, on a daily basis. However, if you have a pilot project in mind, a plentiful selection of tools is already available to develop applications that will help reduce costs, improve information flow, leverage your existing investment in technology, and provide a platform on which to build in the future. Like the Internet, intranets will continue to evolve. They are definitely here to stay.

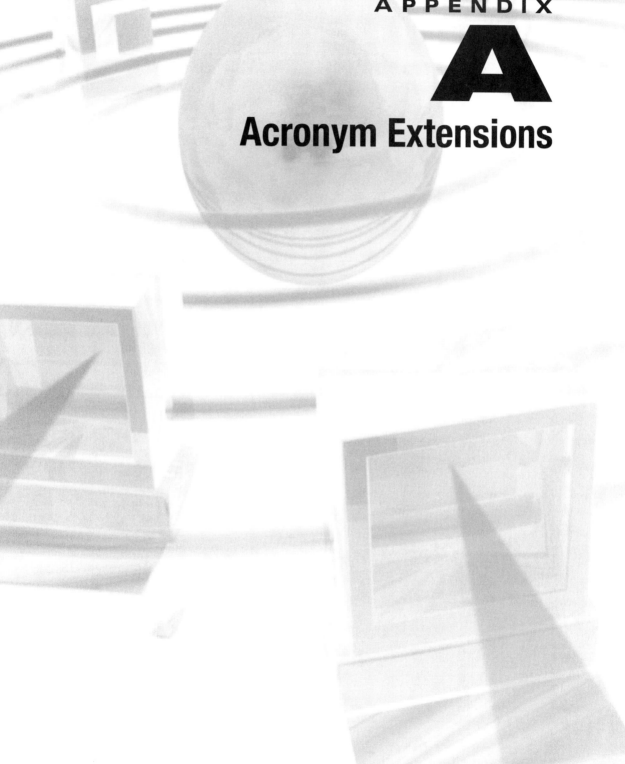

APPENDIX

A

Acronym Extensions

APPENDIX A

Acronym Extensions

A

ACL: Access Control Lists
API: Application Program Interface
ARPANet: Advanced Research Projects Agency Network
ASCII: American Standard Code for Information Interchange
AUI: Attached Unit Interface

C

CD: Compact Disk
CD-ROM: Compact Disk-Read Only Memory
CGI: Common Gateway Interface
CHAP: Challenge Handshake Authentication Protocol
CPU: Central Processing Unit
CSI: Computer Security Institute
CSS: Cascading Style Sheets

D

DBMS: Database Management System
DES: Data Encryption Standard
DLC: Data Link Connection
DNS: Domain Name Services
DOD: Department of Defense

DOS: Disk Operating System
DSM: Distributed Systems Management
DSS: Digital Signal Standard
DSSSL: Document Style Semantics and Specification Language

E

EIDE: Enhanced Integrated Drive Electronics
EISA: Extended Industry Standard Architecture

F

FDDI: Fiber Distributed Data Interface
FTP: File Transfer Protocol

G

GIF: Graphics Interchange Format
GUI: Graphical User Interface

H

HTML: Hypertext Markup Language
HTTP: Hypertext Transport Protocol
HTTPD: Hypertext Transport Protocol Daemon

I

IDE: Integrated Drive Electronics
IEEE: Institute of Electrical and Electronics Engineers
IETF: Internet Engineering Task Force
IGMP: Internet Group Multicast Protocol
IMAP4: Internet Message Access Protocol 4
IO: Input/Output
IP: Internet Protocol
IPX: Internet Packet Exchange
IPX/SPX: Internet Packet Exchange/Sequenced Packet Exchange
ISO: International Standards Organization

J

JPEG: Joint Photographic Experts Group
JPG: see JPEG

L

LAN: Local Area Network
LLC: Logical Link Control

M

MAC: Media Access Control
MAN: Municipal Area Network
MAU: Multi-station Access Unit
MB: Megabyte
MBONE: Multicasting Backbone
MCA: Microchannel Architecture
MHz: Megahertz
MIDI: Musical Instrument Digital Interface
MIME: Multipurpose Internet Mail Extension
MIS: Management Information Services
MPEG: Moving Pictures Experts Group
MPG: see MPEG
MSAU: Multi-station Access Unit

N

NCP: Network Control Protocol
NCSA: National Center for Supercomputing Applications
NDIS: Network Device Interface Specification
NNTP: Network News Transfer Protocol
NOS: Network Operating System
NT: New Technology

O

OCX: OLE Control Extensions
ODBC: Open Database Connectivity

ODI: Open Data-link Interface
OLE: Object Linking and Embedding
OOUI: Object Oriented User Interface
ORB: Object Request Broker
OS: Operating System
OSI: Open Systems Interconnection

P

PC: Personal Computer
PCI: Peripheral Component Interconnect
PDF: Portable Document Format
PEM: Privacy Enhanced Mail
PGP: Pretty Good Privacy, Pretty Good Protection
PIN: Personal Identification Number
POP: Post Office Protocol
POP3: Post Office Protocol 3
PPD: Port Protection Device
PPP: Point to Point Protocol

R

RAID: Redundant Array of Inexpensive Drives
RAM: Random Access Memory
RAS: Remote Access Services
RFC: Request For Comment
RPC: Remote Procedure Call
RSA: Rivest, Shamir, Adleman
RTF: Rich Text Format

S

SATNET: Atlantic Satellite Network
SCSI: Small Computer Systems Interface
SD: Security Descriptors
SGML: Standard Generalized Markup Language
S-HTTP: Secure Hypertext Transport Protocol, Secure-HTTP

SLIP: Serial Line Internet Protocol
SMTP: Simple Mail Transfer Protocol
SNA: Systems Network Architecture
SNMP: Simple Network Management Protocol
SPX: Sequenced Packet Exchange
SQL: Structured Query Language
SSL: Secure Sockets Layer

T

TCP: Transmission Control Protocol
TCP/IP: Transmission Control Protocol/Internet Protocol
TIFF: Tagged Image File Format
TIF: see TIFF

U

URI: Universal Resource Identifiers
URL: Universal Resource Locator
URN: Uniform Resource Name
USENET: User Network

V

VESA: Video Electronics Standards Association
VLB: VESA Local Bus
VRML: Virtual Reality Modeling Language

W

W3: World Wide Web
W3C: World Wide Web Consortium
WAN: Wide Area Network
WWW: World Wide Web
WWW/DBMS: World Wide Web/Database Management System
WYSIWYG: What You See Is What You Get

APPENDIX
B
Intranet Resources

Intranet Resources

This appendix provides additional resources organized by chapter, and includes resource sections of a more general nature.

Chapter 1: Intranet Defined by Form and Function

General Intranet Resources on the World Wide Web

The Intranet Journal
http://www.brill.com/intranet/

The Intranet Information Page
http://www.strom.com/pubwork/intranet.html

InfoWEB Intranet ServicesResources
http://www.infoweb.com.au/intralnk.htm#Articles

The Complete Intranet Resource
http://www.lochnet.com/client/smart/intranet.htm

Yahoo Intranet Resource Listing
**http://www.yahoo.com/Computers_and_Internet/
Communications_and_Networking/Intranet/**

Requests For Comment Archives on the World Wide Web

Nosferatu RFC Archive
http://nosferatu.nas.nasa.gov/rfc/

RFC Archive—Application Protcols
http://www.it.kth.se/docs/rfc/dir/application.html

Dictionary and Glossary

Internet Glossary
http://www.netpart.com/news/articles/glossary.html

The Free Online Dictionary of Computing
http://www.instantweb.com/foldoc/

Sun Glossary
http://www.sun.com/glossary/glossary.html

Chapter 2: Client/Server Computing for the Networked Office

A Tutorial on Client/Server Architecture
http://odo.elan.af.mil/pages/demos/web/cs_arc.html

Strategies for Client/Server Development in C
http://www.pts.co.uk/pts/whtpaper/strat.cs.dev.wp.html

Client/Server FAQ
http://www.mgt.buffalo.edu/orm/Client_Server/csfaq.htm

Chapter 3: Electronic Publishing

About the World Wide Web
http://www.w3.org/pub/WWW/WWW/

World Wide Web FAQ
http://www.boutell.com/faq/

World Wide Web: An Illustrated Seminar
http://www.w3.org/pub/WWW/Talks/General.html

Internet Publishing
http://www.ileaf.com/cyberpaper.html

Chapter 4: Intranets at Work in a Business Environment

Article: The Intranet Rolls In
http://techweb.cmp.com/iw/564/64iuint.htm

A Business Researcher's Interests
http://www.pitt.edu/~malhotra/interest.html

Intranet Articles
http://control.cga.sc.edu/articles.htm

Chapter 5: The Technical Environment

Introduction to PC Hardware
http://www.staffs.ac.uk/pclt/pchw/platypus.htm#contents

BYTE Magazine
http://www.byte.com

LAN Times Online
http://www.wcmh.com/lantimes/index.html

PC Magazine on the Web
http://www.pcmag.com

PC Week Online
http://www.pcweek.com

Windows NT
http://home.sol.no/jgaa/winnt.htm#winnt

Windows NT InfoCenter at Digital
http://www.windowsnt.digital.com/

Windows NT Magazine
http://www.winntmag.com/home/index.dbm

Windows NT Resources
http://wwwnt.robelle.com/winnt.html

MS Windows NT Sites
http://www.warehouse32.co.uk/hotsites/hotsites.htm

Chapter 6: Information Content: The Data Sources

CGI

The Common Gateway Interface
http://hoohoo.ncsa.uiuc.edu/cgi/overview.html

A CGI Programmer's Reference: Existing Gateways
http://www.best.com/~hedlund/cgi-faq/gateways.html

CGI Programming
http://home.sol.no/jgaa/cgi.htm

Yahoo: CGI
**http://www.yahoo.com/Computers/World_Wide_Web/
CGI___Common_Gateway_Interface/**

Selena Sol's Public Domain CGI Script Archive and Resource Library
http://www.eff.org/~erict/Scripts/

WWW Security FAQ: CGI Scripts
http://www-genome.wi.mit.edu/WWW/faqs/wwwsf4.html

FastCGI
http://www.fastcgi.com/

DBMS

DBMS World: Magazines
http://www.worldaccess.nl/~agameren/e_mag.htm

DBMS Online
http://www.worldaccess.nl/~agameren/e_mag.htm

Chapter 7: Developing Web Pages

Composing Good HTML
http://www.cs.cmu.edu/~tilt/cgh/

Hypertext Design Environments and the Hypertext Design Process
http://www.cs.uct.ac.za/Local/CS300W/HCI/nanard.html

Hypertext Design Issues
http://sun1000e.pku.edu.cn/on_line/w3html/DesignIssues/Overview.html

Chapter 8: Protecting an Intranet

AV Center: Virus Info Database
http://www.symantec.com/avcenter/vinfodb.html

CERT Links
http://www.ncsa.com/ncsacert.html

COAST Hotlist—Main
http://www.cs.purdue.edu/homes/spaf/hotlists/csec-top.html

Computer Viruses?
http://www.singnet.com.sg/public/Virus/

CSTC Security Web Site
http://ciac.llnl.gov/cstc/

CIAC Security Web Site
http://ciac.llnl.gov

Electronic Privacy Information Center
http://epic.org

MIT Distribution Site for PGP
http://web.mit.edu/network/pgp.html

EIT Creations: Secure HTTP
http://www.eit.com/projects/s-http/

Netscape: SSL Version 3.0
http://www.netscape.com/newsref/std/SSL.html

Kerberos Users' FAQ
http://www.cis.ohio-state.edu/hypertext/faq/usenet/kerberos-faq/user/faq.html

NCSA Main Menu
http://www.ncsa.com/ncsamain.html

Raptor Systems Security Library
http://www.raptor.com/library/library.html

Crypto-Log: Internet Guide to Cryptography
http://www.enter.net/~chronos/cryptolog.html

Chapter 9: Selecting Software for an Intranet

Dr. Dobb's Web Site
http://www.ddj.com/

inquiry.com: Developer Resources
http://www.inquiry.com/

Web Developer Magazine Online
http://www.webdeveloper.com/

Chapter 10: Working With Web Pages

The Intranet Journal: Design Tools
http://www.brill.com/intranet/design.html

Stroud's CWSApps List
http://cwsapps.cu-online.com

Web Toolz Magazine
http://www.webtoolz.com

Chapter 11: General Purpose and Specialized Programming Tools

Java and JavaScript

Gamelan: Earthweb's Java Directory
http://www.gamelan.com

Introduction to Applets
http://www.ece.sc.edu/students/sanjay/nt/applet.htm

Java Workshop
http://www.sun.com/sunsoft/Developer-products/java/Workshop

JavaScript Index
http://www.c2.org/~andreww/javascript/

JavaScript Resources on the Internet
http://www.dezines.com/dezines/javalinks.htmlJava/

JavaWorld: JavaScript and Netscape Frames
http://www.javaworld.com/jw-04-1996/jw-04-javascript.html

JavaWorld: July 1996—IDG's magazine for the Java community
http://www.javaworld.com

Symantec Café
http://cafe.symantec.com

The Java Developer: Resources
http://www.digitalfocus.com/digitalfocus/faq/resources.html

The Java Sourcebook: Main Java Sites
http://www.wiley.com/Compbooks/javasrbk/javamai.html

The Java Sourcebook User Support Page
http://www.wiley.com/Compbooks/javasrbk/javahome.html

The Java(tm) Language Environment: A White Paper
http://java.sun.com/whitePaper/java-whitepaper-1.html

The JavaScript Authoring Guide
http://home.netscape.com/eng/mozilla/Gold/handbook/javascript/index.html

The Unofficial JavaScript Resource Center
http://www.ce.net/users/ryan/java/

Object-Oriented Programming

Excite NetDirectory: OOP
http://www.excite.com/Subject/Computing/Computer_Science/OOP/

Internet Resources of OOP
http://dolphin.kyungsung.ac.kr/cppres.htm

Object-Orientation FAQ
http://iamwww.unibe.ch/~scg/OOinfo/FAQ/

What is Object-Oriented Software?
http://www.soft-design.com/softinfo/objects.html

OLE and ActiveX

OLE Control/ActiveX FAQ
http://www.sky.net/~toma/faq.htm

Perl

Perl Resources and Reviews
http://www.possibility.com/Perl/

Windows NT Perl 5
http://serverstudent.furman.edu/users/w/wildermike/ntperl/ntperl5.htm

CERN Perl Home Page
http://wwwcn.cern.ch/dci/perl/

Index of Perl/HTML archives
http://www.seas.upenn.edu/~mengwong/perlhtml.html

Perl Meta-FAQ
http://www.khoros.unm.edu/staff/neilb/perl/metaFAQ/metaFAQ.html

REXX

REXX: Yahoo
http://www.yahoo.com/Computers_and_Internet/Languages/Rexx/

The Rexx Language
http://www2.hursley.ibm.com/rexx/

The NetRexx Language
http://www2.hursley.ibm.com/netrexx/

IBM ObjectREXX homepage
http://www2.hursley.ibm.com/orexx/

Quercus Systems Home Page
http://www.quercus-sys.com

Visual Basic

The Visual Basic Community
http://www.apexsc.com/vb/cmmunity.html

Visual Basic Technical Information
http://www.microsoft.com/VBASIC/vbwhite/vbwhite.htm

Windows Development

Windows Developer Magazines on the Internet
http://www.r2m.com/windev/magazines.html

Internet Resources for Windows Developers
http://www.r2m.com/windev/windev.no-frames.html

Chapter 12: The Data: Interfaces, Delivery, and Indexing Tools

Article: ODBC Overview
http://www.pcinews.com/business/pci/sun/features/odbc.overview.html

Accessing a Database Server via the WWW
http://cscsun1.larc.nasa.gov/~beowulf/db/web_access.html

Database Gateways
http://www.channel1.com/Find/Webgate/dataget.html

ODBC: Open Database Connectivity Overview
http://198.105.232.6/KB/deskapps/word/Q110093.htm

Open Database Connectivity
http://www.webbase.com/odbcC.htm

SoftQuad: HTML Resources
http://www.sq.com/htmlsgml/html/h-sites.htm

Understanding and Comparing Web Search Tools
http://www.hamline.edu/library/links/comparisons.html

webreference.com: Programming Databases
http://webreference.com/programming/databases.html

WWW-DBMS Gateways
http://grigg.chungnam.ac.kr/~uniweb/documents/www_dbms.html

Yahoo: Databases and Searches
http://www.yahoo.com/Computers_and_Internet/Internet/ World_Wide_Web/Databases_and_Searching/

Chapter 13: Bundled Solutions for Intranet Development

Netscape Communications
http://home.netscape.com/

SGI
http://www.sgi.com

Sun Microsystems
http://www.sun.com

Chapter 14: Steps and Activities in Constructing an Intranet

IT Reference Manual
http://www.utoronto.ca/utcc/referit/refit_tofc.html

A Practical Guide to Managing Intranet Projects
http://www.justintime.com/intranet/index.htm

Chapter 15: Managing the Web Site: A Necessity, Not an Option

Coast Software
http://www.coast.com/Products.htm

Internet Site Management Tools
http://204.57.196.12/reference/nettools/

Chapter 16: Looking Outwards— Connecting to the Internet

High Bandwidth Web Page
http://plainfield.bypass.com/~gzaret/hiband.html

Index of Infrequently Asked Questions
http://tech.ora.com/iaq/

Internet World Magazine
http://www.internetworld.com/

SMTP Resources Directory
http://www.dns.net/smtprd/

Tools for WWW Providers
http://www.w3.org/pub/WWW/Tools/

Chapter 17: Themes, Trends, and Technologies

CyberAtlas—Intranet
http://www.cyberatlas.com/intranet.html

Forrester Defines the Full-service Intranet
http://www.forrester.com/hp_mar96nsr.htm

InfoHub: A World of High Tech Information
http://www.strategm.com/

Netscape: Intranet White Papers
http://home.netscape.com/comprod/at_work/white_paper/index.html

Other Useful References

Online Magazines

C|Net Online
http://www.cnet.com/

CMP TechWeb
http://techweb.cmp.com/

Communications Week Interactive
http://techweb.cmp.com/cw/current/

CMC Magazine
http://www.december.com/cmc/mag/

Information Week Online
http://techweb.cmp.com/iwk/

Interactive Age Digital
http://techweb.cmp.com/ia/current/

Interactive Week
http://www.zdnet.com/intweek/

Network Computing Online
http://techweb.cmp.com/nwc/current/

PlugIn Datamation
http://www.datamation.com/

SunWorld Online
http://www.sun.com/sunworldonline/common/swol-newbie.html

Searchable Directory of Email Discussion Groups

Liszt
http://wc2.webcrawler.com/select/netinfo.82.html

APPENDIX

C

All Things Hypertext

C

All Things Hypertext

This appendix contains an HTML primer, a summary of the HTML tags, and a list of online resources related to the Hypertext Markup Language.

Writing Great HTML: An HTML Primer

Underneath the slick point-and-click user interface of a Web browser—such as Netscape or Microsoft Internet Explorer—lies an ASCII "markup language" that can easily be composed and edited with any Windows or DOS editor.

As you probably know, the language used by the Web is called HTML, which stands for Hypertext Markup Language. The hypertext part means that a Web page can contain references to other Web pages, or to various Net resources, such as Gophers and FTP sites. The markup part comes from the days when book- and magazine-publishing people made special marks on their authors' manuscripts, to tell typesetters how to format the text. This process was called markup, and the term was adopted when people started inserting formatting instructions into their computer files.

Although we covered many of the basic issues related to Web page content and structure in Chapter 7, this appendix provides a useful guide to most of the HTML features supported by leading Web browsers, such as Netscape and Internet Explorer. As you spend more time creating Web pages, you'll find that this appendix will help you use the HTML tags.

HTML: The Language of The Web

HTML commands are enclosed in angle brackets, like <this>. Most commands come in pairs that mark the beginning and end of a part of text. The end command is often a repetition of the start command, except that it includes a forward slash between the opening bracket and the command name. For example, the title of an HTML document called "Habanero-Mango Chutney" would look like this:

```
<TITLE>Habanero-Mango Chutney</TITLE>
```

Similarly, a word or phrase that Netscape shows in **bold** type would look like this:

```
<B>bold</B> type
```

Using an HTML Editor

Many people prefer using an HTML editor to a word processor like Microsoft Word or a simple text editor, like Windows Notepad. In fact, we've included some handy HTML editors on the companion CD-ROM. It's easier to start writing HTML with an HTML editor than with a basic text editor, because most HTML editors typically offer some sort of menu of tags. This can help you get acquainted with the HTML tag set.

The other advantage of an HTML editor is that when it inserts tags for you, it inserts both the start and the end tags. This feature greatly reduces the chance that your whole document will end up in the **<H1>** (first level header) style, or that a bold word will become three bold paragraphs.

You Still Have to Read HTML

No matter how you create HTML documents, you'll still need to learn how to read them. While an HTML editor may make it easier to insert tags such as **<B>** and **<OL>**, it can't help you decipher a document once it's created. Because an HTML editor lets you start writing without knowing all that much HTML, you could find yourself in a position where you can't even read your own work!

HTML Basics

All HTML files consist of a mixture of text to be displayed, and HTML tags that describe how the text should be displayed. Normally, extra *whitespace* (spaces, tabs, and line breaks) is ignored, and text is displayed with a single space between each word. Text is always wrapped to fit within a browser's window, in the reader's choice of fonts. Line breaks in the HTML source are treated as any other whitespace, and must be specified with a *line break* tag, **
, or a *paragraph break*, **<P>, tag.

Tags are always set off from the surrounding text by *angle brackets,* or the less-than and greater-than signs. Most tags come in "begin" and "end" pairs: for example, **<I>** ... **</I>**. The end tag includes a slash between the opening bracket and the tag name. There are a few tags that require only a start tag; I'll take particular care to point out these tags as they come up.

HTML is *case insensitive:* **<HTML>** is the same as **<html>** or **<hTmL>**. However, many Web servers run on Unix systems, which *are* case sensitive. This will never affect HTML interpretation, but it will affect your hyperlinks: My.gif is not the same file as my.gif or MY.GIF.

Some begin tags can take *parameters,* which come between the tag name and the closing bracket—like this: **<DL COMPACT>**. Others, like description lists, have optional parameters that will alter their appearance, if your reader's browser supports that option. Still others, such as anchors and images, require certain parameters and can also take optional parameters.

The Structure of an HTML Document

All HTML documents have a certain standard structure, but Netscape and most other Web browsers treat any file that ends in .HTML or .HTM on PCs as an HTML file, even if it contains no HTML tags. All HTML text and tags should be contained within this tag pair:

```
<HTML> ... </HTML>
```

<HEAD> ... </HEAD> Tag

All HTML documents are divided into a header that contains the title and other information about the document, and a body that contains the actual document text.

While you should not place display text outside the body section, this is currently optional, since Netscape formats and displays any text that's not in a tag. Also, while you can get away with not using the **<HEAD>** tag pair, we strongly recommend that you do.

<BODY> ... </BODY>

The body of the document should contain the actual contents of the Web page. The tags that appear within the body do not separate the document into sections. Rather, they're either special parts of the text—like images or forms—or they're tags that *say something* about the text they enclose, like character attributes or paragraph styles.

Headings and Paragraphs

In some ways, HTML text is a series of paragraphs. Within a paragraph, text will be wrapped to fit within the reader's screen. In most cases, any line breaks that appear in the source file are totally ignored.

Paragraphs are separated either by an explicit paragraph break tag, **<P>**, a line break tag **
**, or by paragraph style commands. The paragraph style determines both the font used for the paragraph and any special indenting. Paragraph styles include several levels of section headers, five types of lists, three different "block formats," and the normal, or *default*, paragraph style. Any text outside an explicit paragraph style command will be displayed in the normal style.

<ADDRESS> ... </ADDRESS> Tag

The last part of the document body should be an **<ADDRESS>** tag pair, which contains information about the author, and, often, the document's copyright date and revision history. While the address block is not a required part of the document in the same way the header or the body is, official style guides urge that all documents have one. In current practice, while many documents don't use one of the **<HTML>**, **<HEAD>**, or

<BODY> tag pairs, almost all documents have address blocks—perhaps because the address block is visible.

The format for using the **<ADDRESS>** tag is as follows:

```
<ADDRESS>Address text goes here</ADDRESS>
```

Comments

Comments can be placed in your HTML documents using a special tag as shown:

```
<!--Comment text goes here-->
```

Everything between the "<>" will be ignored by a browser when the document is displayed. Be sure to use the exclamation point!

Header Elements

The elements used in the header of an HTML document include a title section and internal indexing information.

<TITLE> ... </TITLE> Tag

Every document should have a title. The manner in which a title is displayed varies from system to system and browser to browser. The title could be displayed as a window title, or it may appear in a pane within the window. The title should be short—64 characters or fewer—and should contain text only.

The title should appear in the header section, marked off with a **<TITLE>** tag pair; for example, **<TITLE>**Lime-Jerked Chicken**</TITLE>**. Netscape is actually such an "easy-going" browser that the title can appear anywhere in the document—even after the **</HTML>** tag—but future browsers might not be quite so clever and accommodating. Including a title is important, because many Web search engines use the title to locate a document.

The format for using the **<TITLE>** tag is as follows:

```
<TITLE>Title text goes here</TITLE>
```

Other <HEAD> Elements

There are a few HTML optional elements that may only appear in the document's header (**<HEAD>** tag pair). The header elements that browsers use are the **<BASE>**, **<META>**, and **<ISINDEX>** tags. Both are *empty,* or *solitary,* tags that do not have a closing **</...>** tag, and thus do not enclose any text.

The **BASE** tag contains the current document's URL, or *Uniform Resource Locator,* browsers can use it to find "local" URLs. For more on **BASE** tags, see *Using URLs.*

The **META** tag specifies a specific act to be performed by the browser. For instance, a **META** tag can specify when the page expires, or can have the browser refresh the page every few seconds.

The **ISINDEX** tag tells browsers that this document is an index document, which means that the server can support keyword searches based on the document's URL. Searches are passed back to the Web server by concatenating a question mark and one or more keywords to the document URL, and then requesting this extended URL. This is very similar to one of the ways in which forms data is returned. (See the section *Form Action and Method Attributes* for more information.)

Other header elements are provided, such as **<NEXTID>** and **<LINK>**, which are included in HTML for the benefit of editing and cataloging software. They have no visible effect; browsers simply ignore them.

Normal Text

Most Web pages are composed of plain, or *normal,* text. Any text not appearing between format tag pairs is displayed as normal text.

Normal text, like every other type of paragraph style except the *preformatted* style, is wrapped at display time to fit in the reader's window. A larger or smaller font or window size results in a totally different number of words on each line, so don't try to change the wording of a sentence to make the line breaks come at appropriate places: You'll be in for a big surprise!

*
 Tag*

If line breaks *are* important, as in postal addresses or poetry, you can use the **
** command to insert a line break. Subsequent text will appear one line down, on the left margin.

The general format for this tag is:

```
<BR [CLEAR=Left|Right]>
```

The section listed between the "[ ]" is optional. This is a feature introduced as an HTML enhancement.

Let's look at an example of how **
** is used. To keep

```
Coriolis Group Books
7339 East Acoma Drive, Suite 7
Scottsdale, Arizona 85260-6912
```

from coming out as

```
Coriolis Group Books 7339 East Acoma Drive, Suite 7 Scottsdale, Arizona
85260-6912
```

you should write:

```
Coriolis Group Books<BR>
7339 East Acoma Drive, Suite 7<BR>
Scottsdale, Arizona 85260-6912<BR>
```

The extended form of the **
** tag allows you to control how text is wrapped. The **CLEAR** argument allows text to be broken, so it can flow around an image to the right or to the left. For example, this tag shows how text can be broken to flow to the left:

```
This text will be broken here.<BR CLEAR=Left>
This line will flow around to the right of an image that can be displayed
with the IMG tag.
```

<NOBR> Tag

This tag stands for **NO BR**eak. This is another HTML extension supported by Netscape. To keep text from breaking, you can include the **<NOBR>** tag at the beginning of the text you want to keep together.

<WBR> Tag

This tag stands for **Word BR**eak. If you use the **<NOBR>** tag to define a section of text without breaks, you can force a line break at any location by inserting the **<WBR>** tag, followed by the **
** tag.

<P> Tag

The **
** command causes a line break within a paragraph, but more often, we want to separate one paragraph from another. We can do this by ending each paragraph with a **<P>** command. Paragraph breaks may be shown with an extra line or half line of spacing, a leading indent, or both. A **</P>** command exists, but it's optional and rarely used.

Logical and Physical Attributes

Character attribute tags let you emphasize words or phrases within a paragraph. HTML supports two different types of character attributes: *physical* and *logical*. Physical attributes include the familiar boldfacing, italics, and underlining, as well as a *tty* attribute for monospaced text.

Logical attributes are different. Logical attributes let you describe what sort of emphasis you want to put on a word or phrase, but leave the actual formatting up to the browser. That is, where a word marked with a physical attribute like **<B>**bold**</B>** will always appear in **bold** type, an **<EM>**emphasized**</EM>** word may be *italicized*, underlined, **bolded**, or displayed in color.

Web style guides suggest that you use logical attributes whenever you can, but there's a slight problem: Some current browsers only support some physical attributes, and few or no logical attributes. Since Web browsers simply ignore any HTML tags they don't "understand," you run the risk that your readers will not see any formatting at all if you use logical tags.

The standard format for using any of the physical attributes tags is as follows:

```
<tag>text goes here</tag>
```

You can nest attributes, although the results will vary from browser to browser. For example, some browsers can display ***bold italic*** text, while others will only display the innermost attribute. (That is, **<B><I>**bold italic**</I></B>** may show up as only italic.) If you use nested attributes, be sure to place the end tags in reverse order of the start tags; don't write something like **<B><I>**bold italic**</B></I>**. This may work with some Web browsers, but it may cause problems with others.

<BLINK> ... </BLINK>

This is an enhanced tag supported by Netscape and Internet Explorer. Text placed between this pair will blink on the screen. This feature is useful for getting someone's attention, but if you use it too much, it could get rather annoying. The format for this tag is:

```
<BLINK>This text will blink</BLINK>
```

<CENTER> ... </CENTER>

This HTML enhancement makes some Web page authors feel like they've died and gone to heaven. Any text (or images) placed between this pair is centered between the left and right margins of a page. The format for this tag is:

```
<CENTER>This text will be centered between the left and right margins
                  </CENTER>
```

<FONT> ... </FONT>

This HTML enhancement allows you to control the size of the fonts displayed in your documents. The format for this tag is:

```
<FONT SIZE=font-size>text goes here</FONT>
```

—where *font-size* must be a number from 1 to 7. A size of 1 produces the smallest font. The default font size is 3. Once the font size has been changed, it will remain in effect until the font size is changed by using another tag.

<BASEFONT>

To give you even greater control over font sizing, you can use the **<BASEFONT>** tag to set the base font for all text displayed in a document. The format for this tag is:

```
<BASEFONT SIZE=font-size>
```

Again, *font-size* must be a number from 1 to 7. A size of 1 produces the smallest font. The default font size is 3. Once the base font size has been defined, you can display text in larger or smaller fonts using the "+" or "-" sign with the **<FONT>** tag. Here's an example of how this works:

```
<BASEFONT SIZE=4>
This text will be displayed as size 4 text.
<FONT SIZE=+2>
This text will be displayed as size 6.
</FONT>
This text will return to the base font size--size 4.
```

Headings

HTML provides six levels of section headers, **<H1>** through **<H6>**. While these are typically short phrases that fit on a line or two, the various headers are actually full-fledged paragraph types. They can even contain line and paragraph break commands.

You are not required to use an **<H1>** before you use an **<H2>**, or to make sure that an **<H4>** follows an **<H3>** or another **<H4>**.

Standard format for using one of the six heading tags is illustrated by this sample:

```
<H1>Text Goes Here</H1>
```

Lists

HTML supports five different list types. Each of the five types can be thought of as a sort of paragraph type. The first four list types share a common syntax and differ only in how they format their list elements. The fifth type, the "description" list, is unique in that each list element has two parts— a tag and a description of the tag.

All five list types display an element marker—whether it's a number, a bullet, or a few words—on the left margin. The marker is followed by the actual list elements, which appear indented. List elements do not have to fit on a single line or consist of a single paragraph—they may contain **<P>** and **
** tags.

Lists can be nested, but the appearance of a nested list depends on the browser. For example, some browsers use different bullets for inner lists than for outer lists, and some browsers do not indent nested lists. However, Netscape and Internet Explorer, which are the most common graphical browsers, *do* indent nested lists; the tags of a nested list align with the elements of the outer list, and the elements of the nested list are further indented. For example:

- This is the first element of the main bulleted list.
    - ◊ This is the first element of a nested list.
    - ◊ This is the second element of the nested list.
- This is the second element of the main bulleted list.

The four list types that provide simple list elements use the *list item* tag, <LI>, to mark the start of each list element. The <LI> tag always appears at the *start* of a list element, not at the end.

Thus, all simple lists look something like this:

```
<ListType>

<LI>
There isn't really any ListType list, however the OL, UL, DIR, and
MENU lists all follow this format.
```

```
<LI>
Since whitespace is ignored, you can keep your source legible by
putting blank lines between your list elements. Sometimes, I like to put
the &lt;li&gt; tags on their own lines, too.

<LI>
(If I hadn't used the ampersand quotes in the previous list element,
the "&lt;li&gt;" would have been interpreted as the start of a new
list element.)

</ListType>
```

Numbered List

In HTML, numbered lists are referred to as ordered lists. The list type tag is <OL>. Numbered lists can be nested, but some browsers get confused by the close of a nested list, and start numbering the subsequent elements of the outer list from one.

Bulleted List

If a numbered list is an ordered list, what could an unnumbered, bulleted list be, but an unordered list? The tag for an unordered (bulleted) list is <UL>. While bulleted lists can be nested, you should keep in mind that the list nesting *may* not be visible: Some browsers indent nested lists; some don't. Some use multiple bullet types; others don't.

Netscape List Extensions

Netscape has added a useful feature, called **TYPE**, which can be included with unordered and ordered lists. This feature allows you to specify the type of bullet or number that you use for the different levels of indentation in a list.

Unordered List with Extensions

When Netscape displays the different levels of indentation in an unordered list, it uses a solid disc (level 1) followed by a bullet (level 2) followed by a square (level 3). You can use the **TYPE** feature with the **<UL>** tag to override this sequence of bullets. Here's the format:

```
<UL TYPE=Disc|Circle|Square>
```

For example, here's a list defined to use circles as the bullet symbol:

```
<UL TYPE=Circle>
<LI>This is item 1
<LI>This is item 2
<LI>This is item 3
</UL>
```

Ordered List with Extensions

When Netscape displays ordered (numbered) lists, it numbers each list item using a numeric sequence—one, two, three, and so on. You can change this setting by using the **TYPE** modifier with the **<OL>** tag. Here's how this feature is used with numbered lists:

```
<OL TYPE=A|a|I|i|1>
```

where **TYPE** can be assigned to any one of these values:

A   Mark list items with capital letters
a   Mark list items with lowercase letters
I   Mark list items with large roman numerals
i   Mark list items with small roman numerals
1   Mark list items with numbers (default)

But wait, there's more: You can also start numbering list items with a number other than one. To do this, you use the **START** modifier as shown

```
<OL START=starting-number>
```

where *starting-number* specifies the first number used. You can use the feature with the TYPE tag. For example, the tag

```
<OL TYPE=I START=4>
```

would start the numbered list with the roman numeral IV.

Using Modifiers with List Elements

In addition to supporting the **TYPE** modifier with the **\<UL\>** and **\<OL\>** tags, Netscape allows you to use this modifier with the **\<LI\>** tag to define list elements for ordered and unordered lists. Here's an example of how it can be used with an unordered list:

```
<H2>Useful Publishing Resources</H2>
<UL TYPE=Disc>
<LI>HTML Tips
<LI>Web Page Samples
<LI TYPE=Square>Images
<LI TYPE=Disc>Templates
</UL>
```

In this case, all of the list items will be displayed with a disc symbol as the bullet, except the third item—"Images"—which will be displayed with a square bullet.

The **TYPE** modifier can be assigned the same values as those used to define lists with the **\<UL\>** and **\<OL\>** tags. Once it is used to define a style for a list item, all subsequent items in the list will be changed unless another **TYPE** modifier is used.

If you are defining **\<LI\>** list elements for ordered lists **\<OL\>**, you can also use a new modifier, named **VALUE**, to change the numeric value of a list item. Here's an example:

```
<H2>Useful Publishing Resources</H2>
<OL>
<LI>HTML Tips
<LI>Web Page Samples
<LI VALUE=4>Images
<LI>Templates
</OL>
```

In this list, the third item would be assigned the number four, and the fourth item would be assigned the number five.

Directory and Menu Lists

The directory and menu lists are special types of unordered lists. The menu list, **\<MENU\>**, is meant to be visually more compact than a standard unordered list: Menu list items should all fit on a single line. The directory list, **<DIR>**, is supposed to be even more compact: All list items should be less than 20 characters long, so that the list can be displayed in three (or more) columns.

I'm not sure if I've ever actually seen these lists in use, and their implementation is still spotty: Current versions of Netscape do not create multiple columns for a **<DIR>** list, and while they let you choose a directory list font and a menu list font, they do not actually use these fonts.

Description List

The description list, or **<DL>**, does not use the **<LI>** tag the way other lists do. Each description list element has two parts—a *tag* and its *description*. Each tag begins with a **<DT>** tag, and each description with a **<DD>** tag. These appear at the start of the list element, and are *not* paired with </DT> or </DD> tags.

The description list looks a lot like any other list, except that instead of a bullet or a number, the list tag consists of your text. Description lists are *intended* to be used for creating formats like a glossary entry, where a short tag is followed by an indented definition, but the format is fairly flexible. For example, a long tag will wrap, just like any other paragraph, although it should not contain line or paragraph breaks. (Netscape indents any **<DT>** text after a line or paragraph, as if it were the **<DD>** text.) Further, you needn't actually supply any tag text: **<DT><DD>** will produce an indented paragraph.

Compact and Standard Lists

Normally, a description list puts the tags on one line, and starts the indented descriptions on the next:

```
Tag 1
Description 1.
Tag 2
Description 2.
```

If you'd like a tighter look, you can use a **<DL COMPACT>**. If the tags are very short, some browsers will start the descriptions on the same line as the tags:

```
Tag 1    Description 1
Tag 2                         Description 2
```

However, most browsers do not support the compact attribute, and will simply ignore it. For example, with current versions of Windows Netscape, a **<DL COMPACT>** will always look like a **<DL>**, even if the tags are very short.

Inline Images

Using only text attributes, section headers, and lists, you can build attractive-looking documents. The next step is to add pictures.

<IMG> Tag

The **<IMG>** tag is a very useful HTML feature. It lets you insert *inline images* into your text. This tag is rather different from the tags we've seen so far. Not only is it an empty tag that always appears alone, but it also has a number of *parameters* between the opening **<IMG** and the closing **>**. Some of the parameters include the image file name and some optional modifiers. The basic format for this tag is:

```
<IMG SRC="URL" ALT="text"
    ALIGN=top|middle|bottom
    ISMAP>
```

Since HTML 3.0 has emerged, and additional Netscape extensions have been added, this tag has expanded more than any other HTML feature. Here is the complete format for the latest and greatest version of the **<IMG>** tag:

```
<IMG SRC="URL" ALT="text"
    ALIGN=left|right|top|texttop|middle|absmiddle|
        baseline|bottom|absbottom
    WIDTH=pixels
    HEIGHT=pixels
```

```
BORDER=pixels
VSPACE=pixels
HSPACE=pixels
ISMAP>
```

The extended version allows you to specify the size of an image, better control image and text alignment, and specify the size of an image's border.

Every **<IMG>** tag must have a **SRC=** parameter. This specifies a URL, which points to a GIF or JPEG file. When the image file is in the same directory as the HTML document, the file name is an adequate URL. For example, **<IMG SRC=**MySmilingFace.gif> would insert a picture of my smiling face.

Some people turn off inline images because they have a slow connection to the Web. This replaces all images, no matter what size, with a standard graphic. This isn't so bad if the picture is incidental to your text—but if you've used small inline images as "bullets" in a list or as section dividers, the placeholder graphic will usually make your page look rather strange. Some people avoid using graphics as structural elements for this reason; others simply don't worry about people with slow connections; still others include a note at the top of the page saying that all the images on the page are small, and inviting people with inline images off to turn them on and reload the page.

Keep in mind that some people use text-only browsers, like Lynx, to navigate the Web. If you include a short description of your image with the **ALT=** parameter, text-only browsers can show *something* in place of your graphic. For example, **<IMG SRC=**MySmilingFace.gif **ALT=** "A picture of the author">.

Since the **ALT** parameter has spaces in it, we have to put it within quotation marks. In general, you can put any parameter value in quotation marks, but you only need to do so if it includes spaces.

Mixing Images and Text

You can mix text and images within a paragraph; an image does not constitute a paragraph break. However, Web browsers, like earlier versions of Netscape, did *not* wrap paragraphs around images; they displayed a single line of text to the left or right of an image. Normally, any text in the same paragraph as an image would be lined up with the bottom of the image, and would wrap normally below the image. This works well if the text is essentially a caption for the image, or if the image is a decoration at the start of a paragraph. However, when the image is a part of a header, you may want the text to be centered vertically in the image, or to be lined up with the top of the image. In these cases, you can use the optional **ALIGN=** parameter to specify **ALIGN=top**, **ALIGN=middle**, or **ALIGN=bottom**.

Using "Floating" Images

With the extended version of the **<IMG>** tag, you can now create "floating" images that will align to the left or right margin of a Web page. Text displayed following the image will either wrap around the right-hand or left-hand side of the image. Here's an example of how an image can be displayed at the left margin with text that wraps to the right of the image:

```
<IMG SRC="limage.gif" ALIGN=left>
This text will be displayed to the right of the image
```

Specifying Spacing for Floating Images

When you use floating images with wrap-around text, you can specify the spacing between the text and the image by using the **VSPACE** and **HSPACE** modifiers. **VSPACE** defines the amount of spacing in units of pixels, between the top and bottom of the image and the text that's displayed. **HSPACE** defines the spacing between the left or right edge of the image, and the text that wraps.

Sizing Images

Another useful feature that has been added to the **<IMG>** tag is image sizing. The **WIDTH** and **HEIGHT** modifiers are used to specify the width and height of an image in pixels. Here's an example:

```
<IMG SRC="logo.gif" WIDTH=250 HEIGHT=310>
```

When a browser displays an image, it needs to determine the size of the image before it can display a placeholder or *bounding box* for the image. If you include the image's size using **WIDTH** and **HEIGHT**, a Web page can be built much faster. If the values you specify for **WIDTH** and **HEIGHT** differ from the image's actual width and height, the image will be scaled to fit.

Using Multiple Images per Line

Since an image is treated like a single (and rather large) character, you can have more than one image on a single line. In fact, you can have as many images on a line as will fit in your reader's window! If you put too many images on a line, the browser will wrap the line and your images will appear on multiple lines. If you don't want images to appear on the same line, be sure to place a **
** or **<P>** between them.

Defining an Image's Border

Typically, an image is displayed with a border around it. This is the border set to the color blue when the image is part of an anchor. Using the **BOR-DER** modifier, you can specify a border width for any image you display. Here's an example that displays an image with a five-pixel border:

```
<IMG SRC="logo.gif" BORDER=5>
```

ISMAP Parameter

The optional **ISMAP** parameter allows you to place hyperlinks to other documents "in" a bitmapped image. This technique is used to turn an image into a clickable map. (See the *Using Many Anchors in an Image* for more detail.)

Horizontal Rules

The **<HR>** tag draws a horizontal rule, or line, across the screen to separate parts of your text. It's fairly common to put a rule before and after a form, to help set off the user entry areas from the normal text.

Many people use small inline images for decoration and separation, instead of rules. While using images in this manner lets you customize how your pages look, it also makes them take longer to load—and it makes them look horrible with inline images turned off.

The original **<HR>** tag simply displayed an engraved rule across a Web page. A newer version of the tag has been extended to add additional features including sizing, alignment, and shading. The format for the extended version of **<HR>** is:

```
<HR SIZE=pixels
    WIDTH=pixels|percent
    ALIGN=left|right|center
    NOSHADE>
```

The **SIZE** modifier sets the width (thickness) of the line in pixel units. The **WIDTH** modifier specifies the length of the line in actual pixel units, or a percentage of the width of the page. The **ALIGN** modifier specifies the alignment for the line (the default is center) and the **NOSHADE** modifier allows you to display a solid line.

As an example of how some of these new features are used, the following tag displays a solid line, five pixels thick. The line is left-justified and spans 80 percent of the width of the page:

```
<HR SIZE=5 WIDTH=80% ALIGN="left" NOSHADE>
```

Hypermedia Links

The ability to add links to other Web pages, or to entirely different sorts of documents, is what makes the Web a *hypermedia* system. The special sort of highlight that your reader clicks on to traverse a hypermedia link is called an *anchor*, and all links are created with the anchor tag, **<A>**. The basic format for this tag is:

```
<A HREF="URL"
   NAME="text"
   REL=next|previous|parent|made
   REV=next|previous|parent|made
   TITLE="text">

text</A>
```

Links to Other Documents

While you can define a link to another point within the current page, most links are to other documents. Links to points within a document are very similar to links to other documents, but they are slightly more complicated, so we will talk about them later. (See *Links to Anchors.*)

Each link has two parts: the visible part—or *anchor*—which the user clicks on, and the invisible part, which tells the browser where to go. The anchor is the text between the **<A>** and **</A>** tags of the **<A>** tag pair, while the actual link data appears in the **<A>** tag.

Just as the **<IMG>** tag has a **SRC=** parameter that specifies an image file, so does the <A> tag have an **HREF=** parameter that specifies the **h**ypermedia **ref**erence. Thus, "**<A HREF=SomeFile.Type>click here</A>**" is a link to "someFile.Type" with the visible anchor "click here."

Browsers generally use the linked document's file name extension to decide how to display the linked document. For example, HTML or HTM files will be interpreted and displayed as HTML, whether they come from an HTTP server, an FTP server, or a Gopher site. Conversely, a link can be to any sort of file—a large bitmap, sound file, or movie.

Images as Hotspots

Since inline images are in many ways just big characters, there's no problem with using an image in an anchor. The anchor can include text on either side of the image, or the image can be an anchor by itself. Most browsers show an image anchor by drawing a blue border around the image (or around the placeholder graphic). The image anchor can be a picture of what is being linked to, or it can just point to another copy of itself:

```
<A HREF=image.gif><IMG SRC=image.gif></A>
```

Thumbnail Images

One sort of "picture of the link" is called a *thumbnail* image. This is a tiny image, perhaps 100 pixels, which is either a condensed version of a larger image or a section of the image. Thumbnail images can be transmitted quickly, even over slow lines, leaving it up to the reader to decide which larger images to request. A secondary issue is aesthetic: Large images take up a lot of screen space, smaller images don't.

Linking an Image to Itself

Many people turn off inline images to improve performance over a slow network link. If the inline image is an anchor for itself, these people can then click on the placeholder graphic to see what they've missed.

Using Many Anchors in an Image

The **<IMG>** tag's optional **ISMAP** parameter allows you to turn rectangular regions of a bitmap image into clickable anchors. Clicking on these parts of the image will activate an appropriate URL. (A default URL is also usually provided for when the user clicks on an area outside one of the predefined regions.) While forms let you do this a bit more flexibly, the **ISMAP** approach doesn't require any custom programming—just a simple text file that defines the rectangles and their URLs—and this technique may work with browsers that do not support forms. For more information about how to create and use image maps, go to:

```
http://sunsite.unc.edu/boutell/faq/imagemap.htm
```

Links to Anchors

When an **HREF** parameter specifies a file name, the link is to the whole document. If the document is an HTML file, it will replace the current document and the reader will be placed at the top of the new document. Often, this is just what you want. But sometimes you'd rather have a link take the reader to a specific section of a document. Doing this requires two anchor tags: one that defines an *anchor name* for a location, and one that points to that name. These two tags can be in the same document, or in different documents.

Defining an Anchor Name

To define an anchor name, you need to use the **NAME** parameter: **<A NAME**=AnchorName>. You can attach this name to a phrase, not just a single point, by following the **<A>** tag with an **</A>** tag.

Linking to an Anchor in the Current Document

To then use this name, you simply insert an **<A HREF=...>** tag as usual, except that instead of a file name, you use a # followed by an anchor name. For example, **<A HREF=#AnchorName>** refers to the example in the last paragraph.

Names do not have to be defined before they are used; it's actually fairly common for lengthy documents to have a table of contents, with links to names defined later in the document. It's also worth noting that while tag and parameter names are not case sensitive, anchor names *are*. **<A HREF=#anchorname>** will not take you to the AnchorName example.

Linking to an Anchor in a Different Document

You can also link to specific places in any other HTML document, anywhere in the world—provided, of course, that it contains named anchors. To do this, you simply add the # and the anchor name after the URL that tells where the document can be found. For example, to plant a link to the anchor named "Section 1" in a file named complex.html in the same directory as the current file, you could use **<A HREF="Complex.html#Section 1">**. Similarly, if the named anchor was in http://www.another.org/Complex.html, you'd use **<A HREF="http://www.another.org/Complex.html#Section 1">**.

Using URLS

Just as a complete DOS file name starts with a drive letter followed by a colon, so a full URL starts with a resource type—HTTP, FTP, GOPHER, and so on—followed by a colon. If the name doesn't have a colon in it, it's assumed to be a local *reference*, which is a file name on the same file system as the current document. Thus, **<A HREF=Another.html>** refers to the file "Another.html," in the same directory as the current file, while **<A HREF=/html/File.html>** refers to the file "File.html" in the top-level directory "html". One thing to note here is that a URL always uses "/", the Unix-style *forward* slash, as a directory separator—even when the files are on a Windows machine, which normally uses " \ ", the DOS-style backslash.

Local URLs can be very convenient when you have several HTML files with links to each other, or when you have a large number of inline images. If you ever have to move them all to another directory, or to another machine, you don't have to change all the URLs.

<BASE> Tag

One drawback of local URLs is that if someone makes a copy of your document, the local URLs will no longer work. Adding the optional **<BASE>** tag to the **<HEAD>** section of your document will help eliminate this problem. While many browsers do not yet support it, the intent of the **<BASE>** tag is to provide a context for local URLs.

The **<BASE>** tag is like the <IMG> tag in that it's a so-called empty tag. It requires an HREF parameter—for example, **<BASE HREF**=http://www.imaginary.org/index.html**>**—which should contain the URL of the document itself. When a browser that supports the **<BASE>** tag encounters a URL that doesn't contain a protocol and path, it will look for it relative to the base URL, instead of relative to the location from which it actually loaded the document. The format for the **<BASE>** tag is:

```
<BASE HREF="URL">
```

Reading and Constructing URLs

Where a local URL is just a file name, a global URL specifies an instance of one of several resource types, which may be located on any Internet machine in the world. The wide variety of resources is reflected in a complex URL syntax. For example, while most URLs consist of a resource type followed by a colon, *two* forward slashes, a machine name, another forward slash, and a resource name, others consist only of a resource type, a colon, and the resource name.

The resource-type://machine-name/resource-name URL form is used with centralized resources, where there's a single server that supplies the document to the rest of the net, using a particular protocol. Thus, "http://www.another.org/Complex.html" means, "use the Hypertext Transfer Protocol to get file Complex.html from the main www directory on the machine www.another.org"; while "ftp://foo.bar.net/pub/www/editors/README" means, "use the File Transfer Protocol to get the file /pub/www/editors/README from the machine foo.bar.net."

Conversely, many resource types are distributed. We don't all get our news or mail from the same central server, but from the nearest one of many news and mail servers. URLs for distributed resources use the simpler form resource-type:resource-name. For example, "news:comp.infosystems.www.-providers" refers to the USENET newsgroup comp.infosystems.www.-providers, which is a good place to look for further information about writing HTML.

Using WWW and Actual Machine Names

In the HTTP domain, you'll often see "machine names" like "www.coriolis.com." This usually does *not* mean there's a machine named www.coriolis.com that you can FTP or Telnet to; "www" is an alias that a Webmaster can set up when he or she registers the server. Using the www alias makes sense, because machines come and go, but sites (and, we hope, the Web) last for quite a while. If URLs refer to www at the site, and not to a specific machine, the server and all the HTML files can be moved to a new machine simply by changing the www alias, without having to update all the URLs.

Using Special Characters

Since < and > have special meanings in HTML, there must be a way to represent characters like these as part of text. The default character set for the Web is ISO Latin-1, which includes European language characters like é and ß in the range from 128 to 255; but it's not uncommon to pass around snippets of HTML in 7-bit email, or to edit them on dumb terminals, so the escape mechanism also has to include a way to specify high-bit characters using only 7-bit characters.

Two Forms: Numeric and Symbolic

There are two ways to specify an arbitrary character: numeric and symbolic. To include the copyright symbol, (©), which is character number 169, you can use ©. That is, &#, then the number of the character you want to include, and a closing semicolon. The numeric method is very general, but not easy to read.

The symbolic form is much easier to read, but its use is restricted to the four low-bit characters with special meaning in HTML. To use the other symbols in the ISO Latin-1 character set, like (®) and the various currency symbols, you have to use the numeric form. The symbolic escape is like the numeric escape, except there's no #. For example, to insert é, you would use é, or &, the character name, and a closing semicolon. You should be aware that symbol names are *case sensitive*: É is É, not é, while &EAcute; is no character at all, and will show up as &EAcute;!

Preformatted and Other Special Paragraph Types

HTML supports three special "block" formats. Any normal text within a block format is supposed to appear in a distinctive font.

<BLOCKQUOTE> ... </BLOCKQUOTE> Tag

The block quote sets an extended quotation off from normal text. That is, a **<BLOCKQUOTE>** tag pair does **not** imply indented, single-spaced, and italicized; rather, it's just meant to change the default, plain text font. The format for this tag is:

```
<BLOCKQUOTE>text</BLOCKQUOTE>
```

<PRE> ... </PRE> Tag

Everything in a *preformatted* block appears in a monospaced font. The **<PRE>** tag pair is also the only HTML element that pays any attention to the line breaks in the source file: Any line break in a preformatted block will be treated just as a **
** elsewhere. HTML tags can be used within a preformatted block; thus you can have anchors as well as bold or italic monospaced text. The format for this tag is:

```
<PRE WIDTH=value>text</PRE>
```

The initial **<PRE>** tag has an optional **WIDTH**= parameter. Browsers won't trim lines to this length; the intent is to allow the browser to select a monospaced font that allows the maximum line length to fit in the browser window.

<ADDRESS> ... </ADDRESS> Tag

The third block format is the address format: **<ADDRESS>**. This is generally displayed in italics, and is intended for displaying information about a document, such as creation date, revision history, and how to contact the author. Official style guides say that every document should provide an address block. The format for this tag is:

```
<ADDRESS>text</ADDRESS>
```

Many people put a horizontal rule, **<HR>**, between the body of the document and the address block. If you include a link to your home page or to a page that lets the reader send mail to you, you don't have to include a lot of information on each individual page.

Using Tables

Features like lists are great for organizing data; however, sometimes you need a more compact way of grouping related data. Fortunately, some of the newer browsers, such as Netscape, have implemented the proposed HTML 3.0 specification for tables. Tables can contain a heading and row and column data. Each unit of a table is called a *cell*. Cell data can be text and images.

<TABLE> ... </TABLE> Tag

This tag is used to define a new table. All of the table specific tags must be placed within the pair **<TABLE> ... </TABLE>**; otherwise, they will be ignored. The format for the **<TABLE>** tag is:

```
<TABLE BORDER= number in pixels
          WIDTH= percentage of page or number
          cellspacing= number in pixels
          cellpadding= number>
table text</TABLE>
```

The **BORDER** tag allows you to define the width of the table's border in pixels. If **BORDER** is not defined, the default setting is no border. **WIDTH** defines the width of the table within the page, as either a percentage of the page or a defined number. It's better to use a percentage, as different people have different sized browser windows, so a defined number may not look right on their screen.

Like it sounds, **CELLSPACING** is the amount of space inserted between individual cells in a table, defined in pixels. The default spacing is 2. **CELLPADDING** is the amount of space between the border of the table cell and the contents of that cell. Setting the **CELLPADDING** at zero is not a good idea, because text from one cell could run into text from the next.

Creating a Table Caption

Creating a title or caption for a table is easy using the **<CAPTION>** tag. This tag must be placed within the **<TABLE> ... </TABLE>** tags. Here is its general format:

```
<CAPTION ALIGN=top|bottom>caption text</CAPTION>
```

Notice that you can display the caption at the top or bottom of the table. By default, the caption will be displayed at the top of the table.

Defining Headings for Cells

In addition to displaying a table caption, you can include headings for a table's data cells. The tag for defining a heading looks very similar to the **<TD>** tag:

```
<TH ALIGN=left|center|right
    VALIGN=top|middle|bottom|baseline
    NOWRAP
    COLSPAN=number
    ROWSPAN=number>
text</TH>
```

Creating Table Rows

Every table you create will have one or more rows—otherwise, it won't be much of a table. The simple tag for creating a row is:

```
<TR ALIGN=left|center|right
    VALIGN=top|middle|bottom|baseline>
text</TR>
```

For each row you want to add, you must place the **<TR>** tag inside the body of the table (between the **<TABLE> ... </TABLE>** tags).

Defining Table Data Cells

Within each **<TR> ... </TR>** tag pair come one or more **<TD>** tags to define the table cell data. You can think of the cell data as the column definitions for the table. Here is the format for a **<TD>** tag:

```
<TD ALIGN=left|center|right
    VALIGN=top|middle|bottom|baseline
    NOWRAP
    COLSPAN=number
    ROWSPAN=number>
text</TD>
```

The size for each cell is determined by the width or height of the data displayed. The **ALIGN** parameter can be used to center, or left or right justify the data displayed in the cell. The **VALIGN** parameter, on the other hand, specifies how data will align vertically. If you don't want the text to wrap within the cell, you can include the **NOWRAP** modifier.

When defining a cell, you can manually override the width and height of the cell by using the **COLSPAN** and **ROWSPAN** parameters. **COLSPAN** specifies the number of columns the table cell will span, and **ROWSPAN** specifies the number of rows to span. The default setting for each of these parameters is one.

Using Forms

The HTML features presented so far correspond with traditional publishing practices: You create a hypermedia document, and others read it. With HTML forms, however, you can do much more. You can create a form that lets your readers search a database using any criteria *they* like. Or you can create a form that lets them critique your Web pages. Or—and this is what excites business people—you can use forms to *sell* things over the Internet.

Forms are easy to create. However, to use them, you'll need a program that runs on your Web server to process the information that the user's client sends back to you. For simple things like a comments page, you can probably use an existing program. For anything more complex, you'll probably need a custom program. While I will briefly describe the way form data looks to the receiving program, any discussion of forms programming is beyond this book's scope.

<FORM> ... </FORM> TAG

All input widgets—text boxes, check boxes, and radio buttons—must appear within a **<FORM>** tag pair. When a user clicks on a submit button or an image map, the contents of all the widgets in the form will be sent to the program you specify in the **<FORM>** tag. HTML widgets include: single and multiline text boxes, radio buttons, check boxes, pull down lists, image maps, a couple of standard buttons, and a *hidden* widget that might be used to identify the form to a program that can process several forms.

Within your form, you can use any other HTML elements, including headers, images, rules, and lists. This gives you a fair amount of control over your form's appearance, but you should always remember that the user's screen size and font choices affect the actual appearance of your form.

While you can have more than one form on a page, you cannot nest one form within another.

The basic format for the **<FORM>** tag is as follows:

```
<FORM ACTION="URL"
      METHOD=get|post>
text</FORM>
```

Notice that text can be included as part of the form definition.

Form Action and Method Attributes

Nothing gets sent to your Web server until the user presses a Submit button or clicks on an image map. What happens then depends on the **ACTION**, **METHOD**, and **ENCTYPE** parameters of the **<FORM>** tag.

The **ACTION** parameter specifies which URL the form data should be sent to for further processing. This is most commonly in the cgi-bin directory of a Web server. If you do not specify an action parameter, the contents will be sent to the current document's URL.

The **METHOD** parameter tells how to send the form's contents. There are two possibilities here: *Get* and *Post*. If you do not specify a method, Get will be used. Get and Post both format the form's data identically; they differ only in how they pass the form's data to the program that uses it.

Get and Post both send the form's contents as a single long text vector consisting of a list of WidgetName=WidgetValue pairs, each separated from its successor by an ampersand. For example:

```
"NAME=Jon Shemitz&Address=jon@armory.com"
```

(Any & or = sign in a widget name or value will be quoted using the standard ampersand escape; any bare "&" and any "=" sign can therefore be taken as a separator.) You will not necessarily get a name and value for every widget in the form; while empty text is explicitly sent as a WidgetName= with an empty value, unselected radio buttons and check boxes don't send even their name.

Where Get and Post differ is that the Get method creates a "query URL," which consists of the action URL, a question mark, and the formatted form data. The Post method, on the other hand, sends the formatted form data to the action URL in a special data block. The Web server parses the query URL that a Get method creates, and passes the form data to the form processing program as a command line parameter. This creates a limitation on form data length that the Post method does not.

Currently, all form data is sent in plain text. This creates a security problem. The optional **ENCTYPE** parameter offers a possible solution: Although currently, this only allows you to ratify the plain text default, in the future, values may be provided that call for an encrypted transmission.

Widgets

From a users' point of view, there are seven types of Web widgets; all of them are generated by one of three HTML tags. Except for the standard buttons, all widgets must be given a name.

<INPUT> Tag

The **<INPUT>** tag is the most versatile, and the most complex. It can create: single-line text boxes, radio buttons, check boxes, image maps, the two standard buttons, and the hidden widget. It's somewhat like the **<IMG>** tag in that it appears by itself—not as part of a tag pair—and has some optional parameters. Of these, the **TYPE=** parameter determines both the widget type and the meaning of the other parameters. If no other parameters are provided, the **<INPUT>** tag generates a text box.

The format for the **<INPUT>** tag is:

```
<INPUT TYPE="text"|"password"|"checkbox"|"radio"|"submit"|"reset"|
  "hidden"|"image"
      NAME="name"
      VALUE="value"
      SIZE="number"
      MAXLENGTH="number"
      CHECKED>
```

The **TYPE** parameter can be set to one of eight values. We'll look at each of these options shortly. Each input must contain a unique name defined with **NAME**. The **VALUE** parameter specifies the initial value of the input. This value is optional. The **SIZE** parameter defines the size of a text line and **MAXLENGTH** is the maximum size allowed for returned text.

Text Boxes

If the **TYPE=** parameter is set to **text** (or no parameter is used), the input widget will be a text box. The **password** input type is just like the text type, except that the value shows only as a series of asterisks. All text areas must have a name. Text areas *always* report their value, even if they're empty.

Check Boxes and Radio Buttons

Check boxes and radio buttons are created by an **<INPUT>** tag with a **checkbox** or **radio** type. Both must have a name and a value parameter, and may be initially checked. The name parameter is the widget's *symbolic name*, used in returning a value to your Web server—not its onscreen tag. For that, you use normal HTML text next to the **<INPUT>** tag. Since the display tag is not part of the **<INPUT>** tag, Netscape check boxes and radio buttons operate differently from their dialog box kin; you cannot toggle a widget by clicking on its text—you have to click on the widget itself.

A group of radio buttons is associated by having identical names. Only one (or none) of the group can be checked at any one time; clicking a radio button will turn off whichever button in the name group was already on.

Check boxes and radio buttons return their value if, and only if, they are checked.

Image Maps

Image maps are created with the **TYPE="image"** code. They return their name and a pair of numbers that represents the position that the user clicked on: The form-handling program is responsible for interpreting this pair of numbers. Since this program can do anything you want with the click position, you are not restricted to rectangular anchors, as with **<IMG ISMAP>**.

Clicking on an image map, like clicking on a Submit button, will send all form data to the Web server.

Submit/Reset Buttons

The **submit** and **reset** types let you create one of the two standard buttons. Clicking on a Submit button, like clicking on an image map, will send all form data to the Web server. Clicking on a Reset button resets all widgets in the form to their default values. These buttons are the only widgets that don't need to have names. By default, they will be labeled Submit and Reset; you can specify the button text by supplying a **VALUE** parameter.

Hidden Fields

A **hidden** type creates an invisible widget. This widget won't appear onscreen, but its name and value are included in the form's contents when the user presses the Submit button or clicks on an image map. This feature might be used to identify the form to a program that processes several different forms.

<TEXTAREA> ... </TEXTAREA> Tag

The **<TEXTAREA>** tag pair is similar to a multiline text-input widget. The primary difference is that you always use a **<TEXTAREA>** tag pair and put any default text between the **<TEXTAREA>** and **</TEXTAREA>** tags. As with **<PRE>** blocks, any line breaks in the source file are honored, which lets you include line breaks in the default text. The ability to have a long, multiline default text is the *only* functional difference between a **<TEXTAREA>** and a multiline input widget.

The format for the **<TEXTAREA>** tag is:

```
<TEXTAREA NAME="name"
          ROWS="rows"
          COLS="cols"> </TEXTAREA>
```

<SELECT> ... </SELECT> Tag

The **<SELECT>** tag pair allows you to present your users with a set of choices. This is not unlike a set of check boxes, yet it takes less room on the screen.

Just as you can use check boxes for 0 to *N* selections, or radio buttons for zero or one selection, you can specify the cardinality of selection behavior. Normally, select widgets act like a set of radio buttons: Your users can only select zero or one of the options. However, if you specify the **MULTIPLE** option, the select widget will act like a set of check boxes. Your users may select any or all of the options.

The format for the **<SELECT>** tag is:

```
<SELECT NAME="name"
        SIZE="rows"
        MULTIPLE>text/option list</SELECT>
```

Within the **<SELECT>** tag pair is a series of **<OPTION>** statements, followed by the option text. These are similar to **<LI>** list items, except that **<OPTION>** text may not include any HTML *markup*. The **<OPTION>** tag may include an optional selected attribute; more than one option may be selected if, and only if, the **<SELECT>** tag includes the **MULTIPLE** option.

For example:

```
Which Web browsers do you use?
<SELECT NAME="Web Browsers" MULTIPLE>
<OPTION>Netscape
<OPTION>Lynx
```

```
<OPTION>WinWeb
<OPTION>Cello
</SELECT>
```

FRAMES

One of the newest HTML features is the ability to have separate frames within a document. Each frame is separate from the others, and is controlled independently. Frames are a way to completely change the look of your Web site without having to learn another, more complicated language.

<FRAMESET>...</FRAMESET>

When you define a set of frames, you enclose your frame code inside the **<FRAMESET>** tags. The **<FRAMESET>** tag replaces the normal **<BODY>** tag, and helps to alert Netscape that the file is a frame file that will set up the overall layout of the screen. Within the **<FRAMESET>** tag, you can have a number of tags, such as:

```
<FRAMESET ROWS="row info, row info, row info..."
  COLS="col info, col info, col info...">
```

The **ROWS** and **COLS** attributes use a comma-separated list of values, either specific pixel values, percentages of the screen (1 to 100), or a relative scaling value. The scaling value is used to divide a section of the screen into separate frames divided into rows or columns. If you leave out the **ROWS** attribute, Netscape assumes you're dealing with a single row, and will automatically size the row to fit. The same applies to **COLS**.

Within the **<FRAMESET>** tags, you can have a number of **<FRAME>** attributes, which define each frame being created. The tag for creating a frame is:

```
<FRAME SRC="url"
  NAME="window_name"
  MARGINWIDTH=value
  MARGINHEIGHT=value
  SCROLLING="YES|NO|AUTO"
  NORESIZE>
```

First, the **<FRAME>** tag specifies a source URL (**SRC=**), which tells Netscape which HTML file or picture to load into the frame. **NAME** gives the frame an internal source, so you can refer to the frame later in your HTML code. **MARGINHEIGHT** and **MARGINWIDTH** define how much border you want between the displayed document and the actual borders of the frame. This value is specified in pixels and can range from zero up to whatever value completely fills the frame. These settings are optional. If you don't use them, Netscape will set the appropriate margin width automatically.

When you define a frame, you can choose to have it scroll or not scroll. The default setting is **AUTO**, which allows the browser to scroll if the document loaded into that frame is bigger than the frame size allows. If you set the scrolling attribute to **YES**, the scroll bar will always appear. If you assign it **NO**, it won't show up. And finally, adding **NORESIZE** to the **FRAME** tag denies the user the ability to resize the frame.

The <TARGET> Tag

The **TARGET** attribute is the main resource Netscape offers that directs exactly which frame is updated by a specific user action. **TARGET** uses the following basic syntax:

```
TARGET="window_name"
```

TARGET can be used in conjunction with several tags, including the **<A>**, **<BASE>**, and **<FORM>** tags. Adding the **TARGET** attribute to the **<A>** tag directs the hyperlink to load the document into a specific frame. Here's an example:

```
<A HREF="myhtml.html" TARGET="mywindow">update my window.</A>
```

You can use the **<BASE>** tag to establish your own default target that's only overridden by other specified targets. This is a good way to set up a list of pictures in one frame that is reserved just for that. Here's an example:

```
<BASE TARGET="pictureframe">
```

When you activate a form using the **<FORM ACTION>** tag, you can add **TARGET** to it, to tell Netscape which frame gets the result from the submitted form, as shown below:

```
<FORM ACTION="/process.cgi" TARGET="verification_window">
```

All **TARGET** names need to begin with an alphanumeric character in order to be valid, except for four, _blank, _self, _parent, and _top, which Netscape calls "magic **TARGET** names."

The CGI

The CGI, or *Common Gateway Interface*, defines how a form-handling program on a Web server should act. This includes the name1=value1&name2= value2 format of the form data vector, as well as how these programs interact with remote Web clients. A CGI program can be any sort of executable code, but on Unix servers, the most common executable seems to be a *Perl* script.

Security

You should be aware that it's always possible for people to intercept forms data bound for your Web server. This means that until forms with encrypted **ENCTYPES** are widely supported, forms data cannot be considered 100 percent reliable—or 100 percent confidential.

The problem is that anyone who loads your form can read the HTML source to see where the forms data goes. If that data includes any tempting information like a credit card number, a thief may be tempted to watch traffic to your server for credit card numbers to steal. Since it can be relatively easy to intercept TCP/IP packets, this is a problem that you shouldn't ignore.

Basically, if you want to do online sales, *don't* use a plain text form to ask for a credit card number unless you have secure sockets (SSL). This means that all transactions between the browser and the server are encrypted, so hackers should be unable to decipher them. If you don't have secure sockets, use a service that lets customers create accounts over the Web, but will only accept credit card numbers and expiration dates via a voice phone call or through "snail mail" (physical letters). When your customers want to place an order, they won't run the risk of having their credit card number stolen; they would only have to supply a name and address to let the order taking system look up their credit card number.

JAVA Applets

To allow Java applets to be played in Java-enabled browsers like Netscape, a new **<APPLET> ... </APPLET>** tag pair has been added. The format for this tag pair is:

```
<APPLET CODE = "appletclassfile"
               WIDTH = pixelwidth
               HEIGHT = pixelheight
               CODEBASE= "URL"
               ALT = "alternatetext"
               NAME = "symbolicname"
               ALIGN = left|right|top|texttop|middle|absmiddle|baseline|
                              bottom|absbottom
               VSPACE = vertspace
               HSPACE = horspace
               <PARAM NAME = parametername VALUE = parametervalue> >
</APPLET>
```

When this tag is encountered, the Java-enabled Web browser loads the applet having the name *appletclassfile*. This will usually be the applet name, with the extension .class at the end. In Java, all applets are created using Java classes. The applet class file that is loaded must be a compiled Java file. To load an applet, you must also specify the width and height of the area you want to run the applet in. These values must be specified in units of pixels.

Here's an example:

```
<APPLET CODE ="TickerTape.class"
  WIDTH = 300
  HEIGHT = 100
  ALIGN = left>
```

If you look closely at the **<APPLET>** tag, you'll see that it includes a **<PARAM>** tag. This tag provides information about optional parameters that can be passed to an applet. For each parameter passed to an applet, a separate **<PARAM>** tag must be provided. The **NAME** attribute specifies the name of the parameter, and the **VALUE** parameter specifies the value assigned to the parameter. Here's an example of an **<APPLET>** instruction that includes a couple **<PARAM>** tags:

```
<APPLET CODE="TickerTape.class" WIDTH=600 HEIGHT=50>
<PARAM NAME=TEXT VALUE="The Java TickerTape Applet...">
<PARAM NAME=SPEED VALUE="4">
</APPLET>
```

HTML Tag Summary

The following tables summarize the HTML tags, and note which new tags, or expanded support, is provided by HTML 3.2

Table C.1   Top-level Document Tags

Element Name	Netscape Extension	Notes
<!DOCTYPE>		Supported by HTML 3.2
<HTML>		
<HEAD>		
<BODY>	BACKGROUND BGCOLOR TEXT LINK VLINK ALINK	Supported by HTML 3.2
<!–A Comment –>		

Table C.2   Document <HEAD> Tags

Element Name	HTML 2.0 Attribute	Netscape Extension	Notes
<BASE>	HREF		
<ISINDEX>		PROMPT	
		ACTION	
<LINK>	HREF METHODS REL REV TITLE URN		
<META>	CONTENT HTTP-EQUIV NAME		
<NEXTID>			
<SCRIPT>			Supported by HTML 3.2
<STYLE>			Supported by HTML 3.2
<TITLE>			

Table C.3   Physical and Logical Style Tags

Element Name	Attribute	Notes
<CITE>		
<CODE>		
<EM>		
<I>		
<KBD>		
<LISTING>		
<PRE>	WIDTH	
<SAMP>		

(Continued)

Table C.3   Physical and Logical Style Tags (Continued)

Element Name	Attribute	Notes
<STRONG>		
<TT>		
<VAR>		
<XMP>		
<DFN>		
<STRIKE>		
<U>		

Table C.4   General Tags

Element Name	HTML 2.0 Attribute	Netscape Extension	Notes
<A>	HREF METHODS NAME REL REV TITLE URN		
<ADDRESS>			Supported by HTML 3.2
<APPLET>			Supported by HTML 3.2
<BASEFONT>		SIZE	
<BLINK>			
<BLOCKQUOTE>			
 		CLEAR	
<CENTER>			Supported by HTML 3.2
<DIV>			Supported by HTML 3.2

(Continued)

Table C.4   General Tags (Continued)

Element Name	HTML 2.0 Attribute	Netscape Extension	Notes
<FONT>		SIZE	Supported by HTML 3.2
<H1>...<H6>			
<HR>		SIZE WIDTH ALIGN NOSHADE	
<IMG>	ALIGN ALT ISMAP SRC	VSPACE HSPACE BORDER WIDTH	Supported by HTML 3.2 ALIGN ALT BORDER HSPACE VSPACE USEMAP ISMAP
<MAP>			Supported by HTML 3.2
<NOBR>			
<P>			
<WBR>			

Table C.5   List Tags

Element Name	HTML 2.0 Attribute	Netscape Extension	Notes
<DIR>	COMPACT*		
<DL>	COMPACT		
<DD>			
<DT>			
<MENU>	COMPACT		
<OL>	COMPACT	TYPE START	

(Continued)

Table C.5   List Tags (Continued)

Element Name	HTML 2.0 Attribute	Netscape Extension	Notes
<UL>	COMPACT	TYPE	
<LI>		TYPE	
		VALUE	

* COMPACT is no longer used and is ignored by most browsers

Table C.6   Forms Tags

Element Name	Attribute	Notes
<FORM>	ACTION	
	ENCTYPE	
	METHOD	
<INPUT>	ALIGN	
	CHECKED	
	MAXLENGTH	
	NAME	
	SIZE	
	SRC	
	TYPE	
	VALUE	
<SELECT>	MULTIPLE	
	NAME	
	SIZE	
<OPTION>	SELECTED	
	VALUE	
	NAME	
	ROWS	

Table C.7   Netscape and HTML 3.0 Table Tags

Element Name	HTML 3.0 Attribute	Notes
\<TABLE\>	BORDER CELLSPACING CELLPADDING WIDTH	
\<CAPTION\>	ALIGN	
\<TR\>	ALIGN VALIGN NOWRAP	
\<TD\>	ROWSPAN COLSPAN ALIGN VALIGN NOWRAP WIDTH	
\<TH\>	ROWSPAN COLSPAN ALIGN VALIGN NOWRAP WIDTH	

Online HTML Resources

Cascading Style Sheets, Level 1

http://www.w3.org/pub/WWW/TR/WD-css1.html

Extensions to HTML 2.0

http://home.netscape.com/assist/net_sites/html_extensions.html

Extensions to HTML 3.0

http://home.netscape.com/assist/net_sites/html_extensions_3.html

HTML3 and Style Sheets

http://www.w3.org/pub/WWW/TR/WD-style

HTML Writers Guild

http://www.hwg.org

Sandia HTML Reference Manual

http://www.sandia.gov/sci_compute/html_ref.html

Introducing HTML 3.2

http://www.w3.org/pub/WWW/MarkUp/Wilbur/

Web Style Sheets

http://www.w3.org/pub/WWW/Style/

D

What's on the CD-ROM

The CD-ROM included with this book contains all the programs needed to set up an entire intranet Web server, produce Web pages, create graphics, and develop CGI scripts. This collection of popular shareware and freeware will enable you to build your first intranet for a $0 investment in software. In addition, these programs are supplemented by the RFCs that define the Internet's protocols, and are accompanied by a companion sub-series to the RFCs called "FYI", as well as the NCSA 1996 Computer Virus Prevalence Survey.

For HTML editors, we've provided tools such as Microsoft Internet Assistant, HTML Editor, and HoTMetaL, all feature-rich editors that can speed up your HTML authoring. If graphics and clip art will be included with your pages, then the tool of choice is Paintshop Pro. This fully functional shareware program is easily one of the best general-purpose graphics tools for Web page authors.

Perl, the CGI scripting language that's the workhorse of the Unix world, is also included on the CD. Two implementations of this popular programming language (including version 5) are available for use on the Windows NT platform, giving you the ability to develop CGI programs for interfacing your pages with local databases.

For server software, you have a choice between the EMWAC (European Microsoft Windows NT Academic Center) HTTPD server and Jigsaw, an innovative new program developed by the World Wide Web Consortium, and written in Java. This particular server program has excited the Web community by offering, among other things, the possibility of eliminating the need for CGI scripting.

Finally, to help your users find and retrieve information from your Web site, you need to provide a search tool. We've provided the Excite search engine, used by Excite Search on the World Wide Web (**http:// www.excite.com**). Their search program will enable you to index your Web page collection and give users both a keyword and concept-based approach to searching for information at your site.

Index